"*Come after me....*" *They immediately abandoned their nets and became his followers.*

Matthew 4:19-20

photo by Don Smith

Catholicism & Reason

Rev. Edward J. Hayes
Rev. Msgr. Paul J. Hayes
& James J. Drummey

Prow Books / Franciscan Marytown Press
1600 W. Park Avenue
Libertyville, IL 60048

MG17231/FRANCISCAN ☐b0 r1

books in this series

CATHOLICISM AND REASON
and **TEACHER'S MANUAL**

CATHOLICISM AND SOCIETY
and **TEACHER'S MANUAL**

CATHOLICISM AND LIFE
and **TEACHER'S MANUAL**

Nihil Obstat:
REV. LAWRENCE GOLLNER
Censor Librorum

Imprimatur:
✝ LEO A. PURSLEY, D.D.
Bishop of Fort Wayne-South Bend

© Copyright by Prow Books/Franciscan Marytown Press, 1981

Cover Design by James E. McIlrath

Second Printing, 1975
Third Printing, 1976
Fourth Printing, 1977
Fifth Printing, 1978
Sixth Printing, 1981
Seventh Printing, 1983
Eighth Printing, 1985
Ninth Printing, 1987

Contents

Introduction	7
Preface	9
1. Grasping for the Truth	13
2. The Search for God	19
3. The Place of Religion in Our Life	29
4. The Gospels in Our Life	39
5. The Man Who Cannot Be Ignored	47
6. The Divinity of Christ	55
7. The Passion of Christ	67
8. The Greatest Miracle of All	81
9. The Church and the Rock	91
10. Where Is Christ's Church Today?	101
11. Christ's Church—Universal and Apostolic	115
12. The Authority of the Church	127
13. The Church and the Bible	137
14. The Church and Ecumenism	147
15. Getting to Know God	155
16. In the Beginning . . .	169
17. The World's Greatest Evil	177
18. Jesus Christ — God and Man	187
19. Grace and the Virtues	193
20. The Bridge to Eternity	203
21. After Death — What?	209
22. Mary, Mother of the Church	219
23. Random Remarks on the Catholic Church	229
The Apostles' Creed	237
The Nicene Creed	237
The Credo of the People of God	237
Bibliography	247
Index	255

Faith does not fear reason.
— *Pius XII to American scholars*

Catechesis seeks to make clear the inner coherence of the truths of faith, their relation to one another and to humanity's final end. Careful attention must be given to the rational bases for faith.
— *"Sharing the Light of Faith"*
National Catechetical Directory
for Catholics of the U.S.

Preface

In our day, looking into the very basis of religion is a fruitful and indeed a vital pursuit, both for those who are Catholic and those who are not.

There are those non-Catholics who have observed the Catholic Church in action — in hospitals, in the care of the poor and homeless, on the battlefield, in the market place — and who have come to respect this institution. On the other hand, there are some who feel an animosity toward the Catholic Church. Again, there are those who are indifferent. For all these this book presents the fundamental convictions of over six hundred million people who belong to the Catholic Church. At the same time it provides for Catholics themselves a needed reaffirmation and re-evaluation of the basic convictions by which they live.

In a spirit of charity and deep conviction this book discusses other religions, so that those who are members of the Catholic Church may have a greater understanding of the Faith that is in them, and those not of the Catholic Faith may gain a deeper understanding of the Catholics with whom they live and work.

A Catholic regards his religion as the one true Faith. To some this may seem a narrow-minded attitude. In point of fact, a man who believes in something must consider it true, and its opposite false; otherwise he does not truly believe. A man's belief represents his convictions. This book presents in popular language the fundamental structure and reasons underlying Catholicism, lists the principal beliefs of Catholics, and explains these beliefs.

In order to accomplish this, *Catholicism and Reason* examines the Apostles' Creed, section by section, and explains it. Particular emphasis is placed on how to find Christ's Church in the world today. Structurally and technically, this would be called a study of the Creed, with particular stress on the theological science known as apologetics.

Catholicism and Reason, however, is anything but dry reading. One of its best features is a light touch. The casual reader will find enjoyment and enlightenment in it. But since solid doctrine underlies every line, it is valuable to adult education groups. It also has an appeal to the searching mind of the modern high-schooler, and is recommended as a one-year high school study of the Creed. To make the book practical for teachers and group leaders, the authors have divided it into 23 chapters, one for each week of a typical High School of Religion year. Or the material can be utilized to provide a full year course for Catholic high school students.

Constant reference is made to the statements of Vatican Council II, as well as to recent papal statements, bringing to space-age man the unchanging teachings of Christ and his Church. Scripture quotations are from the New American Bible.

This book is unique in its use of charts, which are rarely used in the study of faith or morals. The maps of the route of the Passion in Jerusalem and the Holy Land at the time of Christ are the work of Peter Terrafranca and Gabriel Lucas.

In *Catholicism and Reason* the priest-brothers are joined by James J. Drummey, whose writing and teaching experience bring a substantial contribution to the work.

Several years ago, at a time when many of the problems peculiar to our times were beginning to emerge, Pope Pius XII flung out the challenge, "Faith does not fear reason."[1] This same challenge *Catholicism and Reason* gives to its readers.

George Washington once wrote, "The mass of citizens . . . mean well, and I firmly believe they will always act well, whenever they can obtain a right understanding of matters."[2] This book is an endeavor to present such an understanding, such an insight into Christianity.

It is by our efforts in seeking truth, and by following it to its logical conclusions in spite of the sacrifices which this may entail, that we will find the liberty and happiness we seek. "You will know the truth, and the truth will set you free" (Jn. 8:32).

[1] Address to American Fulbright Scholars, Feb. 8, 1958.
[2] To John Jay, May 8, 1796. Writings, Vol. 35, p. 37.

Catholicism & Reason

Chapter 1

Grasping for the Truth

All men are bound to seek the truth. — Vatican II, *Declaration on Religious Freedom*, No. 1.

There is a need today to evaluate once again the place of religion in relation to practical living. An alarming number of people have put religious and ethical principles into a little pigeonhole and have separated such principles from other aspects of life. Some have gone further and perverted the fundamental concept of religion, or have entirely cast aside religious truth as a factor in their lives. Such people reject religion because they do not understand it. They are then at a loss to explain the sense of emptiness in their lives.

The average person will accept the testimony of experts in the field of science. The average person will take for granted many truths he cannot fathom, or which even seem impossible. But as soon as the science of religion comes to the fore, he feels free to propose countless difficulties boldly, even though he is lacking in a knowledge of the very fundamentals of the science of religion. It is as if one who had a grammar-school knowledge of mathematics were to question the principles of geometry and trigonometry. Many a person who has done little more than scratch the surface of religious truth feels free to call into doubt the most sublime doctrines.

Religion from this aspect should be treated in the same way as other sciences, by beginning with fundamental truths and only then going on to a fuller knowledge of the more sublime truths. It is with this thought that we are going to discuss the very fundamentals of religious truth: the existence of God, the fact of a supernatural revelation, and the foundation of a Faith to bring men to eternal salvation.

In days past, men were closer to nature. They would look at the beauty of a tree, the order of the heavens, the wonder of life; and from these things they would perceive the beauty and power and infinite life of God. But the modern man has veered from that approach. His own mind, his own problems, his own existence have become the uppermost concern. Man now is led by a realization of his own inadequacy, or by a vague sense of emptiness in his life, or even perhaps a disorder and confusion in his own mind, to grasp for a higher reality which will give him peace and happiness. The modern man is still seeking God, not through external reality, not through objective truth, but in an oblique way, through a keen awareness of his own insufficiency. The building of a solid foundation of religious convictions upon the bedrock of fundamental objective truth beginning with the very existence of God, and continuing to the logical and inevitable conclusions, will have far-reaching consequences in the modern soul.

In our day there is an extraordinary interest in things religious, and a widespread, intense, and at times, piquant attention to the Catholic Faith. Contributing in no small measure to this interest and attention was the work of the Second Vatican Council (1962-1965). The sixteen pastoral documents that came out of the Council's four years of deliberations have made a significant impression on Catholics and non-Catholics alike.

Shortly after the Council's concluding session, Methodist Bishop Reuben H. Mueller, who was then president of the National Council of Churches, made this comment:

> A great religious community in process of renewal and change, the Roman Catholic Church has, through this Council, won the respectful attention of all who have carefully and prayerfully watched its developments. As the results of the work of the Second Vatican Council now move into dioceses and parishes in response to the admonishment of His Holiness, the world outside will continue to watch with interest and hope. We who are numbered among those whom good Pope John XXIII called "separated brethren" will add our sincere prayers as the evidence of our hopes.[1]

The Catholic Faith, to be rightly understood, must be viewed not merely in its externals. It is something more than an institution responsible for countless hospitals, social agencies and houses of charity; it is not merely the age-old Church which has for centuries fostered education, scholarship and culture. It is indeed more than a church distinguished by its ceremonial, its Mass, its sacraments, its beliefs and its hierarchy. All this is to see Catholicism from without. Catholicism cannot be truly understood as the object of a superficial investigation or the compilation of a mass of scientific findings. Catholicism is a way of life. The purpose of this book is to give, in a spirit of charity, a

---

[1] Bishop Reuben H. Mueller, "An Adventure in Ecumenical Cooperation," *The Documents of Vatican II*, ed. Walter M. Abbott, S.J., New York, New York: America Press, 1966, p. XX.

The intention in the human heart is like water far below the surface, but the man of intelligence draws it forth. —Proverbs 20:5

Religious News Service photo
by John Greensmith

deeper appreciation of the Catholic Faith, and in particular the basic reasoning behind that Faith.

Many renowned scholars, although at times remaining outside the fold, have deplored the widespread ignorance of Catholicism which has been an outstanding factor in the history of the world for two thousand years.

In spite of the apparently widespread interest in things religious, there exists a lack of understanding and at times a misunderstanding of religion in its fullest and truest sense. There is a confusion and uncertainty concerning three all-important realities: God, Jesus Christ, and the Church.

The existence of God is for the most part accepted; but the concept of a personal God and the awareness of the precise relationships between Him and ourselves are shadowy.

The second factor responsible for keeping the roots of religion in shallow soil is a lack of conviction and a vagueness about the Person of Christ. Is He merely a great moral teacher, or is He in truth the Son of God?

A third element that lies at the basis of religious uncertainty is a lack of knowledge and conviction concerning the living voice of Christ in the world today, the institution He established to present his teachings to the world.

In a somewhat vague way countless people today accept the general potentiality for good that is inherent in religion. But many stop there, and do not see the utter necessity of dogmatic principles for personal and social well-being. It was George Washington who proclaimed: "Let us with caution indulge the supposition, that morality can be maintained without religion. Whatever may be conceded to the influence of refined education on minds of peculiar structure; reason and experience both forbid us to expect that national morality can prevail in exclusion of religious principle."[2]

For many years, but especially since the atomic and hydrogen age, deep thinkers on the subject of modern "progress" have realized and at times have spoken out in warning to the world that scientific progress has been overshadowing the moral and spiritual progress necessary to keep a balance for survival.

The late General Douglas MacArthur vigorously insisted on the

---

[2] "George Washington's Farewell Address," *Select Addresses of Washington, Webster, and Lincoln,* ed. James Sullivan, New York: D. Appleton & Co., 1908, p. 21.

need for religious thinking on the occasion of the signing of the surrender of Japan which terminated the hostilities of World War II. Standing on the battleship *Missouri* in Tokyo Bay on September 2, 1945, MacArthur said:

"The problem basically is theological and involves a spiritual recrudescence and improvement of human character that will synchronize with our almost matchless advances in science, art, literature and all material and cultural developments of the past two thousand years. It must be of the spirit if we are to save the flesh."[3]

The necessity of religion for our personal lives is attested to not only by Catholics but by countless non-Catholic thinkers. From whatever aspect we view it, clear-cut thinking on God, on Christ, on the Church is a personal and social necessity.

Many a modern mind is grasping uncertainly for the strong roots of belief and truth. There is a desire for guidance and a rational foundation for the innate code of morality. In the absence of strong religious, dogmatic and moral principles, much of the world is drifting, lacking the knowledge of a goal and purpose in life.

In order to show the solid foundation for the Faith that is in us, we must begin with basic principles. The framework of a dogmatic and moral structure remains tenuous without a solid foundation. It is such a foundation that constitutes our present subject matter.

[3] Douglas MacArthur, *Reminiscences,* New York: McGraw-Hill, 1964, p. 276.

photo by Paul J. Hayes

*The voice of the Lord is
over the waters, the God of glory thunders,
the Lord, over vast waters.*

*The voice of the Lord is mighty;
the voice of the Lord is majestic.*

—Psalms 29:3-4

Chapter 2

The Search for God

> Ask the beasts to teach you, and the birds of the air to tell you; or the reptiles on earth to instruct you, and the fish of the sea to inform you. Which of all these does not know that the hand of God has done this? — *Job 12:7-9.*

"Chemistry is important; God is more important." This is the inscription that a visitor slowly pondered as he read the words appearing on the Mohammedan University in Cairo. We can recall those words now and quote them with a certain amount of envy, indeed with a measure of fond hope that they may become a reality in our modern thinking. We might well take this thought to heart.

Yes, chemistry is needed, and modern science, industry, health and pleasure, all have their places and are necessary. But above all God is needed. It is with this subject, God, that we are going to begin.

A man who says that God does not exist is in the same category as a youngster who denies that he had a grandfather simply because he never saw him.

Why is it that an atheist shows such hatred toward religion and God? Hatred must be directed either against an illusion or against a reality. If it is directed against a figment of a man's imagination, the situation would lead us to question his mental balance. If there is no God, why does the atheist show such hatred? Does anyone vehemently hate Cicero or Hannibal or Napoleon? All were hated when they lived, but hatred for them died with them. Hate ceases when the thing hated ceases. Why then the hatred of God and religion by atheists? If their hatred is directed toward something which does not exist, they are bereft of reason. The other conclusion is that what they hate does exist.

We can clearly show by our own unaided reason that God does indeed exist.

In our daily life we accept without question the fact that our human reason is trustworthy. To deny the reliability of man's reason would be to deny the findings of modern science which are our pride and boast. Therefore, if a number of people looking for the answer to a problem all come to the same conclusion, we would be inclined to agree with that answer.

It is a fact that men at all times and in all countries have believed in the existence of God. True, there have been individuals who doubted it, but these are rare exceptions which prove the rule. Every race and tribe, civilized and uncivilized, whether in connection with the rest of the world or isolated in a remote area, profess belief in some sort of god.

From ancient times to the present day all races have believed in a deity. At the very dawn of civilization along the Nile, primitive peoples worshiped a supreme being, leaving behind them evidence of their faith that is studied by the scholar in his library and examined by the visitor to modern museums. The Greeks called their supreme god Zeus; among the Romans Jupiter was the supreme deity; and so it goes down to our own day, all races believing in some sort of supreme deity. No race has yet been found which did not believe in some supreme being.

Perhaps one may object: "Travelers *have* reported tribes without any belief or religion." Yes, but *scientific investigation* has definitely proved the contrary. As recently as June, 1971, for example, a primitive tribe was discovered in the Philippines which believed in a god called Diwata, whom their ancestors had told them would someday come to help the tribe.[1]

In brief, a belief in God has existed among all races, in all times and places, and exists, too, universally among all peoples today. A belief so universal that it cannot be attributed to any one nation, that is present among tribes which have no contact with the rest of the world, cannot be due to chance. If we accept human reason as trustworthy, we must recognize the fact of the existence of God.

We can verify the existence of God in another way, by using the principle that there must be a cause for everything which exists. The fact that we see an egg on the breakfast table is a sign that a chicken exists or did exist; when we see a typewriter, we know that a man with intelligence designed it. The philosophic principle is as simple as that. We can find in the world nothing that is the cause of itself. Everything we observe in the world was caused by something. If we see a book, we know it did not just happen; it was made by a man out of paper and

---

[1] "A Filipino Tribe Leaves Stone Age," *New York Times,* July 18, 1971, p. 15.

ink; but the paper was made of pulp from wood, which in turn came from trees; the trees grew through the light of the sun. And so we must go back. In everything we can observe in the world there is a long line of causes, each dependent on a higher one before it. Search as we may, no evidence can be found to contradict this assertion. We cannot go back through a line of causes indefinitely. The only conclusion we can reach is that at the beginning of the line there is an Uncaused Cause.

If there were ever a moment at which nothing existed, nothing could ever exist. Nowhere in the world can we find a thing which was not caused. Men believe that nothing can proceed from nothing in the natural world, but when it comes to God's creation, some proclaim, "This is an exception." Yet they do not prove the exception, they merely deny the fact. They do not believe because they do not want to believe.

A man, for instance, was caused by his parents; they in turn by their parents. It does not solve the problem to become vague by going to the distant past. Some have summed up the problem vaguely with such an assertion as this: "The first living being came from lower beings." Then we must ask where these came from. A being cannot cause itself. Perhaps one may say that the sun is responsible for life. Where then does the sun get the power to give life? You cannot give money to a man in need if you simply have no money.

The idea, too, that life just sprang up in the beginning and developed in the course of ages is scientifically unsound, and we might add that Pasteur through his scientific findings proved the impossibility of spontaneous generation many years ago. We must look for another answer. Blind chance is ruled out by all reputable scientists. We are back to one solution: Life could have been originally produced only by a Living Cause, which is merely another name for God.

It is not a question of time, nor does it help to add a few million years to the age of the world. Either the last thing in your series of causes was caused or it was not. If it were caused, then we must ask the same question of that thing. If it were not, it is an Uncaused Cause. Everything in the world is caused, but this cannot go on *ad infinitum;* there must be an Uncaused Being at the beginning. This Being we call God.

Briefly: We observe in the world that everything which exists has a cause. A series of causes cannot go on indefinitely; it must have a beginning. Therefore, at the beginning there must be an Uncaused Cause. This Uncaused Cause we call God.

There is a third way in which we can prove the existence of God.

Look at your watch. What a marvelous device! Does it not presuppose a watchmaker? Even if you had never seen a watch before, you would conclude immediately and definitely that someone made it. Observe the intricate mechanism with springs and wheels all working together — the minute hand traveling precisely sixty times faster than the hour hand; the second hand sixty times faster than the minute hand. You know that such a mechanism did not happen by chance, just several pieces of metal happening together to work in this way, any more than chance could explain the composition of a color television, a computer, or a spaceship that can carry men to the moon and back. Even a child would see the absurdity of such a statement. If you were to argue the point, people would think you either insane or joking.

If a person were to walk along the seashore and come across a word written in the sand, he would conclude that someone had been there. No one would say that such a thing happened by chance, that the wind and waves and sand just formed the word by accident. Obviously it was done by some person with intelligence. Upon seeing a beautiful picture, no one in his right mind would say that it came about by throwing several colors of paint on the wall. Anyone recognizes that a beautiful picture is the product of a man with intelligence, the result of a plan in someone's mind.

Every time we see an object with order or design, we immediately know there was an intelligent designer.

In the great Strasbourg Cathedral there was at one time a huge clock. It showed not only hours and minutes but seconds, days, months, and seasons of the year. In addition, its mechanism moved many small figures, so that the quarter-hours were heralded by a child striking a bell with a hammer; the half-hours by a youth; the three-quarter-hours by a middle-aged man; the hours by an old man. Suppose a person were to say of this intricate mechanism: "There is nothing extraordinary about it; there is a pendulum which turns wheels, which in turn brings about movement of the dials."

No, a person viewing such a mechanical masterpiece instinctively exclaims: "What a clever engineer it took to produce this!"

The human body is a greater masterpiece than the clock in France. All parts of the body concur in a wonderful manner to bring about one complete effect. Look at the eye, for example. The act of seeing supposes each time the simultaneous presence of thirteen different conditions. Each of these presupposes many others. Did it all happen by chance? Scientists have calculated that, by the law of chance, without any designing cause, there would be 9,999,985 chances against 15 that all the conditions would concur to make seeing possible. Why, in examining such things which give evidence of order and plan far beyond that found in any man-made mechanism, should we attribute it to chance? An Intelligent Planner is the only answer behind it all.

In the development of a child in the womb and the birth process numerous conditions must be present and major physiological changes must take place in order to bring forth a healthy baby. One of these involves the circulation of blood. In an adult heart, two completely separate circulatory systems keep pure and impure blood from mixing. This separation is not present in the heart of an unborn child, however. There is an opening in the wall of the fetal heart, protected by flaps of tissue, that allows blood to flow uninterrupted through the right auricle and left auricle. But at the time of birth — or shortly thereafter — the flaps close and seal the opening shut, thus preventing for a lifetime any mixing of pure and impure blood. This circulatory adjustment is absolutely essential if the baby is to survive. It must occur at the time of birth — and it almost always does. Any attempt to ascribe this remarkable adaptation to chance raises more questions than it answers. Wise planning and intelligent design are the only sensible explanations.

In every aspect of our life, whenever we observe orderliness, we know that there was an intelligent planner. Consider the universe, arranged as it is in a marvelous order and design. The earth rotates on its axis once every twenty-four hours; it revolves around the sun once a year. The stars move in their orbits with a precision which far overshadows any chronometer made by man. The most accurate clock made by man is not perfect, but falters and must be corrected by the clock of the stars.

As the clock implies an intelligent clockmaker, as the word written in the sand supposes a person with intelligence, as a picture supposes an artist, so the universe, so complex, vast and precise in its working, supposes a Being with greater power and intelligence; so also the intricate working of the human body cannot be attributed to chance, but supposes an Intelligent Being behind it. "Show me a watch without a watchmaker," said G. K. Chesterton, the famous English convert, "then I'll take a universe without a Universe-Maker."

In every part of the animate world we might observe things working out according to a finely detailed plan and order. We may consider just two examples. The bat, in order that its flimsy wings may not become too easily torn, has a gland near its nose containing an oil with which it can lubricate its wings. How does the bat know when it is necessary to oil its wings? Like the bird building its nest or the beaver its dam, the bat operates according to an intelligent plan. As does the one spider, the *Argyroneta aquatica,* which builds its home underwater. This amazing insect spins an oval-shaped web just beneath the surface of the water, leaving an opening at the bottom for entrance and egress. Its specially designed hind legs enable it to carry an air bubble down into the water underneath the web. When the bubble is released, it rises and displaces an equal amount of water. The spider continues this process until the web, which resembles a diving bell, is filled with air. Eggs are then laid in the upper part of this airtight and watertight bell and food is gathered and stored for the mother and her soon-to-be-hatched progeny. Once this has been completed, the spider closes the opening and spends the winter in this safe and well-stocked home. Who taught the spider how to carry bubbles of air? What made the spider decide to live underwater in the first place? The only logical answer is that there is some Intelligent Designer behind it.

A visit to a planetarium will give a vivid picture of the universe with its innumerable stars and planets and their precise movements. There the technical skills of engineers and astronomers have depicted for us the order and precision of the heavenly bodies which we see at night. The images of the stars and planets are projected upon the ceiling. It is a wonderful work of skill and engineering genius. Suppose a person, after seeing this, were to say, "This does not point to any designer; it just happened by chance — concrete, metal, wire, lights, all came together to form this." That statement is patently absurd. But is it any worse than saying that the universe, of which the planetarium is only a small picture, is the result of chance? If we are to be logical, we must say that not only is the planetarium the result of a designer, but that the world, which is a much greater masterpiece, is also the result of a Designer.

Strong testimony for the order and precision in the universe comes from America's space pioneers, the men whose missions could never have been planned down to the minutest detail unless scientists and astronomers could be sure of the unchanging and exact conditions of the universe. For those who have rocketed through space, there is no doubt about the existence of an Intelligent Planner whom we call God. Astronaut Gordon Cooper, a veteran of two space flights, has commented:

> In my opinion there is no rift between science and religion; the more one learns about scientific endeavors, the more one is convinced of the wonders of God's creation. The more one contemplates the complex workings of millions of planetary bodies, and the unknown immensity of space, the more one realizes what a fantastic miracle it all is. History bears this out. Today I see evidences that scientists are turning more and more to a belief in God; they have almost been forced to recognize the Creator who made this magnificent, precise universe we live in.[2]

From July 30 to August 2, 1971, astronaut James B. Irwin spent 67 hours on the surface of the moon. Following his return to earth, he made this observation:

> I have encountered nothing on *Apollo 15* or in this age of space and science that dilutes my faith in God. While I was on the moon, in fact, I felt a sense of inspiration, a feeling that someone was with me and watching over me, protecting me. There were several times when tasks seemed to be impossible. But they worked out all right every time. We were able to accomplish almost all of our objectives, and I believe it helped to have someone there watching over me.[3]

Gordon Cooper's statement that scientists are turning more and more to a belief in God has been amply demonstrated by Dr. John Clover Monsma, an ordained Presbyterian minister, who has brought together in two books (*The Evidence of God in an Expanding Universe* and *Behind the Dim Unknown*) the views of 66 prominent and widely-respected natural scientists about God and his awesome presence in the world. These scientists have set forth briefly and clearly their reasons for believing in a Divine Creator of the universe.

But what of evolution — the theory regarding the growth and development of plants, animals, and human beings from earlier and more primitive organisms? Must one who accepts this theory reject the concept of God? Not at all. While a substantial body of evidence has been amassed by scientists in support of evolution, an equally substan-

---

[2]L. Gordon Cooper Jr., "God and Man in Space," *Friar*, November, 1969, p. 27.
[3]James B. Irwin, "In Mountains: 'I Felt Right at Home,' " ©*New York Times*, August 14, 1971, p. 16. Reprinted by permission.

tial body of evidence is still required to remove the issue completely from the realm of theory, especially as far as the evolution of man's body from pre-existing and living matter is concerned. But even if all the questions are answered, and all the hypotheses are proved, no explanation will make sense unless room is left for the existence of a Creator who got everything started.

God, if He so chose, could have fashioned the universe through an evolutionary process. But whether He did it that way or by direct creation, He still must be acknowledged as its Maker. With this basic premise established, the Church positively encourages diligent investigation and study of the problem by scientists and scholars so that someday we may know with certainty the method which God used to bring men and the universe to their present state of development.[4] The ultimate answer will involve no conflict between scientific and religious truth, for God is the Author of both.

It is said that a certain woman expressed the opinion that there can be no God because, if God existed, He would write his Name in the heavens for all to see. Apparently this woman would have huge letters in the sky. In what language, so all could understand? Actually God has written his Name in a universal language: the language of order, of law, of purpose, of design. We have but to open our eyes to see it.

I see His blood upon the rose
And in the stars the glory of His eyes,
His body gleams amid eternal snows,
His tears fall from the skies.

I see His face in every flower;
The thunder and the singing of the birds
Are but His voice — and carven by His Power,
Rocks are His written words.

All pathways by His feet are worn,
His strong heart stirs the ever-beating sea,
His crown of thorns is twined with every thorn,
His cross is every tree.[5]

---

[4] Pope Paul VI, "Address to Theologians and Scientists Attending a Symposium on Original Sin," July 11, 1966. Included in *The Catechism of Modern Man,* Boston, Massachusetts: Daughters of St. Paul, 1968, pp. 649-656.

[5] Joseph Mary Plunkett, "I See His Blood Upon the Rose," *The Catholic Anthology,* ed. Thomas Walsh, New York: The Macmillan Company, 1927, p. 428. Reprinted with permission of The Talbot Press Limited, Dublin, Ireland.

No matter what way we turn, we are faced with the same conclusion — the world does have a Maker. No matter where we look in the world, we see perfect order and plan. The only conclusion is that there is a Planner.

To put it briefly: Wherever we see a thing in perfect order or acting according to plan, our common sense tells us that there is an Intelligent Planner behind it. All over the earth there are things working in perfect order. Therefore these things demand some Intelligent Planner. This Intelligent Planner we call God.

The disciples came up to Jesus with the question, "Who is of greatest importance in the kingdom of God?" He called a little child over and stood him in their midst and said: "I assure you, unless you change and become like little children, you will not enter the kingdom of God. Whoever makes himself lowly, becoming like this child, is of greatest importance in that heavenly reign."

—Matthew 18:1-4

photo by Paul J. Hayes

Chapter 3

The Place of Religion in Our Life

In all his activity a man is bound to follow his conscience faithfully, in order that he may come to God, for whom he was created. It follows that he is not to be forced to act in a manner contrary to his conscience. Nor, on the other hand, is he to be restrained from acting in accordance with his conscience, especially in matters religious. For of its very nature, the exercise of religion consists before all else in those internal, voluntary, and free acts whereby man sets the course of his life directly toward God. — Vatican II, *Declaration on Religious Freedom,* No. 3.

A good many people have an attitude something like the painter in Don Quixote. This particular painter was one day asked what he was painting. To this question he casually replied: "Whatever it turns out to be."

Many people are that way about religion. They belong to a particular denomination because their family has traditionally belonged to that sect. It never occurs to them to think much about the subject. They are content to continue in the way in which they were brought up: Lutheran, Presbyterian, Catholic, no religion at all. But the subject is more important than that, and we ought to take time out to consider the fundamental truth: "Just how necessary is religion?"

We must begin by first discussing the term "religion."

There are three elements in this concept: God, myself, and the relation between God and myself.

We know that God exists; He is infinitely perfect. He is a personal Being and the cause of every other existing thing. So much for the first element.

We know that man is a personal being, created by God. He depends far more on God than upon his fellow men, because he owes his very existence to God. Thus man's relation to God is one of dependency. This dependence upon God and its expression we call *religion*. Religion then may be said to be the collection of truths and duties which arise from man's dependence upon God.

Is religion necessary for the human race?

There was once an old fisherman who took a young man out in his small boat. The young man noticed that on one of the oars was written the word "Prayer" and on the other, "Work." "Well," said the youth, "that idea is all right for those who wish to depend upon prayer, but it is out of date. Work is the thing needed in the world; we can get along without prayer and religion." The old man said nothing, but let go of the oar on which "Prayer" was written, and rowed with the other. He rowed and rowed, but they only went around in a circle and made no progress. The youth understood the old fisherman's lesson: that besides the oar of "Work" we also need that of "Prayer." Religion is necessary for men.

Suppose a man paid taxes according to his individual conscience and nothing else? What then? Perhaps a few would pay more than their share; some would give what they pay now; but the vast majority would pay little or nothing. The government could not function. Private judgment and individual opinion are just as unreliable in determining whether worship is to be paid to God, as in determining the taxes to be paid to the government. There are standards outside ourselves regulating religion, governing our relations to God.

As we have said, God is responsible for our existence. Certainly we should thank Him. If a boy scout helps a feeble woman across a busy thoroughfare, she would rightly be considered ungrateful if she merely took this for granted without a word of thanks. There is a true story of an unfortunate man who was quite destitute. A family down the street heard of the man's plight, and so the mother began to send one of her children down to him every day with soup and food. She did this for quite some time. Then one day something happened, and the mother neglected to send the soup to the man. Before long the man came and, knocking on the door, demanded, "Where's my soup?" It does not take much to see the ungrateful attitude of that man. We expect to hear a "thanks" in return for a favor. And should it be any different in our relations with God? God is our benefactor, and we ought by our own standards to say "thanks."

Our relationship with God might be analyzed from another aspect. Dominion and subjection are complementary. Wherever there is one, the other must be present. For example, one man is an employer, and his employees are subject to him. Or, in a more complete way, a slave presupposes a master. Now, God's dominion over us is total.

He created us and preserves us in existence. Therefore, our subjection is total. Expression or recognition of this we call *adoration*.

We know that God is infinite, and we are finite. We know, too, that we have need of many things. What does a teen-age girl do when she needs a new coat? The natural thing for her is to ask for it from those who can and will take care of her — her mother and father. The natural thing is to ask for what we need from one who can give it to us. Petition to God is rooted in our very nature, and He, being infinite, can grant us favors which can be obtained from no other source.

We have come to a realization, then, of our obligation of thanks, adoration and our need for petition to God, on the basis of our own human standards. This is a fundamental phase of what we mean by religion, or the expression of our relation to God.

We may see this in another way. If all men of all times have had some sort of religion, then it would appear that religion is not merely accidental but rather rooted in man's very nature.

All nations, even the most primitive, have had some sort of beliefs, some religious ceremonies and some sort of moral code. It is difficult to find the beliefs of savage people, but investigation has proved that some notion of a deity is always there. At first glance it may seem to us that there is no moral law but, although the ideas of primitive people may be somewhat different from ours, there are some moral standards of right and wrong. Is there a country where the betrayal of a friend would be praised? Where blasphemy of the deity is commended? True, there may be persons here and there who seem to practice no religion. But a more than superficial glance will indicate that all people of all nations do have some beliefs concerning a deity, some moral standards and some religious ceremonies.

A soldier during World War II was on a Pacific island. One of the natives took out a Bible. The soldier said, "We have gotten away from that sort of thing back home." The native simply replied: "Lucky for you that we have not gotten away from it here — otherwise your life would have been in danger soon after we saw you." Try as we may or turn where we might, we cannot escape religion. Even Plutarch, the pagan Greek philosopher and historian who lived in the last half of the first century and first part of the second, A.D., echoed this sentiment:

> If you travel from country to country, you may find cities . . . without science and arts, without kings and palaces, without riches; cities where money is unknown or not in use; cities without

public buildings and theaters; but no one has ever seen, and no one will ever see, a city without temples, gods, prayers.

History and scientific investigations have entirely borne this out. *There is no nation entirely without religion.* The list of godless nations drawn up by some men to disprove our opinion has dwindled to nothing in the light of recent scientific investigations. Every nation possesses at least some primitive form of religion.

Religion is part of man's very nature. Otherwise people would long ago have abolished it as unnecessary.

Religion, as we have seen, is really an integral and necessary part of man's very life, not merely a satisfying experience for those who find consolation therein. It is a matter of justice; it gives God his due.

If God exists and if religion and subjection to Him are necessary, it is quite possible that He would reveal some aspects of this relationship to us. Any sensible man will stop to ask himself, "Where did I come from?" and "Where am I going?" Perhaps the answer will be, "I came from an ape and I am going to end at the grave." That is one possible answer. In any case, every man ought to stop to ask himself the questions. First we must pause to consider where we will find the answers to some of these fundamental questions. God *could* have revealed to us some of the answers we are seeking, and it is possible that He did. If a teacher can communicate to his pupils things which they do not know, is there any reason to believe that God could not do the same with us, either by speaking to us himself or by choosing other men to tell us?

It is then at least possible that God has told us something about things supernatural. Why not then look around to find out? — for, after all, *if* He has, it is a thing of the utmost importance in our life. If He has not, we are at least none the worse for our investigation.

For years an unbeliever, John L. Stoddard, who spent a good part of his life thinking out the subject, finally reasoned: "As for the inherent probability of a revelation being made by God to man, I asked myself if it were rationally conceivable that such a God as I had come to believe in would set in motion this amazing piece of mechanism, called the earth, and then deliberately leave it to its fate, neglecting in particular the finest and most delicate portion of it all, the human soul. It absolutely contradicts the character of such a Being that He should let this human colony rush aimlessly through space upon a relatively short-lived globe, with no instruction from Him whatsoever, and no revelation of His will concerning it. *If man has been created for some definite purpose, as is to be supposed from an intelligent Creator, how can he learn the nature of that purpose, the goal assigned to him, and the conditions of attaining it, unless he has received from God some indication of His wish and some commands as to man's line of conduct?*"[1]

As a matter of fact, millions of people today — Christians and Jews, to name two groups — maintain that such a revelation was made by God to man.

The necessity of divine revelation was alluded to many centuries ago in the thought expressed by Seneca, the Roman statesman and philosopher who lived at the time of Christ: "No man is in a condition to help himself; *someone above him must stretch forth his hand and raise him up.*"[2]

The same thought re-echoes through the ages to our twentieth century.

More people than we suspect prefer to go to any extremes to avoid the trouble of thinking. The majority of people always seek the easier way out. One reflection of this attitude is shown by the members of a town called "Nameless." The people of that community could not decide on a name, and so authorities simply called it "Nameless." In the same way, the fact that there are a vast number of religions has led a good many people to throw up their hands, to raise aloft a white flag, surrendering before what seems to them a hopeless task. It is the easier way to declare that all religions are equally good and that it does not matter what a man believes so long as he lives a good life. This is the *easier* solution. But is it the correct one?

The majority of people today will admit that religion is quite necessary and useful. But many are of the opinion that God does not care just what form that religion takes provided that we admit our dependence upon God and lead a clean, upright life. The teaching that any type of religion is all right is well worth examining. If it is true, it should be propagated and instilled in the minds of all; if it is false, it should be unmasked and rejected. If it is true, it is convenient; if it is false, it is dangerous.

Do not worry whether two and two make four or five; it is all the same! Let the children drink brandy or milk; it does not make any difference.

[1] John L. Stoddard, *Rebuilding a Lost Faith,* (New edition with index), New York: P. J. Kenedy & Sons, n.d., p. 63.
[2] Ibid., p. 64

"Wait a minute," you say. "That is nonsense. Two plus two equals four, not five. It does make a difference whether you bring up a child on milk or brandy."

Yes, all people admit the sense of that, but many stop there. Religion, they say, is the one exception. It does not make much difference which religion a person follows. Is it logical to admit the truth of a principle in all fields but religion? If we are to be consistent, we must admit that in religion, as in everything else, it does make a difference which course we follow.

If the principle is admitted that one religion is as good as another, that we all have the same objective in view but are simply going by different roads to the same place, we must eventually say that vice and virtue are equally good, that error is as good as truth. How is this so? The principle that one religion is as good as another places pagan religions which condone polygamy and concubinage on an equal footing with the Christian religion. Some religions practiced the slaying of children as part of their rites. To adherents of the "one-as-good-as-another" principle such things cannot be condemned; to them such things as worship of the sun instead of the true God may not be criticized. Is not such an opinion the same as saying that vice is as good as virtue; idolatry as good as true worship?

Perhaps the proponents of the theory of indifferentism mean to exclude such things as paganism and Mohammedanism. Perhaps what they mean is that we are all followers of Christ, and so one *Christian* religion is as good as another. Let us see how such a theory works out in practice.

Most Christian religions believe that Christ is God and worship Him as such. Some, however, teach that Christ is mere man and refuse to adore Him. Either Christ is God or He is not. If He is not, then most Christian religions are giving adoration to some being who is not God and are practicing idolatry; if Christ is God, then some religions are blasphemous in denying it and refusing to adore Him. Thus, one who holds to the principle that one religion is as good as another says that idolatry is all right or that blasphemy is a good thing.

Many will still say that they cannot see how one Christian religion is not as good as the next: all have the same end, and their members are all trying to live good lives. Even here the principle does not hold. There are many Christian religions and no two agree exactly. What one holds true and good another rejects as false and evil.

Some teach that infant baptism is right; others teach that it is wrong. Some teach that hell exists, and maintain that God is just and punishes those who disobey Him; others deny that hell exists, saying that a merciful God would not permit it. Now, obviously two contradictory statements cannot be true at the same time. A thing cannot be a square and a circle at the same time. So too, if one group is right, another cannot be.

As is evident, many religions today teach contradictory things. Therefore it is evident that all of them cannot be right, that some are not in possession of all the truth. We are speaking here only of objective truth, not of the subjective consciences of the people involved. There are good and sincere men in all religions, and God will reward them accordingly. However, their sincerity cannot change what is objectively false.

Respect and love should be shown toward those whom we believe to be in objective error about religious matters, but, in the words of Vatican II, "this love and good will, to be sure, must in no way render us indifferent to truth and goodness. Indeed love itself impels the disciples of Christ to speak the saving truth to all men. But it is necessary to distinguish between error, which always merits repudiation, and the person in error, who never loses the dignity of being a person, even when he is flawed by false or inadequate religious notions. God alone is the judge and searcher of hearts; for that reason He forbids us to make judgments about the internal guilt of anyone" *(Pastoral Constitution on the Church in the Modern World,* No. 28).

It is true that we all must lead clean and upright lives and keep our conduct above reproach. But to say that all religions aim at the same thing does not change the fact that of two religions that hold contradictory doctrines one is in error. Two men may both lead exemplary lives. One denies hell; the other says it exists. Clearly one is in error. The fact that both are virtuous men does not change the situation. To say that the views of both men are equally correct is to say that truth and error are equally pleasing to God.

There is also widespread disagreement among Christian religions on such moral issues as abortion, divorce, and homosexuality. Some say that taking the life of an unborn child is murder; others say that it is not. Some say that a man and a woman cannot terminate their marriage; others say that they can. Some say that a sexual relationship between members of the same sex is contrary to the law of God; others say that it is not. To say that both sides are right on each of these issues is to say that there is no such thing as objective truth, or that anyone's approach to the truth is as good as that of anyone else. The chaotic results of this false philosophy are only too apparent today.

It is interesting to note that those who say that one religion is as good as another are not as tolerant if you substitute some other word for religion. For instance, one car is as good as another. Or one newspaper is as good as another. Or one football team is as good as another. In each case, you will get a strong argument against such a statement. How ironic it is, then, that religion, which is far more important than any car, newspaper, or football team could ever be, provokes no such reaction.

As we have shown, it is possible that God has revealed to us how He wants to be worshiped. No one teaches without wishing to be believed, or without being hurt by simple indifference to his teaching. Is not this equally true with God? If God has revealed some truths to us, do you think that He will look with approval on those who say that it does not matter what you believe, what religion you are in, as long as you try to be good? No, if God has spoken to us, He wants to be heard and does not want his words looked upon with indifference or the gift of his revelation refused. It does make a difference to Him what men believe. Pope John XXIII made this statement on the danger of religious indifference:

> To reckon that there is no difference between contraries and opposites has surely this ruinous result, that there is no readiness to accept any religion either in theory or in practice. For how can God, who is Truth, approve or tolerate the heedlessness, neglect, and indolence of those who, when it is a question of matters affecting the eternal salvation of us all, give no attention at all to the search for and the grasp of the essential truth, nor indeed to paying the lawful worship due to God alone?[3]

We may give the following thumbnail sketch of the position of the man who holds that all religions are equally right. If he just sits down to think, he will find himself in one of the following categories:

1. *Either* he believes that *all* religions are true and thus must say that contradictions are true. Christ is mere man and Christ is God; Christ was the Messiah and Christ was not the Messiah. This leaves the one who believes that all religions are equally true in a peculiar position.

---

[3]Pope John XXIII, "Near the Chair of Peter" (*Ad Petri Cathedram*), June 29, 1959.

2. *Or* he believes that only *one* religion is true, and then he is simply a hypocrite when he approves the others as being equally good.

3. *Or* he believes *none* is true and his only alternative here is to follow none. But we have seen that religion is, as a matter of fact, necessary for man.

SUMMARY

1. We have seen that God exists.

2. He *could* have revealed to us certain truths which we are to follow, and this millions of Christians, Jews, and innumerable others believe He actually did.

3. We have shown that religion is not only good but necessary.

4. There is a confusing picture today because of the number of different religions. We have agreed that it does make a difference which one you follow.

5. If it makes a difference which religion we follow, then we ought to investigate some of them and weigh their claims.

Where shall we begin, since there are so many religions — about 250 in the United States alone? Two are certainly outstanding because of their age and numbers — Judaism and Christianity. Christianity by dint of numbers alone has wielded a great influence. If we wish to form an idea of what reforms Christianity made in the world, remember the attitude of even the best pagans. For Plato, the Greek philosopher who lived four centuries before Christ, justice consisted in doing as much good to his friends and as much harm to his enemies as possible; and the truly happy man could say on his deathbed that no one had treated his friends better or his enemies worse!

In the ancient world much was made of Caesar's clemency, but he could not be happy unless the joy of vengeance was there; we read the life of a pupil of Aristotle who dragged alive one of his most heroic enemies behind his chariot. These and other qualities of the pagans are summed up by St. Paul in the words, "without conscience, without loyalty, without affection, without pity" (Rom. 1:31). It was on such a world that Christianity left its indelible stamp. It has been said that *there is not and there never was on this earth a work so well deserving of examination as Christianity.* We might then look into this body which has exerted such an influence. What are its claims and credentials?

The book called the New Testament is the historic sourcebook dealing with the founding of Christianity, and so we ought to look first at this book and weigh it as we would any history book before reading it, to decide whether or not it is reliable, who the authors are, when it was written. This we shall do in the following chapter.

Chapter 4

The Gospels in Our Life

> Holy Mother Church has firmly and with absolute constancy held, and continues to hold, that the four Gospels just named, whose historical character the Church unhesitatingly asserts, faithfully hand on what Jesus Christ, while living among men, really did and taught for their eternal salvation until the day He was taken up into heaven. — Vatican II, *Dogmatic Constitution on Divine Revelation,* No. 19.

When we take up the collection of books called "The New Testament," we may consider that collection from either of two different points of view. We may consider the New Testament books as a group of works written by men under the inspiration of God. On the other hand, we may look upon them merely as books of history. Catholics, as Catholics, accept these books as divinely inspired. For our present purposes, however, we will confine our scrutiny to an analysis of their value as history. Just as we might ask, "Was Tacitus a reliable historian?", here we are going to ask, "Were Matthew, Mark, Luke and John reliable historians?"

Suppose, in 1850, a man wrote a history of the United States. It would not be too difficult to find out whether it is reliable or not, because we can easily verify his statements. In the case of the Gospels of the New Testament, the process of verification is a little more involved because the writers of these books are relating facts now two thousand years old.

In investigating the reliability of any book, especially an old one, we will have to consider several questions:
 1. When was the book written?
 2. Who was the author?
 3. Was he honest? Or did he wish to deceive?
 4. Was he well informed about the events which he is describing?
 5. Could he have been deceived about the events he is relating?
 6. Could the writer deceive, even if he wished to?
 7. Is the book substantially the same today as when it was written, or did some changes creep in?

When we answer these questions about a history book, we will easily be able to decide whether what is related therein is true history or not.

Now, let us apply these questions to the book called the New Testament and see for ourselves whether it is a reliable history book or not. For the sake of greater simplicity we shall focus our special attention on the Four Gospels, leaving further study to more advanced scholars.

1. When were the Four Gospels written?

Of course, no date of publication appears on the Gospels, but we can ascertain the date by examining the books themselves. Suppose we were trying to discover the date of a history of the United States the title page of which was missing. We would read the book and perhaps find mention of President Taft as the current President. We would know within a few years when the book was written. So with the Gospels; some years ago, certain scholars thought they were written in the second century. At present most are in substantial agreement that they were written in the last half of the first century.

Speaking broadly, the books of the New Testament were written between 50 and 100 A.D., some of them before the destruction of Jerusalem in 70 A.D. They were written well within the lifetime of many who knew Christ, who certainly was the great figure of the period. They were written by men who listened to Christ or who had known his contemporaries.

2. Who were the authors?

St. Irenaeus of Lyons, one of the greatest writers in the early Church, speaks of the authorship of the New Testament. He had a personal knowledge through a man named Polycarp, who was a personal friend of John himself, one of the very authors in question. Irenaeus says that Matthew, Mark, Luke and John were the writers. The writers of the second century who tell us this were merely recording the opinion of people earlier, many of whom were living at the time of the writers themselves, and could make no mistake about the authorship. At the time, John himself was alive, and if the popular opinion were wrong as to the authors, he would certainly have said so. In short, the writings were always attributed to these four men and never to anyone else.

3. Were they honest? Did they wish to deceive?

No scholar nowadays would accuse the Gospel writers of conscious fraud. It is clear that they were plain, honest men. Moreover,

photo by Don Smith

All Scripture is inspired of God and is useful for teaching — for reproof, correction, and training in holiness. —II Timothy 3:16

they had nothing to gain by telling what they did. Like the soldiers set to guard the tomb of Christ, they might expect pay if they testified *against* Christ. For relating Christ's doctrines they were persecuted, scourged, and even put to death. There was no possible reason to lie concerning the things they were relating. It was to their disadvantage to write as they actually did. People may be ready to lay down their lives for truth, but not for a lie. Even the Jews who crucified Christ did not accuse them of lies, for the truth was too well known.

4. Were the Gospel writers well informed about the events they were relating?

We have in the Gospels a chronicle of the historical figure Christ and a record of his works and teachings. The men who wrote this were well informed on the subject. Matthew and John were particular friends, indeed Apostles, of Christ, and were with Him all during his public life. There is no doubt that they were qualified to write about the events. Matthew and John were actual witnesses of nearly all they relate.

Mark was a kind of secretary and companion of Peter, who was very close to Christ. Mark wrote down what Peter spoke orally. Clearly, then, Mark had reliable information.

Luke was a companion (today we would call him a "secretary") of Paul who knew Peter and the other Apostles firsthand. There is no question about their reliability. They were certainly competent and qualified. These writers had access to information on their subject as few other historians have had.

5. Could the authors of the Four Gospels have been deceived about the facts related?

There are certain things about which even the dullest of men cannot be mistaken. It does not take a scholar to see an event and simply relate it as he saw it. The writers in question knew Christ too well to be deceived about the facts.

Some have proposed this idea: Myths grow up in time around all great and popular men. Incidents are distorted, words are changed. So too, they say, in the case of Christ. This was the theory of some rationalists, and that is why they placed the date of the writings in the second century, to allow sufficient time for the myths to grow up. But, as we have seen, now the dates are definitely established as earlier, and exclude the theory of myths. Christ died in 30 A.D. The first writings of the New Testament date from twenty or thirty years after the death of Christ, and later ones perhaps some ten years more distant. Clearly, it is impossible for any widespread myths to grow up within forty years, especially in the case of a well-known personage and facts which were viewed by many thousands, some still alive at the time of writing.

6. Could they deceive even if they wished to?

They could not possibly have deceived. The people would not have permitted it. What the writers were relating had been seen by many thousands besides themselves. Christ and his followers had many enemies among the pagans and Jews who would have leaped at the opportunity to expose any falsehood. As an example of how false writings were exposed, look at the fate of the apocryphal books, which were immediately rejected as false. These were writings that resembled the New Testament in subject matter and title — the Gospel of Peter, for example — but were so lacking in historical accuracy that the Church has never recognized them as authentic.

We might note, too, that wherever there are places where we can test the accuracy of the events narrated in the New Testament with other histories of the time, such as those by Tacitus or Josephus, the New Testament is always in agreement with them. The *Annales* of Tacitus, the Roman historian who wrote early in the second century, refers to a group of people living in 64 A.D. called *Crestiani* and says that "the author of this denomination, Christ, in the reign of Tiberius, had been condemned to death by Pontius Pilate. . . ."[1] Josephus, the Jewish historian who was born seven or eight years after the death of Christ, wrote in the *Antiquities of the Jews:*

> Now about this time there was a certain Jesus, a wise man, if indeed he must be called a man. He was in fact the worker of extraordinary things, the teacher of men who accept the truth with pleasure. And he drew to himself many of the Jews and many Greeks also. This man was the Christ. And when Pilate, because the principal men among us denounced him, had punished him on the cross, those who had loved him from the beginning did not cease. In fact, he appeared to them on the third day alive once more, the divine prophets having already spoken these and thousands of other wonderful things concerning him. And even today the tribe of those who from him are called Christians has grown no less.[2]

In other words, despite the fact that the New Testament has been subjected to the most intense scrutiny and painstaking investigation —

---

[1] Giuseppe Ricciotti, *The Life of Christ,* Milwaukee, Wisconsin: © Bruce, 1947, p. 83.
[2] *Ibid.*, pp. 81-82.

44   CATHOLICISM AND REASON

more so than any work ever written, not a single contradiction has ever been found between a statement made by the first Christian writers and a fact taken from other historical sources.

Still more convincing evidence of the reliability of the New Testament — and the Old Testament — has been uncovered by archaeologists excavating the sites of cities and towns mentioned in the Gospels. H. V. Morton, who visited all of the localities associated with the birth of Christianity, has compiled an impressive summary of these archaeological findings and shown how they have corroborated down to the smallest details places and events described in the Gospels. "One has to visit Palestine," he said in his book, "to understand how meticulously accurate is the Bible."[3] Morton found that he could read pertinent passages from the Gospels while visiting Jacob's Well, or the Inn of the Good Samaritan, or the Garden of Gethsemani, and feel as if he had been transported back to the days of Christ, so accurately did the evangelists describe these places.

Archaeological exploration continues apace in the Holy Land even today, spurred on by the discovery in 1968 of the skeleton of a man crucified about 2,000 years ago.[4] The skeleton, uncovered when a bulldozer sliced into an ancient cemetery in northeastern Jerusalem, provides the first definite physical evidence of crucifixion at the time of Christ. The man's heel bones had been pierced by a single nail and his legs had been broken in order to hasten the death of the victim. There were also scratches on the wrist bones indicating that nails had been driven through the wrists. This find is of considerable significance since the only previous evidence of crucifixion came from literary sources. It is also further confirmation of the historical reliability of the New Testament.

7. Have the New Testament books been altered since they were written?

Suppose the President of the United States gives a speech and it is reported in ten newspapers. If we were carefully to compare the accounts in each, we would find that there were slight variations, such as *in* for *into;* but that *substantially* they are all correct. Now, if this is so in printing, how much more should we expect certain variations in writing. If you were to get five people to copy by hand a chapter of a

---

[3] H. V. Morton, *In the Steps of the Master,* New York, New York: © Dodd, Mead, 1971, p. 171.
[4] Peter Grose, "Israelis Find a Crucifixion Skeleton," *New York Times,* January 3, 1971, p. 1. Also: George W. Cornell, "Time of the Cross," *Boston Globe,* April 5, 1971, p. 1.

book, you would usually find all five a bit different, but all *substantially* the same.

Now, in the case of the New Testament, we obviously do not have the original. Printing was not invented until 1450, so before that time copies were made by hand. These copies are called manuscripts. We might expect to find some slight variations due to human frailty of the writers, and indeed such is the case. But we have a great number of New Testament manuscripts. Through the work of scholars we definitely possess today the New Testament in its correct form. There are indeed doubts concerning such words as *and*, and *in* for *into,* and some minor differences which do not affect the sense. However, in the whole New Testament there are only four principal places where scholars are in disagreement. Not a single point of Catholic doctrine depends for its proof on a variant reading.

Obviously the more manuscripts we have in agreement and the closer they are to the original, the surer we may be of the correctness of our book. For Tacitus we have only about two manuscripts, and no one thinks of denying that we have his work substantially the same as he wrote it. For the New Testament there are over 4,370 manuscripts in substantial agreement. In other words, we have that much more reason to trust the accuracy of the New Testament than of Tacitus.

In the case of Herodotus, the fifth century B.C. Greek historian, we do not have an original copy, and not one of the manuscripts for his work goes beyond the tenth century A.D., leaving a gap of some 1,500 years between the date he wrote and our oldest copy of his work. On the other hand, in the case of the book we are talking about, the New Testament, we can trace it back step by step to the fifth, fourth, and then to the second and first centuries. The process is a work for scholars, and we rest with their conclusion that our New Testament today is substantially the same as when it was written.

Concerning the New Testament, and particularly for our purposes the books written by Matthew, Mark, Luke, and John, scholarly investigation discloses that the authors were competent and honest and undeceived, and that we have their work in its correct form. There is only one conclusion: The Gospels are reliable history books. In our future endeavors we can feel perfectly safe in using them as such.

Present day site of the synagogue at Capernaum where Christ's listeners were held "spell bound by his teaching, for his words had authority" — Luke 4:32.

photo by Dorothy E. Kelly

Chapter 5

The Man Who Cannot Be Ignored

> He dwelt among us, full of grace and truth. . . . He gave us his new commandment to love one another as He loved us. He taught us the way of the beatitudes of the Gospel: poverty in spirit, meekness, suffering borne with patience, thirst after justice, mercy, purity of heart, will for peace, persecution suffered for justice sake. — Pope Paul VI, *Credo of the People of God.*

No figure has made a greater impact or had a more powerful influence on human history than Jesus Christ. The year in which we live is measured from the date of his birth. Nearly one-third of the people of the world call themselves followers of Christ. It has been estimated that tens of thousands of books have been written about his life and teachings, some 60,000 of them in the past century alone.

It was an unknown author, however, who provided a most striking summary of Jesus' life and its effect on the history of the past 2,000 years. The anonymous writer said it this way:

> Here was a man born in an obscure village, the child of a peasant woman. He grew up in another obscure village. He worked in a carpenter shop till He was thirty and then for three years He was an itinerant preacher. He never wrote a book. He never held an office. He never owned a home. He never had a family. He never went to college. He never put his foot inside a big city. He never travelled two hundred miles from the place where He was born. He never did one of the things that usually accompanies greatness.
>
> While still a young man, the tide of public opinion turned against Him. His friends ran away. One of them betrayed Him. Another denied he ever knew Him. He was turned over to his enemies. He went through the mockery of a trial. He was nailed to a cross between two thieves. While He was dying, his executioners gambled for the only piece of property He had on earth and that was his coat. When He was taken down, He was laid in a borrowed grave through the pity of a friend.
>
> Nineteen wide centuries have come and gone and today He is

still the centerpiece of the human race and the leader of the column of true progress.

I am far within the mark when I say that all the armies that ever marched, and all the navies that ever sailed, all the parliaments that ever sat, and all the kings that ever reigned, put together have not affected the life of man upon this earth as powerfully as this one solitary life.

Whenever we are called upon to listen to what a person has to say in any field, we must reasonably begin by considering who the person is before giving full credence to his statements. If one is seeking legal advice in an important aspect of his life, he will be very careful to whom he goes and not simply seek advice from any man on the street.

Is my would-be advisor worthy of trust? Does he know what he is talking about? What authority has he in his field? What are his credentials? It is only after a person has satisfied himself as to the answers to these questions that he would then go on to listen to what his advisor has to say.

We may apply the same norms of acceptability in apologetics. We are interested in what Christ had to say and what his credentials were.

If Mohammed were sent by God as a messenger, and if this can be proved, then that religion which he founded, namely Islamism, is divine. We are going to begin by studying the founder of Christianity, Christ. What did He say and do, and what were his credentials? It is reported that Napoleon once remarked of Christ, "I know men; and I tell you this is more than man."

It is of fundamental importance at this point that we propose and discuss two basic questions:
Did Christ actually claim to be a divine legate, a messenger from God?
Just what is the value of his claims?
Christ did actually claim to be a divine messenger, as is evident in many places in the Gospels. You may recall the occasion on which Jesus was in the synagogue at Nazareth. It was an accepted Jewish custom to have one of the men from the congregation stand before the group, read a passage from the Scriptures, and then comment on this selection. On this particular day, Jesus was requested to read, and He chose a section from Isaiah the prophet. The section was a prophecy of

the Messiah and was known as such to all the Jews. When Jesus finished, He rolled up the scroll and said, "Today this Scripture passage is fulfilled in your hearing" (Lk. 4:21). In other words, the passage they all considered to be a prophecy concerning the promised Savior, Christ declared applied to himself. There is no mistaking his meaning, for the people clearly knew what He meant and vocally opposed Him. Jesus in return remarked, "No prophet is without honor except in his native place, among his own kindred, and in his own house" (Mk. 6:4). There is no doubt that Christ claimed to be sent by God and that the people understood this claim.

On another occasion, as Jesus was travelling through Samaria on his way to Galilee, He met a Samaritan woman at Jacob's Well. During the course of their conversation, He told the woman that everyone who drank the water from the well would be thirsty again, "but whoever drinks the water I give him will never be thirsty" (Jn. 4:14). He also told her that the day was coming when Jews and Samaritans, who were very hostile to each other, would worship God in the same way. The woman said to Him: "I know there is a Messiah coming. When he comes, he will tell us everything." Jesus replied: "I who speak to you am He" (Jn. 4:25-26).

Remember, too, the words of Christ to his followers: "He who hears you, hears Me. He who rejects you, rejects Me. And He who rejects Me, rejects Him who sent Me" (Lk. 10:16). Jesus claims to be more than an ordinary man. He claims to be sent on a special mission from God.

Jesus said similar things over and over again, claiming to be sent by God, and indeed to be Divine.

Speaking to His disciples: "Whoever acknowledges me before men I will acknowledge before my Father in heaven." (Mt. 10:32)

At the feast of the Dedication, Christ spoke in unmistakable terms: "The Father and I are one." (Jn. 10:30)

Christ standing before the highest court of the Jews, the Sanhedrin, is charged with the crime of claiming divine honors for Himself. There are two things worthy of note: He is put under oath and is asked if he is the Messiah, the Son of God. Jesus declares unequivocally, "It is you who say it," (Mt. 26:64) the brief Hebrew phrase expressing an affirmative answer. The High Priest understood the claim to be God, for he tore his garments and exclaimed: "He has blasphemed."

CHRIST SAID THAT HE WAS A MESSENGER FROM GOD

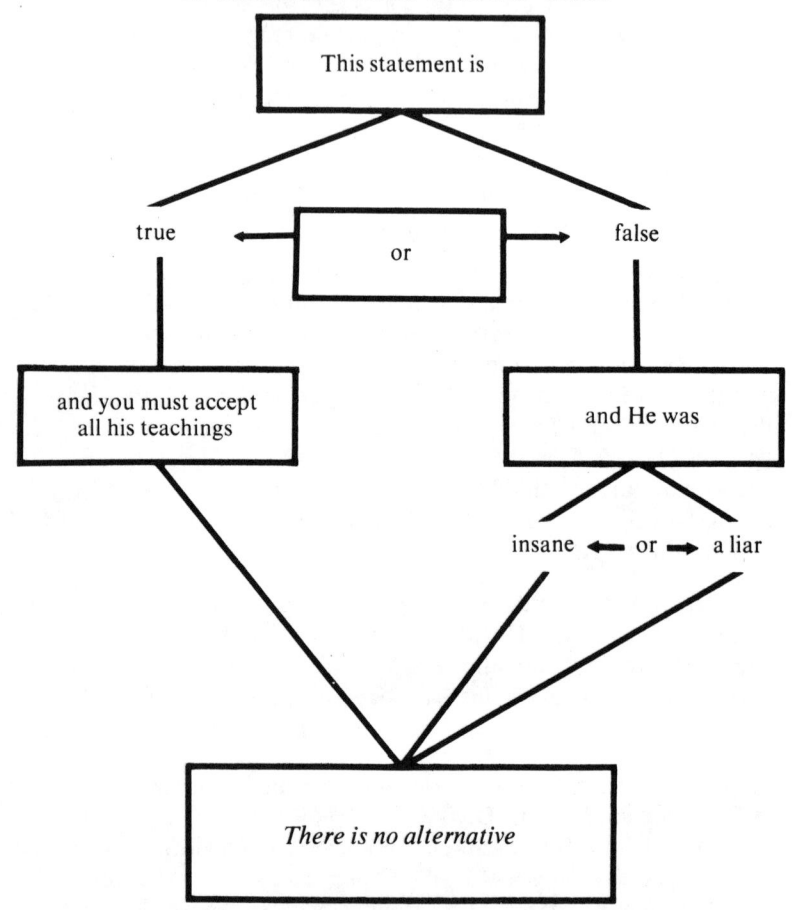

```
          This statement is
         /                 \
     true  ←—  or  —→  false
      |                    |
and you must accept      and He was
all his teachings         /        \
      |            insane  ←  or  →  a liar
      |                    |
       \                  /
        There is no alternative
```

What conclusion must we draw? Either Christ was God or He was not. If He were not, either He was mentally unbalanced or He was a liar. There is no other alternative.

It is obvious that Christ was not mentally incompetent. Indeed, few would be willing to propose this. It is clear from the account of his life that He was by no means retarded mentally. Even the temple guards who had been sent to apprehend Jesus while He was preaching in the temple area were impressed with his eloquence. When asked by the chief priests and Pharisees why they had not arrested Christ, the guards replied: "No man ever spoke like that before" (Jn. 7:46).

Some of the best examples of Jesus' mental competence and quick-wittedness involved those occasions when the Pharisees asked Him questions designed to trap Jesus and embarrass Him in front of the people. There was the time, for instance, when the enemies of Christ asked Him if it was lawful to pay taxes to Caesar. If Jesus said that it was lawful, He would invite the wrath of the people who despised the Romans who occupied their land and extracted tribute from them. If He answered that it was unlawful, He could be reported to the authorities as an agitator and an enemy of Rome.

The Pharisees thought that they had Jesus cornered. But He recognized what they were doing and said to them: "Why are you trying to trip Me up, you hypocrites? Show Me the coin used for the tax." When they handed Him a Roman coin, He asked them: "Whose head is this, and whose inscription?" Surprised, they answered: "Caesar's." At that, Jesus said to them: "Then give to Caesar what is Caesar's, but give to God what is God's." According to the evangelist, they were "taken aback by this reply" and went off and left Jesus (Mt. 22:15-22).

On another occasion, the Pharisees brought to Jesus a woman who had been caught in adultery. The penalty for such an offense was death by stoning and they asked Jesus for his opinion of the case. If He said that the woman should not be stoned, He would be accused of undermining the Mosaic Law. If He told them to proceed with the stoning, He would lose those of his followers who had been attracted by his mercy and kindness.

Jesus did not respond immediately and the Pharisees probably thought that they had trapped Him. He bent down and began writing in the dust with his finger. After a few moments, they repeated the question. Jesus straightened up and said to them: "Let the man among you who has no sin be the first to cast a stone at her." Having said this, He bent down and began writing on the ground again. The crowd began drifting away slowly until Jesus was left alone with the woman. He finally straightened up and said to her: "Woman, where did they all disappear to? Has no one condemned you?" When she answered, "No one, Sir," He told her: "Nor do I condemn you. You may go. But from now on, avoid this sin" (Jn. 8:1-11).

As for Jesus being a liar and a deceiver, just read over his life and see if He looks like a deceiver. No one, not Pilate, nor the Jews, nor his enemies, nor modern unbelievers, has proved Christ to be a sinner.

Nor may one logically declare that he is willing to accept Christ as a great moral teacher and an outstanding figure, but not as one sent by God. One who was merely a man and said the things Christ said could not be an outstanding moral teacher. He would be a lunatic or a liar, for time after time He claimed to be a divine messenger. It is impossible that this Man, so wise and so holy as his contemporaries testify, could be either mentally unbalanced or a calculating deceiver.

Consider the moral code that Jesus preached. Its core was love — love of God and love of neighbor. He even went one step further and urged love of enemies. "My command to you is: love your enemies, pray for your persecutors," He said in the Sermon on the Mount. "This will prove that you are sons of your heavenly Father, for his sun rises on the bad and the good, He rains on the just and the unjust. If you love those who love you, what merit is there in that? Do not tax collectors do as much? And if you greet your brothers only, what is so praiseworthy about that? Do not pagans do as much? In a word, you must be made perfect as your heavenly Father is perfect" (Mt. 5:44-48).

He called upon his followers to help those in need — to feed the hungry, clothe the naked, give drink to the thirsty, visit the sick and imprisoned, saying to them that as often as they performed these acts of love "for one of my least brothers, you did it for Me" (Mt. 25:40). He asked them to forgive the faults of others and laid down the Golden Rule: "Treat others the way you would have them treat you" (Mt. 7:12).

Jesus' moral standards were high. He forbade murder and stealing, adultery and impurity, anger and hatred, revenge and rash judgment, and false oaths. He encouraged prayer and fasting and sacrifice. "If a man wishes to come after Me," He said, "he must deny his very self, take up his cross, and follow in my steps. . . . If anyone in this faithless and corrupt age is ashamed of Me and my doctrine, the Son of Man will be ashamed of him when He comes with the holy angels in his Father's glory" (Mk. 8:34-38).

Jesus' reputation as a great moral teacher was due in large part to his unsurpassed ability as a storyteller. He held thousands spellbound as He presented his teachings, illustrating them with examples and parables that could be understood by the wisest intellectual and the simplest peasant. He used persons, places, and things that were familiar to the people to unfold his message. He spoke of fishermen casting their nets, sowers going out to plant seed, farmers harvesting their fields, laborers working in the vineyards, shepherds chasing after lost sheep, and the pompous Pharisee lording it over the humble publican.

Who can forget the parable of the Good Samaritan? Jesus had been asked how a person might recognize his neighbor, and He told the story of a man who was waylaid and beaten by robbers on the road from Jerusalem to Jericho. The story had an authentic ring to it because much of the 20-mile stretch between the two cities passed through uninhabited and mountainous regions which provided ideal conditions for the robbers who infested the area. The dangers of travelling this highway were well known to those listening to the story.

Shortly after the robbery, Jesus said, two travelers — first a priest and then a Levite — came along the road but passed by the injured man. Then a third traveler — a Samaritan — arrived at the place, took pity on the victim, bound up his wounds as best he could, and took him to an inn where he cared for him. On the following day, the Samaritan gave the innkeeper some money for the injured man's expenses and promised to pay any additional charges on his return trip. "Which of these three, in your opinion, was neighbor to the man who fell in with the robbers?" Jesus asked after completing the story. The answer came: "The one who treated him with compassion." Jesus concluded: "Then go and do the same" (Lk. 10:30-37).

The point of the parable was clear. The priest and the Levite were religious men who should have shown some compassion for their half-dead countryman. But they did not. The Samaritan, on the other hand, who was a hated foreigner, took pity on his enemy, thus demonstrating Christ's lesson that a neighbor can be anyone who shows love and concern for his fellow man.

Another well-known parable is that of the Prodigal Son. A father had two sons, Jesus said, the younger of whom asked for his share of the estate and went off to a distant land, where he quickly squandered all his wealth on dissolute living. A famine broke out in that country and the only work the son was able to get was taking care of pigs. But he did not even have as much food as the pigs. Finally, in desperation, he decided to return home, beg his father's forgiveness, and ask no more than to be treated as a hired hand. As we know, the father was overcome with joy at the son's return. He welcomed him back into the family and ordered a celebration to begin. Meanwhile, the other son — sober, conscientious, and loyal to his father — returned from a hard day's work in the fields and heard the sounds of music and dancing. When a servant told him the reason for the party, he was furious and refused to enter the house. His father came out and pleaded with him, saying: "My son, you are with me always, and everything I have is yours. But we had to celebrate and rejoice! This brother of yours was dead, and has come back to life. He was lost, and is found" (Lk. 15:31).

Again, the lesson was obvious. Jesus was illustrating the attitude of God toward a sinner who repents. He was saying that his merciful Father would always welcome a sinner back into the fold if that sinner humbly asked forgiveness. The parable, despite its simplicity and brevity, contained a profound message of hope. It is recognized today for this reason but also because it is a literary masterpiece. It could not have come from the mind of a man who was unbalanced or deceitful.

We cannot conclude this chapter without touching briefly on the personal qualities of Christ, those traits which have drawn so many millions of people to Him. There was his tenderness and compassion for the sick and the suffering. "Come to Me, all you who are weary and find life burdensome, and I will refresh you," He said. "Take my yoke upon your shoulders and learn from Me, for I am gentle and humble of heart. Your souls will find rest, for my yoke is easy and my burden light" (Mt. 11:28-30).

There was the mercy and forgiveness He showed toward sinners. He was frequently criticized by the Pharisees for his association with sinners. "People who are healthy do not need a doctor; sick people do," He told them. "I have come to call sinners, not the self-righteous" (Mk. 2:17).

There was also his courage and fearlessness — characteristics of Jesus that are sometimes overlooked. It took courage to chase the money changers out of the temple. It took fearlessness to condemn the hypocrisy of the Scribes and Pharisees, to call them "frauds," "blind guides," "blind fools," men who were like "white-washed tombs — beautiful to look at on the outside but inside full of filth and dead men's bones" (Mt. 23:1-39).

There is no virtue or admirable quality that Jesus did not possess to the fullest possible degree. No man with all of these attributes could possibly be a liar or a deceiver or an unbalanced person. Jesus was the perfect Man. His flawless personality is one of the strongest arguments in support of his claim to be a divine legate, a messenger from God.

Chapter 6

The Divinity of Christ

> We believe in our Lord Jesus Christ, who is the Son of God. He is the Eternal Word, born of the Father before time began, and one in substance with the Father . . . and through Him all things were made. — Pope Paul VI, *Credo of the People of God.*

If the only indications of Jesus' divinity were his impeccable character and extraordinary holiness, a convincing case could be made in support of his claim to be God. However, the Gospels afford us even more impressive evidence. This evidence can be broken down into three categories: (1) the prophecies concerning the Messiah which were fulfilled by Jesus; (2) the accurate prophecies which He himself made about future events; and (3) the numerous miracles which He performed.

Few men ever have their biographies written, even after they are dead; fewer still have their biographies written during their lifetime. One Man had his biography written centuries before He was born. That Man was Jesus of Nazareth.

Many years before Jesus was born, certain events of his life were predicted. These prophecies were fulfilled in no one but Christ, and He fulfilled them perfectly.

Prophecies Concerning the Messiah	*Fulfillment in Christ*
The Messiah would be born of the tribe of Judah. (Gen. 49:10)	Christ was born from the tribe of Judah. (Mt. 1:3; Lk. 3:33; Heb. 7:14)
He would be born of the House of David. (Is. 11:1-2)	". . . the gospel concerning his Son, who was descended from David according to the flesh." (Rom. 1:3; Lk. 1:32; Mt. 1:1; Lk. 3:31)

He would be born in Bethlehem. (Mi. 5:1)	"After Jesus' birth in Bethlehem of Judea . . ." (Mt. 2:1; Lk. 2:4)
He would be born of a Virgin mother. (Is. 7:14)	"Now this is how the birth of Jesus Christ came about. When his mother Mary was engaged to Joseph, but before they lived together, she was found with child through the power of the Holy Spirit." (Mt. 1:18; Lk. 1:35)
Kings would come with presents and adore. (Ps. 72:10)	"They were overjoyed at seeing the star, and on entering the house, found the child with Mary his mother. They prostrated themselves and did Him homage. Then they opened their coffers and presented Him with gifts of gold, frankincense, and myrrh." (Mt. 2:10-11)
He would perform great miracles. (Is. 35:5-6)	"Jesus toured all of Galilee. He taught in their synagogues, proclaimed the good news of the kingdom, and cured the people of every disease and illness." (Mt. 4:23)
He would be a man of sorrows. (Is. 53)	History confirms this of Christ.
He would be betrayed. (Ps. 41:10)	"Then one of the Twelve whose name was Judas Iscariot went off to the chief priests and said, 'What are you willing to give me if I hand Him over to you?'" (Mt. 26:14-15)
He would be sold for thirty pieces of silver. (Zec. 11:12-13)	"They paid him thirty pieces of silver. . . ." (Mt. 26:15)

© Holy Shroud Guild, Esopus, N.Y. The Face of Christ as it appears photographically. This is a positive image, proof that the image on the cloth is a negative image, unknown before the advent of photography.

He would suffer willingly for our sins. (Is. 50:6)	Jesus Christ willingly and meekly goes through his sufferings and death. (Mt. 27)
He would be led like a sheep to the slaughter. (Is. 53:7)	The expression is most apt for the events of Christ's passion and death.
He would have his hands and feet pierced. (Ps. 22:17)	Christ's hands and feet were nailed by soldiers.

If the prophecies of the Messiah were not fulfilled in Christ, they never will be fulfilled.

"It seems to me," one might declare, "that anybody who knew these prophecies could adapt his life to them and pass as the One who was to come." Such a thing is impossible. What man could be born of a virgin? Who could pick the town of his birth? What has the unborn to say about the tribe in which he will be born? The prophecies concerning the Messiah are more than mere biographical data. They are so unusual as to stand as proof against fraud. When they are fulfilled, they point with certainty to the object for which they were intended, to a manifestation of the hand of God.

CHRIST'S PROPHECIES AS CREDENTIALS OF HIS MISSION

Christ predicted future events which in fact were fulfilled and which could not possibly have been known by natural means. Christ, too, appealed to these prophecies as credentials of his divine mission.

Christ appealed to his prophecies as credentials certifying that He was sent by God with a message: "I tell you this now, before it takes place, so that when it takes place you may believe that *I am*" (Jn. 13:19).

It is unmistakable that Jesus did predict future events. Subsequent history tells us that these predictions were fulfilled. We have no choice but to listen to one with such credentials.

The following are a few of Christ's prophecies and their fulfillment:

Prophecy	Fulfillment
1. Christ predicted that He would be handed over to the priests and scribes: Christ said He "will be handed over to the chief priests and scribes, who will condemn Him to death" (Mt. 20:18).	1. "Those who had apprehended Jesus led Him off to Caiaphas the high priest, where the scribes and elders were convened" (Mt. 26:57). "They all concurred in the verdict 'guilty' with its sentence of death" (Mk. 14:64).
2. Christ predicted that He would be handed over to the Gentiles, who would mock Him, spit upon Him, scourge and crucify Him: "They will turn Him over to the Gentiles, to be made sport of and flogged and crucified" (Mt. 20:19). (Note the details; there is no vagueness in the prediction.)	2. Jesus is led to Pilate, a Gentile, who hands Him over to soldiers who scourge, spit upon Him and mock Him (Mt. 27:26, 29-30). He is crucified (Lk. 23:33).
3. Christ foretold that Judas would betray Him: " 'I tell you solemnly, one of you will betray Me. . . . The one to whom I give the bit of food I dip in the dish.' He dipped the morsel, then took it and gave it to Judas, son of Simon Iscariot" (Jn. 13:21-26).	3. "Then Satan took possession of Judas, the one called Iscariot, a member of the Twelve. He went off to confer with the chief priests and officers about a way to hand Him over to them" (Lk. 22:3-4).
4. Christ predicted the threefold denial of Peter: "I give you my word, before the cock crows tonight you will deny Me three times" (Mt. 26:34).	4. "I do not even know the Man" (Mt. 26:69-75). Peter denies Christ three times.

5. Christ foretold the destruction of Jerusalem: "The people will fall before the sword; they will be led captive in the midst of the Gentiles. Jerusalem will be trampled by the Gentiles, until the times of the Gentiles are fulfilled" (Lk. 21:24).

5. Forty years later (70 A.D.) this prediction is accurately fulfilled. We read in the works of the secular historian of the time, Flavius Josephus, that the Romans (Gentiles) besieged Jerusalem: "The entire city [of Jerusalem] was leveled to the ground . . . so that a later visitor could hardly have believed that it was ever inhabited."

Christ's prediction that Jerusalem would be destroyed was his most striking prophecy because of the utter devastation wreaked upon the city by the Romans four decades later. The Jewish historian, Josephus, was an eyewitness to the six-month siege, and he has reported the incredible atrocities that occurred during that time. He tells of thousands of dead bodies stacked in the cellars and houses of the city and thousands more which were hurled over the walls by the inhabitants. He says that five hundred deserters and captives were crucified each day until the hills around Jerusalem were literally covered with crosses, and wood became scarce. He even relates the grisly incident of a woman maddened by hunger who killed her infant son, roasted him, and ate half of him, saving the other half for another meal.

Finally, after months of trying to starve the inhabitants into submission, the Roman general, Titus, gave the order to burn and plunder the city. H. V. Morton, the famous travel writer, gives this summary of the last assault on Jerusalem:

> Once more the battering-rams were pushed to the walls. Once more the ramps were built up. Once more the *ballistae* flung their stones and the bows their burning brands upon the gallant defenders. Then eventually the Romans poured over the wall and grew sick of slaughter. They ran about the city in search of plunder, but, breaking into houses, they retreated horror-stricken, for every house was piled with rotting corpses.
>
> So Jerusalem, after a siege of nearly six months, was beaten to the dust. The prophecy that Jesus had delivered in the Temple forty years before had come true. . . . The Legion left in occupation of the smoking ruin was the Tenth, "Fretensis." Their camp

was the only sign of life on the brown hills that had once been Jerusalem. Everything that Christ had known, and every site that the disciples and the first Christians had associated with the Passion, the Trial and the Crucifixion, had been levelled to the ground, with the exception, of course, of the rise of ground known as Golgotha.[1]

Thus was fulfilled Jesus' prediction about the temple that "not one stone will be left upon another — all will be torn down" (Mk. 13:2). Not only that, but future attempts to rebuild the temple were frustrated by violent winds and fire spewing forth from the earth. Three centuries after the destruction of the temple, Julian the Apostate, a Roman emperor noted for his fierce hatred of Christianity, tried to rebuild it. According to the pagan writer Ammianus Marcellinus:

> Julian committed the accomplishment of this task to Alypius of Antioch, who before that had been Lieutenant of Britain. Alypius therefore set himself vigorously to the work and was seconded by the governor of the Province. Fearful balls of fire, breaking out near the foundations, continued their attacks, till the workmen, after repeated scorchings could approach no more and thus, the fierce elements obstinately repelling them, he gave over his attempt.[2]

CHRIST'S MIRACLES AS CREDENTIALS OF HIS MISSION

Many a modern man approaches the subject of miracles with an air of incredulity, remarking that belief in them is a sign of ignorance in the light of modern science. In reality, if we accept belief in God, we should have no difficulty accepting miracles, for God is infinite and can work beyond the sphere of nature.

For our purposes we may set down the definition of a miracle in the following terms:

A miracle is a happening beyond or outside the course of nature, perceptible to the senses, and whose existence is explainable only through the direct intervention of God.

A miracle is undeniable proof of the divine origin of the truth in testimony of which it has been worked. In examining a miracle and its

---

[1] H. V. Morton, *In the Steps of the Master,* New York, New York: © Dodd, Mead, 1971, pp. 36-37.
[2] Peter Sullivan, *Christ the Answer,* Boston, Massachusetts: © St. Paul Editions, Daughters of St. Paul, 1964, p. 115.

relation to the proof of a truth presented by God, several points should be considered: (1) Did the occurrence actually take place? (2) Was it indeed beyond the power of nature? (3) Was this miracle worked in support of the truth of some teaching? It is through thoroughly investigating these points that the truth of a miraculous happening may be ascertained and (what is important for our purposes) the fact of its confirmation of some doctrine determined.

To say that science has shown that there can be no miracles is baseless. How can science forbid men to believe that which it does not profess to investigate? Science is the study of the physical laws. It cannot prove that those laws can never be suspended by something above them. It is as if we were to say that a lawyer was so deeply learned in the American Constitution that he knew there could never be a revolution in America. The Constitution follows a certain course, so long as the course is there to follow. Nature follows a certain course, so long as there is nothing to stop it. But that fact throws no light on *whether there is* anything to stop it. That is a question not of physics but of metaphysics. To answer it one must leave the realm of material science and enter that of philosophy.

Now, in the light of this, let us go beyond science to investigate whether miracles are possible or not.

If miracles are impossible, the impossibility must be on the part of God who is the cause of a miracle, or on the part of nature which is the subject of a miracle. There is no third possibility.

There is no impossibility on the part of God. Even man can act above and beyond laws inferior to himself.

A man can pump water uphill, when by its nature it should flow downhill. He can hold up a stone or send a rocket to the moon, thus suspending the law of gravity. What man can do, certainly God can do. Certainly God can suspend laws inferior to himself.

There is no impossibility of miracles on the part of nature. The laws of nature are not immutable. They admit exceptions, and even men can intervene in the laws of nature. A doctor operates on a man and saves his life by the operation; the course of nature would have led to death, but the doctor suspended the course of nature. If man can do such things with ordinary laws of nature, God, who is infinitely more powerful than man, must be able to intervene in many laws which man knows nothing about, or over which he has no control.

It is evident that many things are beyond the power of natural forces. If a blind man is healed by mud, or a fractured bone healed by water, there is obviously some higher and greater power at work.

For a century, at Lourdes in France, similar things have been happening. These phenomena do not merely involve ignorant or simple people, led on by blind faith. For many years there has been maintained at Lourdes a medical institute, in which there is conducted strict scientific inquiry into alleged cures. The bureau is open to all doctors who care to study the evidence. For many years, visiting physicians totaled one thousand annually. The cases in the files are open to the inspection of any qualified person who desires to see them. Doctors of all faiths (as well as those with no faith) confess that these cures are beyond any natural explanation. No one has successfully impeached the bureau's scientific character.

The evidence is there for those who have an open mind. Those who look into the matter with the attitude that they will not be convinced will never be persuaded. It is evidently not God's purpose to *compel* men to believe in the supernatural. Miracles are not intended to have the effect of a ton of bricks falling upon a man to physically reduce him to subjection. They are *invitations to faith*.

If God is admitted as the Creator, there should be no difficulty in accepting the possibility of miracles. To deny the possibility of God's intervention in his own world is to make matter independent of its maker, the machine superior to its constructor.

Now, if we admit that miracles are possible, that there are some things beyond any natural forces which can be done by God alone, what is the reason for them?

First of all they show the work of an omnipotent God.

Second, if they are accompanied by some doctrine, they show the divine origin of that doctrine, for God cannot attest to an error or lead men to a false belief. They are credentials attesting to the fact that God is speaking.

We have shown that the book called the New Testament is a true historical work and that the authors of it are trustworthy historians. We have also shown that such things as miracles are possible. Now, these authors tell us of the miraculous character of some of Christ's acts. Strange or difficult as this may be to believe, we have no choice, for the authors, as we know, related what they saw or were sure of. The historical reality of these miracles is guaranteed by the authors, who were trustworthy witnesses. Besides, they were public facts, and if what the writers of the Gospels said were false, Christ's enemies would have exposed the fraud. As a matter of fact, even Christ's personal enemies never denied that the facts happened; rather, they admitted the facts which the writers of the New Testament relate and tried to account for them in some other way. Therefore we have little difficulty as to the fact that Christ did do some marvelous deeds. Now these could only be attributed to the forces of nature, or to demons, or to God.

The forces of nature could not be the cause of fever, paralysis, blindness being cured by the use of some mud, a touch of the hand, or merely a word. These means are entirely out of proportion and entirely incapable of producing such results, as medical science will testify.

Some opponents point to the overwhelming personality of Christ and maintain that the cures were wrought by hypnotic suggestion. Indeed, such suggestion may have an effect on nervous diseases, but again the medical profession will agree that it is powerless in the case of certain organic maladies.

The Jews may have been hasty in burying their dead, and perhaps this fact increased the possibility of burying someone alive, but to conclude from this that the three persons Jesus raised to life were not really dead is putting far too much on chance. Besides, as we know, Lazarus was in his grave four days, and already the odor of corrupting flesh was there. Yet he appeared alive again.

In the case of miracles worked in connection with nature there can be no doubt — the changing of water into wine, the calming of a storm by mere words clearly indicate a higher power at work.

Suppose one were to take some alphabet-soup letters, throw them into the air, and they were to come down to form a sentence. It would be strange indeed, and hard to believe. Suppose the process is repeated and again a sentence is formed. This would be too much for anyone to believe. If the unusual continues repeatedly, people demand an explanation and refuse to accept chance as a solution. It is the same with miracles which Jesus performed. Time after time, day after day, there were wonderful works. Chance is no explanation.

Nor can the deeds of Christ be attributed to evil spirits. It is admitted by all that Jesus was a good and holy man. His whole life is opposed to the work of the devil. Would the evil spirits then help Him in this cause? It is the same as saying that the United States received official aid from the Japanese in the war against Japan. The idea is no different from Christ's being aided by the forces of evil to defeat those forces.

There is one miracle — the cure of the man born blind (Jn. 9:1-41) — that is worthy of extended discussion because it answers all of the usual objections to the miracles of Christ. It happened one Sabbath as Jesus was walking through Jerusalem. He passed a beggar who had been blind from birth, and his disciples asked if the man's blindness was a result of either his own sin or that of his parents. Jesus replied: "Neither. It was no sin, either of this man or of his parents. Rather, it was to let God's works show forth in him."

Christ then spat on the ground, made mud with his saliva, smeared the mud on the man's eyes, and told him: "Go, wash in the pool of Siloam." When the man returned, he could see. His neighbors and those who had been accustomed to see him begging asked if he were the same fellow. "I am the one," he said. They asked how it was that he could now see, and the beggar responded: "That Man they call Jesus made mud and smeared it on my eyes, telling me to go to Siloam and wash. When I did go and wash, I was able to see."

At this point, the man was taken to the Pharisees, who questioned him carefully. He told them the same story, but they did not believe it. They said that Jesus must have been a sinner because He performed the cure on the Sabbath. Others objected, saying that if Jesus were a sinner, He could not have been the author of "signs like these."

The Pharisees then summoned the beggar's parents and asked if he was their son, if he had been born blind, and if they could explain why he was now able to see. They answered the first two questions in the affirmative, but they replied to the third: "... we have no idea. Ask him. He is old enough to speak for himself."

Angered because they could not discredit the miracle, the Pharisees resumed their interrogation of the man born blind and tried to get him to say that Jesus was a sinner. Instead he told them: "We know that God does not hear sinners, but that if someone is devout and obeys his will, He listens to him. It is unheard of that anyone ever gave sight to a person blind from birth. If this Man were not from God, He could never have done such a thing."

This lecture so infuriated the Pharisees that they threw the beggar out bodily. Jesus sought him out and asked him: "Do you believe in the Son of Man?" The man answered: "Who is He, Sir, that I may believe in Him?" Jesus replied: "You have seen Him. He is speaking to you now." "I do believe, Lord," he said, bowing down to worship Christ.

The points to be noted in the account of this miracle are these: (1) The man was *born* blind, so his blindness was an organic malady. It was not caused by an emotional shock and could not be cured by hypnotic suggestion. (2) The use of mud to restore the man's sight is outside the course of nature and indicates some higher power at work. (3) The results of the miracle were witnessed by a crowd of people, many of whom knew the beggar and that he had been blind from birth. There could be no concealing or explaining away the cure. Even the enemies of Christ did not deny that it happened. They tried instead to condemn Christ for working the miracle on the Sabbath. (4) Jesus performed the miracle to show that He was doing the work of God and also as an invitation to faith.

There are only three alternatives or explanations for the deeds of Christ: they were due either to the forces of nature, or to the powers of evil, or to God. Now, the first two of these, as we have just seen, are impossible.

Christ said that He was sent by God and had credentials, and these miracles were his credentials: "These very works which I perform testify on my behalf that the Father has sent me" (Jn. 5:36). Clearly, if He was truthful and holy and good, we must take his word. But we need not stop here. Christ had as credentials all his extraordinary works which must be attributed to a higher cause, God.

There is no other alternative — the facts are there; they are the work of God; Christ appealed to them as a sign that He was sent by God. We must listen to what He has to say.

One cannot reject Christianity if he accepts the New Testament as authentic history.

Chapter 7

The Passion of Christ

> Besides, as the Church has always held and continues to hold, Christ in his boundless love freely underwent his passion and death because of the sins of all men, so that all might attain salvation. — Vatican II, *Declaration on the Relationship of the Church to Non-Christian Religions,* No. 4.

It was shortly after midnight when Jesus and his Apostles left the city of Jerusalem, crossed the Kidron Valley, and made their way up the Mount of Olives to a grove of olive trees known as the Garden of Gethsemani. The Last Supper had been concluded and Jesus, as was his custom prior to all the major events in his life, wanted to spend some time alone in prayer.

Leaving eight of his followers just inside the entrance to the garden, Jesus walked further into the grove with his favorite Apostles — Peter, James and John. "My heart is nearly broken with sorrow," He told them. "Remain here and stay awake with Me" (Mt. 26:38). He then moved a short distance away, prostrated himself on the ground, and prayed in these words: "Father, if it is your will, take this cup from Me; yet not my will but yours be done" (Lk. 22:42).

The "cup" referred to the tremendous mental and physical suffering Jesus would undergo over the next fifteen hours. His human nature at first rebelled against the impending trial and He pleaded with his heavenly Father to spare Him the ordeal. But then, in an act of perfect obedience, He subordinated his will to that of his Father.

The bright moon shining through the gnarled olive trees enabled Peter, James, and John to see that their Master was involved in a terrible struggle. "An angel then appeared to Him from heaven to strengthen Him. In his anguish, He prayed with all the greater intensity, and his sweat became like drops of blood falling to the ground" (Lk. 22:43-44). It is significant that the only evangelist to record the bloody sweat was a physician. The phenomenon, known to medical men as hematidrosa, occurs when the subcutaneous capillaries expand and burst upon coming into contact with the millions of sweat glands which are distributed over the body. The blood is exuded with the sweat, coagulates outside the skin, and falls as drops to the ground.

According to medical authorities, hematidrosa is caused by physical exhaustion accompanied by profound emotion or fear and violent mental disturbance. All of these conditions were present during Jesus' agony in the garden. He was physically worn out and there was the natural fear of death — both consequences of his humanity. But the predominant consideration in the mind of Jesus was not physical pain but the horror of sin. To fulfill his mission, the pure and sinless Christ would have to take upon his shoulders all the sins that had been committed from the time of Adam and all the sins that would be committed until the end of the world. Bishop Fulton J. Sheen once summed it up this way:

> From the North, South, East, and West, the foul miasma of the world's sins rushed upon Him like a flood; Samson-like, He reached up and pulled the whole guilt of the world upon himself as if He were guilty, paying for the debt in our name, so that we might once more have access to the Father. He was, so to speak, mentally preparing himself for the great sacrifice, laying upon his sinless soul the sins of a guilty world. To most men, the burden of sin is as natural as the clothes they wear, but to Him the touch of that which men take so easily was the veriest agony.[1]

Three times during his agony, Jesus returned to Peter, James, and John and found them sleeping. Twice He chided them and urged them to remain awake and pray lest they succumb to temptation. On the third occasion, however, He said: "Sleep on now. Enjoy your rest! The hour is on us when the Son of Man is to be handed over to the power of evil men. Get up! Let us be on our way! See, my betrayer is here" (Mt. 26:45-46).

While Jesus was speaking, a great crowd armed with swords and clubs stormed into the garden. Leading the mob was Judas Iscariot, the Apostle whose love of money had caused him to enter into a conspiracy with the enemies of Christ. He had gone straight to the chief priests after leaving the Last Supper, told them where Jesus could be found, and even arranged a special sign by which the temple guards would be able to recognize Him.

Everything had gone according to plan. When the guards saw Judas embrace Jesus, they stepped forward to seize Him. Peter, however, drew his sword and cut off the ear of one of the men. But Jesus

---

[1] Fulton J. Sheen, *Life of Christ,* New York, New York: © McGraw-Hill, 1958, p. 339. Reprinted by permission.

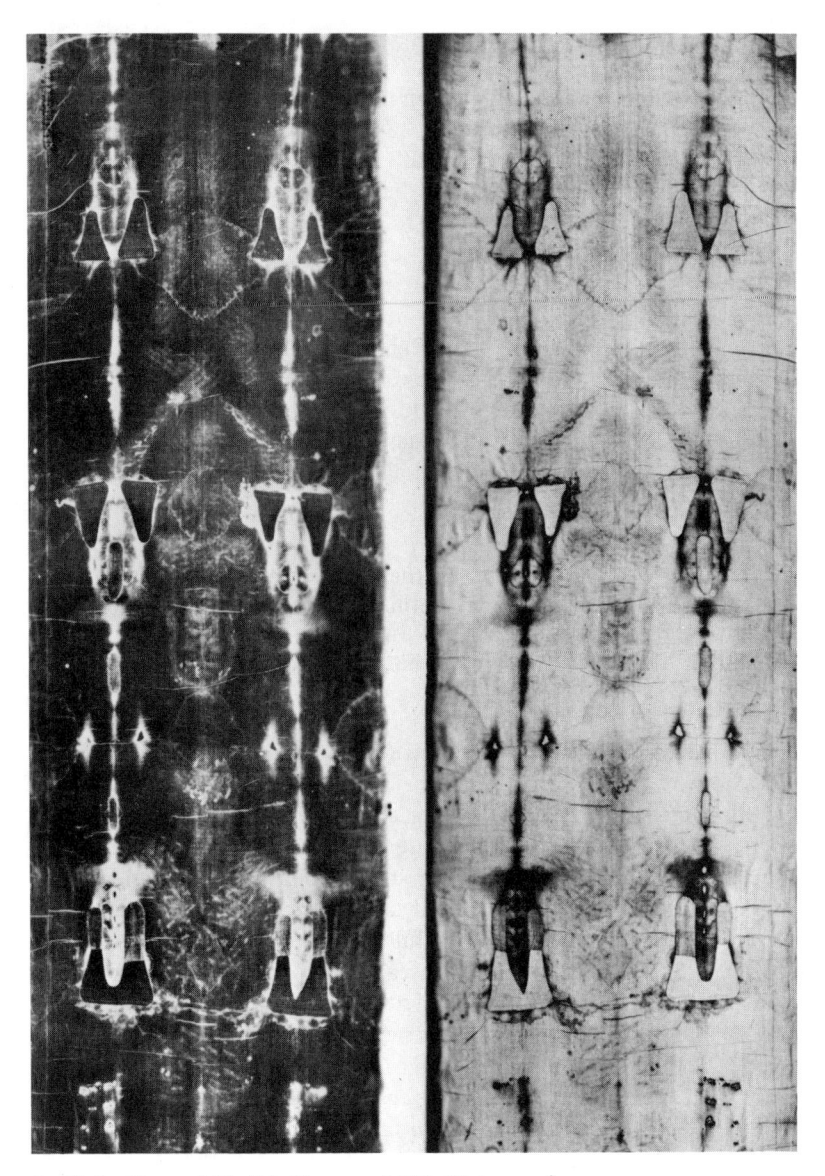

© Holy Shroud Guild, Esopus, N.Y. Picture of the Shroud of Christ as it appears to the eye (light background and dark figure) and also the cloth as it appears on photographic negative (dark background and white image).

told Peter: "Put your sword back in its sheath. Am I not to drink the cup the Father has given Me?" (Jn. 18:11). After healing the man's ear — his last miracle before his death — Jesus was arrested, bound with ropes, and forcibly marched back to Jerusalem. His Apostles, fearful for their own lives, deserted their Master and fled into the night.

It was about two o'clock in the morning when Jesus was brought to the house of Annas, the father-in-law of Caiaphas, the high priest at the time. Although Annas had been deposed as high priest by the Romans fifteen years before, he was still a powerful figure and probably masterminded the plot to kill Jesus. He opened the interrogation by questioning Jesus about his teachings in an attempt to come up with a charge which could be used against Christ. Jesus stopped him cold, however, by saying:

> I have spoken publicly to any who would listen. I always taught in a synagogue or in the temple area where all the Jews come together. There was nothing secret about anything I said. Why do you question Me? Question those who heard Me when I spoke. It should be obvious that they will know what I said (Jn. 18:20-21).

At this unimpeachable reply, one of the guards, perhaps detecting annoyance on the part of Annas, struck Jesus in the face and said: "Is that the way to answer the high priest!" Jesus responded: "If I said anything wrong produce the evidence, but if I spoke the truth why hit Me?" (Jn. 18:22-23). This time there was no answer. The session was concluded and Jesus was sent bound to Caiaphas, who also questioned Him. But this interrogation lasted only a short time and Jesus was turned over to the guards until the full Sanhedrin could be convened.

The guards, tired and angry because they had to stay up all night on account of Jesus, now had Him at their mercy. They dragged Him into an underground room and for nearly two hours they vented their rage by slapping and punching Him, spitting in his face, and directing every kind of insult at Him. They even amused themselves by blindfolding Jesus and then striking Him savagely in the face, saying: "Play the prophet for us, Messiah! Who struck You?" (Mt. 26:68).

Finally, about 5 a.m., the full Sanhedrin having been assembled, Jesus was brought before the 71-member council, which was empowered to decide any religious or civil case in any way connected with the Jewish law. His appearance must have startled some of them. The vicious beatings had taken their toll. His face was bloodied and bruised and his beard was covered with spittle. Yet He demonstrated no emotion as a string of witnesses paraded before the council giving false testimony about the things He had said and done during his brief public life.

But the testimony was so confusing and contradictory and the stories were so obviously untrue that even the hostile Sanhedrin must have felt uneasy. Seeing his case falling apart, Caiaphas, in desperation, rose to his feet and spoke directly to Jesus: "I order You to tell us under oath before the living God whether You are the Messiah, the Son of God" (Mt. 26:63).

The issue had been put squarely up to Jesus. If He replied in the negative, there was a possibility that He would be granted his freedom. If He replied in the affirmative, He would be signing his own death warrant. For more than two years, He had almost constantly hidden the fact that He was the Messiah primarily because his followers were looking for a political leader, a king who would lead them in battle against the Roman forces occupying their land. But now Jesus' time had come. He turned to the high priest and answered: "I am; and you will see the Son of Man seated at the right hand of the Power and coming with the clouds of heaven" (Mk. 14:62).

At that, Caiaphas tore his robes and shrieked in horror: "He has blasphemed! What further need have we of witnesses? Remember, you heard the blasphemy. What is your verdict?" The Sanhedrists, all of whom were on their feet now, shouted in unison: "He deserves death!" (Mt. 26:65-66).

And so the religious trial was ended and the sentence decreed. The trial had been a farce. It had featured hypocrisy, perjury, and violation of the Sanhedrin's own rules of conduct. The question posed by Caiaphas constituted a completely illegal maneuver. A man could not be convicted on his own testimony, according to the Sanhedrin's regulations. The testimony of at least two witnesses was required. But the enemies of Christ were not interested in legal niceties. They had plotted for a long time to kill Jesus and nothing was going to stand in their way.

However, there was another obstacle. Because their country was under the control of Rome, the chief priests had to obtain the approval of the Roman procurator in order to carry out the death sentence. The post of procurator, or governor, was held at that time by a man named Pontius Pilate. It was about 6 a.m. then when the entire Sanhedrin led Jesus, who was still bound, to the other side of the city, to the fortress

Antonia, where Pilate was staying. It is interesting to note that the leaders of the Jews, who had no scruples about condemning an innocent Man to death, refused to enter the residence of Pilate, who was

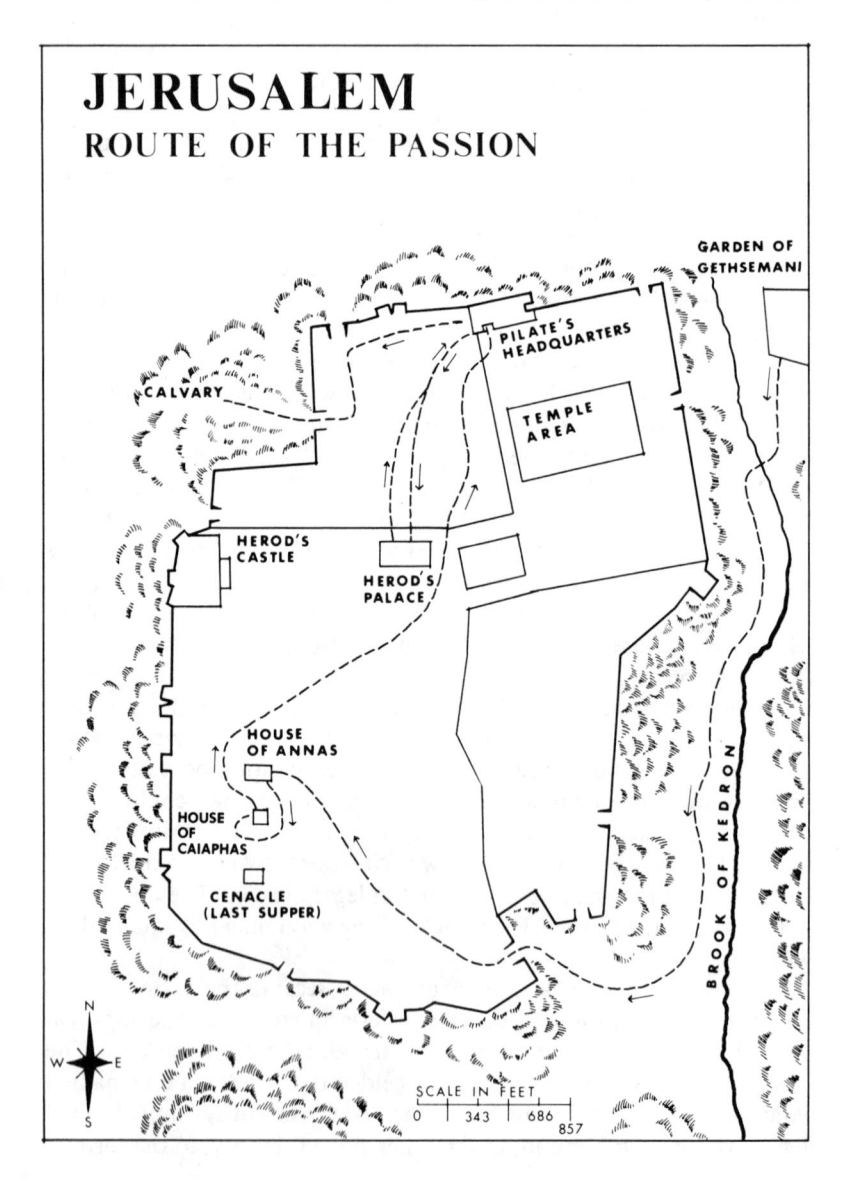

JERUSALEM
ROUTE OF THE PASSION

a Gentile, lest they be defiled and not be able to celebrate the Passover. Jesus had often criticized the Pharisees for such hypocrisy and it eventually led them to plot against Him.

Pilate came out to meet the Sanhedrists and asked them what charges they were bringing against Jesus. "We found this Man subverting our nation, opposing the payment of taxes to Caesar, and calling himself the Messiah, a king" (Lk. 23:2), they replied. There was no mention of blasphemy or of any other religious crime, for the enemies of Christ knew that Pilate would not be interested in matters involving religion. No, it would have to be a political charge, one accusing Jesus of being a revolutionary, an enemy of Caesar and of Rome.

The charges, of course, were completely false, and Pilate must have realized this. If Jesus had been the enemy of Rome that the chief priests described, the Roman magistrate would certainly have known of Him. Nevertheless, Pilate was cautious. He had Jesus brought into the praetorium and he asked Him if He were the King of the Jews. Making clear the distinction between a religious and political kingship, Christ replied: "My kingdom does not belong to this world. If my kingdom were of this world, my subjects would be fighting to save Me from being handed over to the Jews. As it is, my kingdom is not here" (Jn. 18:36).

Pilate, convinced that Jesus was not a political threat, went back outside and told the crowd: "Speaking for myself, I find no case against this Man" (Jn. 18:38). But the crowd persisted, saying: "He stirs up the people by his teaching throughout the whole of Judea, from Galilee, where He began, to this very place" (Lk. 23:5). On hearing the mention of Galilee, Pilate saw a chance to shift the problem of Jesus to a man who had jurisdiction over Galilee, Herod Antipas, who happened to be in Jerusalem for the Passover.

This Herod, the murderer of John the Baptist, was the son of Herod the Great, who had ordered the slaughter of the Holy Innocents shortly after the birth of Jesus. He had wanted to meet Jesus for a long time, having heard many reports about the wondrous deeds performed by Him. So when Christ was brought to his palace, Herod questioned Him at great length, but Jesus uttered not a word. Not even when Herod and the chief priests goaded and insulted Jesus did He favor them with a reply. Herod gave up and sent Jesus back to Pilate.

The procurator, still looking for a way to release Jesus but also wishing to placate the mob, hit upon what he thought was a way out of the dilemma. It was customary during the Pasch to release to the crowd some prisoner. So Pilate called for a notorious murderer and revolutionary named Barabbas, feeling quite sure that the multitude would choose Jesus rather than a dangerous criminal. But when Pilate asked them, " 'Which one do you wish me to release for you?' they said, 'Barabbas.' Pilate said to them, 'Then what am I to do with Jesus, the so-called Messiah?' 'Crucify Him!' they all cried. He said, 'Why, what crime has He committed?' But they only shouted the louder, 'Crucify Him!' Pilate finally realized that he was making no impression and that a riot was breaking out instead. He called for water and washed his hands in front of the crowd, declaring as he did so, 'I am innocent of the blood of this just Man. The responsibility is yours.' The whole people said in reply, 'Let his blood be on us and on our children.' At that, he released Barabbas to them" (Mt. 27:21-26).

Pilate, shaken by the reaction of the mob, had still another idea, however. He would have Jesus tortured and then perhaps the crowd would be satisfied and would not insist that He be executed. The form of torture was known as scourging and it was a horrible punishment. Men frequently died from it. At Pilate's order, the guards took Jesus to a dungeon below the praetorium, stripped Him of his clothes, and tied Him, naked, to one of the stone pillars. The instrument used, the *flagellum,* resembled a whip, except that the leather thongs were tipped with balls of lead or pieces of bone. Giuseppe Ricciotti, in his *Life of Christ,* gave this graphic description of scourging:

> Usually whoever underwent the Roman scourging was reduced to a sickening and terrifying monstrosity. At the first blows the neck, back, hips, arms, and legs grew livid, and then became streaked with bluish welts and swollen bruises; then the skin and muscles were gradually lacerated, the blood vessels burst and blood spurted everywhere, till finally the prisoner, every one of his features disfigured, was nothing but a bleeding mass of flesh. Very often he fainted under the blows, and sometimes he died.[2]

Although Jesus had been reduced to a bleeding mass of flesh, the soldiers were not through with Him. They revived Him, placed a scarlet military cloak over his shoulders, and then fashioned a crown of thorns from some bushes that had been left in the hall and jammed it down on Jesus' head. It was not a crown, really, but a cap. They twisted and turned the branches until there was hardly a spot on his scalp that was not pierced by a long and sharp thorn. The pain was agoniz-

---

[2]Giuseppe Ricciotti, *The Life of Christ,* Milwaukee, Wisconsin: ©Bruce, 1947, p. 621

ing and the flow of blood was substantial. The soldiers then placed a reed in his hand as a symbol of authority and began to mock Him by bowing before Him and saying: "All hail, King of the Jews!" (Mt. 27:29). They also spit at Him, took the reed from his hand, and kept hitting Him on the head with it, driving the cap of thorns deeper into his scalp.

Several hours had now passed since Jesus was first brought before Pilate, and it was around eleven o'clock when the Roman official ordered that He be taken out in front of the crowd again. One can only imagine the horrible sight that Jesus presented when He came out into the daylight wearing the cap of thorns and the scarlet cloak. "Look at the Man!" Pilate said to the crowd, expecting some sign of sympathy or compassion. But they shouted back, "Crucify Him! Crucify Him!" (Jn. 19:5-6). Pilate was still eager to release Jesus until he heard the Jews shout: "If you free this Man you are no 'Friend of Caesar.' Anyone who makes himself a king becomes Caesar's rival" (Jn. 19:12). This struck fear into Pilate's cowardly heart. The last thing that he wanted was to have reports get back to Rome that he had set free an enemy of Caesar. Unable to summon the courage to resist the pressure of the howling mob, Pilate handed Jesus over to be crucified.

The prisoner was taken back down to the dungeon and the cloak was ripped from his body, opening up all the wounds that had dried and causing blood to flow once more. He was given his own clothes, which quickly became stained with blood, and the horizontal beam of his cross was placed on his lacerated shoulder. The vertical portion of the cross was already in the ground at the spot selected for the execution, which was always a high plot of ground outside the city gates near a well-travelled road. The purpose of choosing such a conspicuous place was to give the greatest number of people an opportunity to see what savage punishment opposition to Rome would bring.

The place for Jesus' crucifixion met all of these conditions. Called Golgotha, which meant "Skull Place," it was about half a mile from the residence of Pontius Pilate. It would not have been a long walk under ordinary circumstances. But these were not ordinary circumstances. The Man carrying the heavy crosspiece through the winding, crowded city streets had not slept in more than twenty-four hours. He had had nothing to eat or drink in more than twelve hours. He had suffered violent damage to his body through a bloody sweat, mistreatment and beatings by the soldiers, the scourging, and the crowning with thorns. Now He was faced with a painful journey to execution.

Jesus fell at least three times on the way to Golgotha, causing more bruises and lacerations. It took a superhuman effort for Him to rise each time. The soldiers, concerned that He might die on the way and thus cheat his enemies of their satisfaction, took a man named Simon out of the crowd and forced him to help Jesus carry the crosspiece.

It was nearly noon when Jesus and the two men who were to be crucified with Him arrived at the Skull Place. They were about to undergo the cruelest and most vicious form of punishment ever devised by man. It was considered such a vile method of execution at the time of Christ that it was reserved for criminals and slaves. A Roman citizen, no matter his crime, was rarely crucified.

The Gospels say very little about the sufferings of Christ during his passion and offer scarcely a hint about the physical effects of the punishment inflicted upon Him. Luke, the physician, does not even mention the scourging, and the other three evangelists each devote only one sentence to this horrible torture, stating simply that Pilate had Jesus scourged. So we must turn to other sources to understand fully the meaning of the words scourging and crucifixion.

One of the most authoritative books on the physical aspects of the Passion, especially the crucifixion, was written by a French surgeon and teacher of anatomy, Pierre Barbet, M.D. In his book, *A Doctor at Calvary,* Dr. Barbet presents a medical description of Christ's sufferings. It is based on extensive laboratory experimentation on cadavers and amputated limbs and also on a careful study of photographs of the Holy Shroud, which many authorities believe to be the winding sheet in which the body of Jesus was wrapped after He was taken down from the cross. The image on the shroud bears all of the marks that you would expect to find on the body of Christ in view of the brutalities recorded in the Gospels. We are indebted to Dr. Barbet for his scholarly research and moving treatment of the Passion, and we shall rely heavily on him in discussing the crucifixion.

Jesus had barely stumbled up the hill of Calvary when his executioners began their cruel task. They first stripped Him of his garments, again ripping open his wounds and causing thousands of painful shocks over his entire body. Anyone who has ever removed a dressing that was stuck to a wound has a very remote idea of the pain Jesus experienced at that moment. The victim was then shoved to the ground, his bleeding body quickly becoming caked with dust, and his shoulders were placed on the rough wood of the crosspiece. With one executioner holding his arm outstretched, the palm facing upwards, the other took a nail (perhaps six or seven inches long and one-third of an inch thick), placed it on his wrist, and then drove it home with a few blows from a hammer.

Dr. Barbet found through experimentation that a nail placed in the palm of the hand would not support a man's weight. He soon discovered, however, that there was a spot where the palm meets the wrist that would take a nail and would support the body of a man. But his most startling finding was that when a nail pierced this spot, it partially severed the median nerve, causing unbelievable pain but also causing the thumb to jerk inward against the palm. This corresponded exactly to the stain on the shroud. Not only did the bloody wound appear on the wrist in the pictures of the shroud, but the image of the hands — with the palms downward — showed no sign of thumbs.

Doctors know that the greatest pain that a man can experience is that caused by wounding the main nervous centers. Usually it causes fainting and this is fortunate. But Christ did not lose consciousness. To sever a nerve is one thing. But in the case of the nails in the wrist of Jesus, the raw nerve remained in contact with the nail and as the body sagged with weakness, the nerve was stretched against it like a violin string and it vibrated with each movement. This process went on for three hours.

The same process was repeated with the other arm, with the same indescribable pain, and Jesus was dragged to his feet. The beam was carried to the place where the vertical portion of the cross stood, hoisted up on top on it, and nailed in place. His body now hung suspended off the ground, supported only by the nails in his wrists. The next step was to fix the feet. Contrary to the form of most crucifixes, there was no block on which the feet rested. Rather, the executioners bent the right knee and placed the right foot flat against the cross; the left knee was then bent and the left foot brought around in front of the right. One nail, driven through the middle of both feet, fixed them firmly to the cross. This was a more ordinary pain, and Jesus was now crucified, as were the two thieves on either side of Him. The whole process had taken only a few minutes.

Jesus was offered a drink of wine flavored with gall, which was designed to help lessen the pain, but He refused it, choosing instead to suffer his agony to the fullest. As He hung on the cross, the sky suddenly grew dark, and He began to experience a strange phenomenon.

The muscles of Christ's arms became rigid, his biceps strained; his fingers contracted. Cramps set in. The stomach muscles, respiratory mechanis, solar plexus were all affected. Air entered but could scarcely escape. He thirsted for fresh air. It is like a person with an intense asthma attack. Christ was asphyxiating. His lungs took in air but could no longer let it out.

But Jesus was not ready to die. There was only one way, however, one agonizing, excruciating way, that He could prevent death by asphyxiation, which is how the crucified always died.

Dr. Barbet, in his classic book, speaking as a medical man describes how Christ put off his death by asphyxiation through an almost superhuman effort. Christ used the nail through his feet as a fulcrum. By pressing on his open wound, He gradually lifted his body and some breathing became possible.

The purpose of this violent, painful struggle was to enable Jesus to speak his first words from the cross. They were very different from the curses and blasphemies that were usually screamed by those nailed to the cross. With the soldiers and the people jeering and mocking Him and challenging Him to save himself if He is God, Jesus looked up to heaven and said: "Father, forgive them; they do not know what they are doing" (Lk. 23:34).

Having spoken, his body began to slump forward again, the cramps returned, and the inexorable process of strangulation reoccurred, as it would many times over the three hours. And each time that Jesus wished to breathe or to speak, He would have to push down on the nail in his feet and pull on the nails in his wrists — aggravating those median nerves — until his raw, bruised shoulders were level with the crosspiece. In so doing, his head would continually hit against the cross, driving the thorns again and again into his scalp.

The seconds and minutes and hours dragged slowly by until it was nearly three o'clock. The soldiers had just raised to Jesus' lips a sponge dipped in common wine. After taking the wine, He said: "Now it is finished" (Jn. 19:30). The mission on which his Father had sent Him — the redemption of mankind — had been completed. What had been lost at the tree in the Garden of Eden had been won back on the tree of the cross. Jesus was the new Adam and his goal had been achieved.

The Savior would die, however, only when He willed it. Reaching back for his last ounce of strength, Jesus drew himself slowly and painfully up the cross and cried out in a loud voice: "Father, into your hands I commend my spirit" (Lk. 23:46). Then He bowed his head, slumped forward, and died. Strange things began to happen at that moment. The earth quaked, boulders split, and many tombs were opened, freeing the bodies of the saints. In the darkened city, one of the two great curtains hanging in the temple was torn in two from top to bottom. The events had a profound effect on the centurion who was keeping watch over Jesus, causing him to exclaim: "Clearly this was the Son of God" (Mt. 27:54).

Following the death of Christ, Joseph of Arimathea, a distinguished member of the Sanhedrin who had had no part in the vendetta against Jesus, went to Pilate and asked permission to take the body down from the cross and place it in a nearby tomb which he had built for himself. Pilate granted the permission but ordered a group of soldiers to go to Calvary to make sure that the three men were dead. When the soldiers reached the Skull Place, they broke the legs of the two thieves with an iron bar to hasten their death by asphyxiation. Jesus' legs they did not touch because He was already dead. But one soldier took his lance, thrust it into Jesus' side, "and immediately blood and water flowed out" (Jn. 19:34).

The flow of blood and water, Dr. Barbet has explained, indicated that the lance pierced the right auricle of the heart, in which blood was present, and the pericardium, a sac which encloses the heart and which contains a fluid that resembles water. Thus there can be no doubt that Jesus was dead when He was taken down from the cross.

The body of Jesus was then placed in the arms of his mother, who had sorrowfully witnessed the brutal murder of her Son. After a hundred pounds of spices had been applied to the body, it was wrapped in fine linen and laid in the tomb which had been cut out of rock. Joseph then rolled a huge stone across the entrance of the tomb and he, the Blessed Mother, and a few other loyal followers of Jesus walked slowly and sadly away.

I am the resurrection and the life. — John 11:25

EGO SUM RESURRECTIO ET VITA

Interior of present day Franciscan church at the site of the tomb of Lazarus.

photo by Paul J. Hayes

Chapter 8

The Greatest Miracle of All

> He was buried, and, of his own power, rose on the third day, raising us by his resurrection to that sharing in the divine life which is the life of grace. — Pope Paul VI, *Credo of the People of God.*

Jesus performed many miracles during his brief public life. Some of them were witnessed by hundreds and even thousands of people. Others only by his Apostles. But each extraordinary wonder provided still more evidence that Jesus Christ was God. When John the Baptist, from his prison cell, sent two disciples to ask Jesus if He was the Messiah, Jesus told them: "Go back and report to John what you hear and see: the blind recover their sight, cripples walk, lepers are cured, the deaf hear, dead men are raised to life, and the poor have the good news preached to them" (Mt. 11:4-5).

But the greatest miracle of all, and the crowning proof of Christ's divinity, was his resurrection from the dead. On this miracle rests the whole case for Christianity. St. Paul said it best some years later when he told the people of Corinth that "if Christ has not been raised, our preaching is void of content and your faith is empty, too" (1 Cor. 15:14).[1]

Jesus certainly gave plenty of advance notice that He would rise from the dead. On six different occasions, He predicted his resurrection. One of these predictions occurred in the district of Caesarea Philippi shortly after Peter, in response to a question by Christ, declared that "You are the Messiah, the Son of the living God" (Mt. 16:16). Jesus then commanded the Apostles not to tell anyone that He was the Messiah, saying that "the Son of Man must first endure many sufferings, be rejected by the elders, the high priests, and the scribes, and be put to death, and then be raised up on the third day" (Lk. 9:22).

On another occasion, as Jesus was going up to Jerusalem, He took the Apostles aside and told them that "the Son of Man will be handed over to the chief priests and the scribes. They will condemn Him to death and hand Him over to the Gentiles, who will mock Him

---

[1] In some cases, the Bible speaks of Christ as *being raised* from the dead, in other cases *rising* from the dead. This presents no problem, since Christ is both God and man.

and spit at Him, flog Him, and finally kill Him. But three days later, He will rise" (Mk. 10:33-34).

It is interesting to note that while the Apostles apparently paid little heed to Jesus' numerous predictions of his resurrection from the dead, the enemies of Christ took Him at his word. The Gospel tells us that on the day after the crucifixion, the chief priests and the Pharisees went to Pontius Pilate and asked that a guard be placed at the tomb of Christ, because "we have recalled that that imposter while He was still alive made the claim, 'After three days I will rise' " (Mt. 27:63). Pilate told them to secure the tomb themselves; so they sealed the stone across the entrance and placed a guard in front of it.

What actually happened on that Easter morning nearly 2,000 years ago? For this information, we must turn to the Gospels, which provide us with a reliable historical account of the momentous events which took place on the third day after the crucifixion and death of Jesus Christ.

It was shortly after sunrise on that Sunday when Mary Magdalene arrived at the tomb. Although she had set out with several other women to anoint the body of Jesus and give it a more fitting burial, Mary impatiently left her slow-moving companions and ran on ahead to the sepulchre. But what she saw as she reached it puzzled her and filled her with dismay. The huge stone had been rolled aside and the tomb was empty. Unable to comprehend what had happened, she decided to return to Jerusalem to inform the Apostles of her startling discovery.

While Mary Magdalene was on her way back to the city, the other women — including Mary, the mother of James, Salome, and Joanna — reached the sepulchre and saw that the stone had been rolled back. On entering the tomb, they saw an angel (two of them according to Luke) who said: "Do not be frightened. I know you are looking for Jesus the crucified, but He is not here. He has been raised, exactly as He promised. Come and see the place where He was laid. Then go quickly and tell his disciples: 'He has been raised from the dead and now goes ahead of you to Galilee, where you will see Him.' That is the message I have for you" (Mt. 28:5-7).

Matthew also informs us that while the women were returning to Jerusalem to tell the Apostles what the angel had said, "Suddenly, without warning, Jesus stood before them and said, 'Peace!' The women came up and embraced his feet and did Him homage. At this Jesus said to them, 'Do not be afraid! Go and carry the news to my brothers that they are to go to Galilee, where they will see Me' " (Mt. 28:9-10).

At about this time, the soldiers who had been guarding the tomb were relating their terrifying experience to the chief priests in Jerusalem. They told of a mighty earthquake, the dazzling appearance of the angel, and the wide open and empty tomb. The chief priests, after consulting with the elders, paid the soldiers a large sum of money and instructed them to say that the Apostles had stolen the body of Christ while the soldiers were sleeping. "The soldiers pocketed the money and did as they had been instructed. This is the story that circulates among the Jews to this very day" (Mt. 28:15).

Meanwhile, Peter and John had heard Mary Magdalene's incredible story and had sped to the tomb with her to see for themselves. What they saw was an empty grave with the burial cloths lying on the ground and the cloth which had covered the head rolled up in a place by itself. There was apparently something special about the condition of the burial wrappings that caused John to say that he "saw and believed" (Jn. 20:8). Some scholars suggest that Jesus had passed through the wrappings without disturbing them. In any case, the two men hurried back to the city to consult with the other disciples.

Mary Magdalene, however, remained at the tomb, weeping. As she wept, she stooped to peer inside and saw two angels. When they asked her why she was crying, Mary replied: "Because the Lord has been taken away, and I do not know where they have put Him" (Jn. 20:13). She had no sooner said this when she turned around and caught sight of Jesus, but did not recognize Him. Thinking He was the gardener, she asked if He knew what had happened to the body. Jesus then called her by name, and Mary exclaimed, "Rabbouni!" or Teacher. Christ instructed her not to cling to Him, "for I have not yet ascended to the Father. Rather, go to my brothers and tell them, 'I am ascending to my Father and your Father, to my God and your God' " (Jn. 20:16-17).

It is not difficult to imagine Mary's excitement as she raced back to tell the Apostles that Jesus was alive, that she had seen and talked to Him. How disappointed she must have been at the reaction of the disciples: "But when they heard that He was alive and had been seen by her, they refused to believe it" (Mk. 16:11).

Several hours had now passed since the empty tomb was discovered, but the only ones to whom Jesus had appeared were women, and no one believed their stories. Meanwhile, two of Jesus' disciples, despondent over the events of the past few days, were on their way to Emmaus, a village about seven miles from Jerusalem, when Jesus approached and began to walk with them. They did not recognize Him.

He asked them why they were sad and they replied that Jesus of Nazareth, "a prophet powerful in word and deed in the eyes of God and all the people" whom they had hoped "would set Israel free," had been put to death by the chief priests. (Lk. 24:19-21). The two men also told Jesus that they had heard reports of the empty tomb but that no one had seen the body.

Jesus then scolded them, saying: "What little sense you have! How slow you are to believe all that the prophets have announced! Did not the Messiah have to undergo all this so as to enter into his glory?" (Lk. 24:25-26). He proceeded then to interpret for them all the scriptural passages from the Old Testament which referred to Him. The lesson lasted to the end of the journey.

It was late in the day when Jesus and the two disciples arrived in Emmaus. They invited Him to stay with them and while they were eating, "He took bread, pronounced the blessing, then broke the bread and began to distribute it to them. With that their eyes were opened and they recognized Him; whereupon He vanished from their sight" (Lk. 24:30-31).

The disciples immediately got up and returned to Jerusalem, reaching the city after nightfall. Before they could report their own experience to the Apostles, they were greeted with, "The Lord has been raised! It is true! He has appeared to Simon" (Lk. 24:34). The Gospels give us no details of Jesus' appearance to Peter, but it is undoubtedly the same appearance which Paul sets first in his list of the resurrected Christ's appearances (1 Cor. 15:5).

All doubts were resolved, however, while they were discussing these things. For "even though the disciples had locked the doors of the place where they were for fear of the Jews, Jesus came and stood before them. 'Peace be with you,' He said" (Jn. 20:19). It is interesting to note the reaction of the Apostles, who obviously had paid no attention to Jesus' predictions that He would rise from the dead on the third day. They were panic-stricken because they thought He was a ghost.

Jesus showed them the wounds in his hands and feet and said, "Touch Me, and see that a ghost does not have flesh and bones as I do" (Lk. 24:39). However, it was not until they handed Him a piece of cooked fish, which He took and ate in their presence, that they believed that He had truly risen from the dead. One of the Apostles,

Thomas, was not present that night and he refused to believe that Jesus had risen unless he could put his fingers into the wounds. Eight days later, Jesus again appeared to the Apostles and Thomas was present. He instructed the doubter to probe the wounds, but Thomas could only respond: "My Lord and my God!" (Jn. 20:28).

So much for the events of that first Easter Sunday. There would seem to be sufficient evidence that Jesus Christ did in fact rise from the dead on the third day after his crucifixion and death on the cross. However, there are millions of people who neither believe that Jesus is God nor that He rose from the dead. Many of these are simply unaware of the historical facts. Others, who are aware of the historical facts, choose to deny them and to offer objections or other explanations for these events. Let us examine some of the major objections to the resurrection and see if they have any merit.

Many explanations have been advanced to account for the indisputable historical fact that on the third day after the death of Jesus, his corpse was missing from the tomb. We will consider four of them: (1) The Apostles stole the body. (2) Jesus really did not die. (3) The earthquake swallowed up the body. (4) Jesus truly rose from the dead.

The Apostles Stole the Body

This was the only explanation offered by the Jews at the time of Christ. They were faced with an empty tomb and a totally vanished corpse. The best story that they could come up with, as we noted earlier, was that the Apostles had stolen the body while the Roman soldiers were sleeping. The chief priests paid the guards to spread this story.

There are many flaws in this explanation. The most obvious one is that a sleeping person is in no position to witness anything. If the guards were asleep, how could they have seen the disciples steal the body? And why were they never punished for sleeping at their post? Second, Peter and John discovered while inspecting the tomb that the burial cloths were still there, a fact that apparently convinced them that the body had not been stolen (Jn. 20:6-8). What person or persons trying to steal the body would take the time to unwind the cloths or roll up the headpiece and place it to one side?

Third, we must consider the attitude of the Apostles at the time. Had they demonstrated the courage and daring that would be necessary to carry out such a venture against a heavily-guarded tomb? Far from it. They were frightened, disillusioned, and fearful for their lives. They were afraid to leave their hiding place, as John has pointed out.

Is it likely that these terrified and grief-stricken men could have planned such a coup? Who would lead them? Peter, who only a few hours earlier had denied Jesus three times? And even if they had been capable of engineering the theft, what could they gain by it? Would they champion the cause of Christ now that He was dead? Would they invite persecution and death over a broken corpse? It is not likely. They probably would have returned to the pursuits that filled their time before they met Christ.

Jesus Really Did Not Die

This explanation and the following one were offered long after the resurrection, notably by nineteenth-century German biblical commentators. This objection is also known as the "swoon theory." It contends that Christ was not really dead but only in a faint when He was taken down from the cross, that this horribly wounded Man somehow extricated himself from the sepulchre by moving the huge stone, eluded the guards, and rejoined his disciples on the third day.

No one who has read the preceding chapter, or Dr. Barbet's book, could for a single moment even allow the possibility of such a theory. The brutal beatings, the scourging, the crowning, the crucifixion itself, and finally the spear thrust which pierced the heart could only have resulted in death. Further confirmation came from the Roman soldier, who did not break the legs of Jesus for the simple reason that He had already died.

Second, the body of Christ passed through the hands of his mother, the holy women, Joseph of Arimathea, and Nicodemus before it was laid in the tomb. Can the proponents of this theory really believe that if there was a spark of life left in Jesus, his mother and his friends would not have exhausted every possible measure to fan it into a flame? They certainly never would have packed the body in a hundred pounds of spices, wrapped it in a suffocating sheet, and sealed it in an airless tomb. Indeed, if Jesus had survived his passion and the forty hours in the tomb, it would be a miracle comparable to the resurrection.

Finally, in the words of Leo J. Trese,[2] "it was not a limping, agonized Christ who greeted Mary Magdalene in the garden early Sunday morning. It was not an exhausted, stumbling Christ who walked with the disciples on the road to Emmaus. It was not a tor-

---

[2] Leo J. Trese, *Wisdom Shall Enter,* Notre Dame, Indiana: © Fides, 1954, p. 73

tured, pain-twisted Christ who appeared to the Apostles on Easter Sunday night."

The Earthquake Swallowed Up the Body

If this were true, why did not the earthquake also swallow up the burial cloths and the handkerchief that had been wrapped around the head of Jesus? And why did not Peter or John, or any of the many other persons who subsequently inspected the tomb, report any signs of a fissure that might have swallowed up the body?

Jesus Truly Rose from the Dead

Having shown that the Apostles could not have stolen the body, that Jesus really died on the cross, and that an earthquake could not have swallowed up the body, we are left with only one sensible explanation: Jesus Christ rose from the dead by his own power, and therefore He is God. However, we do not have to accept this explanation simply because the other three have been ruled out. There is considerable evidence which we can cite to convince any reasonable person that the resurrection actually occurred. Let us review this evidence under three separate categories: (1) The empty tomb. (2) The apparitions of Christ. (3) The transformation of the Apostles.

The Empty Tomb

As we noted earlier, the primary and undisputed fact of the whole incident is the empty tomb. No reasonable person can deny that the tomb was empty on Easter Sunday morning. The fact was mentioned by all the evangelists. It was attested to by Mary Magdalene, the holy women, and Peter and John, as well as the Roman soldiers who had been guarding the grave. There are only two plausible explanations: the Apostles stole the body, or Jesus rose from the dead. We have demonstrated that the first explanation is inadequate. Therefore, the second must be true.

The Apparitions of Christ

We know that Jesus appeared to his disciples many times during the forty days after his resurrection: "In the time after his suffering, He showed them in many convincing ways that He was alive, appearing to them over the course of forty days and speaking to them about the reign of God" (Acts 1:3). We have already mentioned his appearances to Mary Magdalene, the holy women, Peter, the two men on their way to Emmaus, and to the Apostles in Jerusalem on two occasions.

Jesus' other recorded appearances were to the disciples at the Sea of Tiberias (Jn. 21:1-23), in Galilee (Mt. 28:16-20), and on Mount Olivet (Lk. 24:50-51), and, according to St. Paul, to a group of five hundred, to James, and much later to Paul himself (1 Cor. 15:6-8).

The appearance at the Sea of Tiberias was noteworthy because Jesus performed a miracle. He was standing on the shore as a boat carrying seven of the Apostles approached. They had been out fishing all night but had caught nothing. "Cast your net off to the starboard side," He suggested, "and you will find something." The Apostles, although they did not know it was Jesus speaking, followed his instructions "and took so many fish they could not haul the net in" (Jn. 21:6).

John then recognized Jesus and told Peter, "It is the Lord!" On hearing this, the impulsive Peter dived into the water and swam to shore to greet Jesus. John says that "this marked the third time that Jesus appeared to the disciples after being raised from the dead" (Jn. 21:14).

The usual objection to the apparitions is that the disciples were having hallucinations, that they were seeing things. Shattered by the death of Christ, the theory goes, they wanted to believe that He was still alive, and over a period of time, their overactive imaginations transformed a myth into a reality.

There might be some substance to this theory if the appearances of Jesus had always taken place under a definite set of conditions, or in a certain area, or at the same time of day, or to a certain group of people — women, for example. But this is not the way it happened. Some of the apparitions occurred in Jerusalem, others at a distance of seventy miles away in Galilee. Some took place in the open, others behind closed doors. One was by the Sea of Tiberias, another on Mount Olivet. Jesus appeared to his friends in the morning, at noon, and at night. He appeared to individuals (both men and women), to small groups (two, three, seven), to larger groups (ten, eleven), and to a crowd (about five hundred). He showed them his wounded body, dined with them, and instructed them in their mission. To suggest that all of these people, in all of these places, at all of these times, were seeing things is to put a severe strain on one's own credulity.

Further, if the appearances of Jesus were imaginary on the part of those who claimed to have seen Him, why did the hallucinations last only forty days? Since when do deluded minds display such unanimity?

Finally, the disciples were not hallucination-prone fanatics. They were farmers, fishermen, and housewives. They knew that dead people stayed dead. How else can we explain the initial reaction of Mary Magdalene and the Apostles at the sight of Jesus? They showed surprise, disbelief, doubt, and even fear. Hardly the reactions of people hallucinating. The disciples were practical, down-to-earth people. They would not have believed that Christ had risen from the dead and appeared to them unless it actually happened.

The Transformation of the Apostles

Only the bodily resurrection of Christ could have transformed the Apostles from timid, frightened, and simple men to zealous, courageous, and articulate missionaries, who, along with their disciples, converted the hostile Roman Empire to Christianity in less than three-hundred years. As we pointed out earlier, men do not suffer persecution and death for a lie. The Apostles would never have preached the risen Christ openly and fearlessly, at the risk of their lives, unless they truly believed that Jesus had overcome death.

What else could have inspired the Apostles to submit willingly to torture and death? At his own request, Peter was crucified with his head downward. James the Less was hurled from the pinnacle of the temple. Andrew and Philip were also crucified. Bartholomew was flayed alive and then beheaded. Thomas suffered death by the sword. Paul was a man of tremendous courage. Rather than renounce Christ, he endured at least five floggings, one stoning, three shipwrecks, numerous imprisonments, hunger and thirst, cold and nakedness, before he was finally beheaded.

The Apostles could have denied Christ and escaped persecution and violent death. But none of them ever wavered. They preached the word of Christ, performed miracles in his name, and changed the course of human history. Millions upon millions of Christians have followed their example down through the centuries — cheerfully giving up their lives as a witness to the risen Christ. They offer the greatest testimony to Jesus' promise: "I am the resurrection and the life: whoever believes in Me, though he should die, will come to life; and whoever is alive and believes in Me will never die" (Jn. 11:25-26).

Frank Smoczynski Photo

"I have come to you to speak of salvation in Jesus Christ. I have come to proclaim it anew: to proclaim this message to you and with you and for you — and for all the people. As the successor of the apostle Peter speaking in the Holy Spirit, I too proclaim: 'There is salvation in no one else, for there is no other name under heaven given by which we must be saved.'" — *Pope John Paul II.*

Chapter 9

The Church and the Rock

> Our Lord made Simon Peter alone the rock and key-bearer of the Church, and appointed him shepherd of the whole flock. — Vatican II, *Dogmatic Constitution on the Church,* No. 22.

Jesus was here with revolutionary ideas. Love your enemies . . . Blessed are the meek . . . Fast in secret . . . Jesus meant these teachings for everyone, not merely for those who listened to Him. Yet, He himself wrote nothing. How was He to accomplish his purpose? He established a society, an organization to carry on his work.

Henry Ford and Thomas Edison knew that they were going to die. Before that time came, each had a well-organized corporation to carry on the work that he had started. The telephone company was not to be disbanded after Alexander Graham Bell died. No. A head and a vice-president, and other officers stepped into place. The function and authority of each department was determined.

Christ did a somewhat similar thing. He knew that He was going to die. Before that time He made plans for an organization to carry on his work in the world after his death. Without even going further, this seems to be the natural course of action.

Christ, when speaking of his society, referred to it as "the kingdom of God" or "the kingdom of heaven" because of its religious nature.

In establishing a society there are several points which require attention.

First of all, members would have to be recruited. Whether you are establishing a recreational group, or a charitable society to help the poor, or a literary group, you would begin by speaking of it and promoting it among those with whom you came in contact. Christ did the same thing for his society, the Church which He founded. He proclaimed it in towns, with friends, in the temple.

The next step would be to tell your associates of the object of your society. If it did not have a specific purpose, it would be a society in name only. Christ made clear to his little group what the purpose of his society, his Church, was. Just as Henry Ford and Thomas Edison organized corporations to carry on their work after them, Christ's society was to have a specific purpose. It was to carry on the work He had been doing: "As the Father has sent Me, so I send you" (Jn. 20:21).

The next logical step would be to choose a small group who would be reliable enough to form the backbone of the society: a committee, or, in the case of a corporation, a board of directors. Christ gathered such a group (Mt. 10:1-4), and trained them for over two years. They became the backbone of his society. Instead of calling them a board of directors, He called them his "flock." They were to have authority in the group: "If anyone does not receive you or listen to what you have to say, leave that house or town, and once outside it shake its dust from your feet. I assure you, it will go easier for the region of Sodom and Gomorrah on the day of judgment than it will for that town" (Mt. 10:14-15).

Just as a society has a president to make decisions and to see that things run smoothly, Christ appointed Peter as head of his Church: "I will entrust to you the keys of the kingdom of heaven" (Mt. 16:19).

Christ established a religious society, a Church, and only one Church. He always spoke of his Church, not churches — "I will build my Church" (Mt. 16:18); He compared it to a sheepfold, a kingdom, a city — words which imply unity of rule or administration.

Since we know that Christ founded a Church, and Christ was sent as a messenger from God, then the one Church which He founded is the one with which we ought to become associated. The question is to find which church is the one founded by Christ, since many today claim this distinction. The thing to do is look at some of the essential qualities of Christ's Church and to see if today some church still has those qualities. If so, that is the same Church which was founded by Christ.

The book called the New Testament is a reliable history book, and it is as such that we shall use it in discussing the subject at hand.

We know from the New Testament that Christ established an organization, a Church. This, He said, was going to continue after He was gone. If we want to find out which is his organization in the world today, among all those that claim to be such, we will have to see first what the characteristics of the Church were as Christ established it. We will have to look for the Church with those characteristics today. When this Church is found, we will have an unmistakable indication of the Church of Christ.

First we are going to look at one main feature of the Church which Christ established, namely, the fact that Christ determined that there was to be one supreme head in his organization.

Every properly operating organization has a head. The United States, for instance, has a president. If there were no such head to govern with authority, the nation would become an unwieldy mob, and confusion would be inevitable. Such a simple thing as a family, if it is to be well ordered, requires that someone preside. Children may not all do as they please. There must be someone to keep things in order.

Christ's Church is a society composed of human beings. It has a spiritual purpose, to be sure, but, being composed of men, it must have some leader, just as any well-ordered society. Can we attribute any less common sense to Christ than to human leaders, saying that He left his society, his Church, to be governed without a head?

"But," some may say, "I do not deny that the Church has a head. God himself is its ruler." This is merely side-stepping the true issue. Is not God the ruler of all governments? "By me kings reign, and lawgivers establish justice; by me princes govern, and nobles; all the rulers of earth" (Prv. 8:15-16).

God is the head of each country, and of every Christian family in it; but, nevertheless, there must always be in the country a *visible* head who represents God in the civil sphere. So also the Church, besides having an invisible head in heaven, must have a visible head on earth. The members of the Church are visible; why not also the head? The Church without a supreme ruler would be like an army without a general, a corporation without a president, a sheepfold without a shepherd, or like a human body without a head.

From the fact that a supreme head is necessary in any government, in any family, in any corporation, in any society composed of human beings we might expect likewise to find a head in the society which Christ founded. This would be true even if other evidence were lacking. But such evidence is not lacking. There is hardly a truth clearer in the New Testament than that Peter was made the supreme head of Christ's organization, the Church, and that Christ willed to have a supreme headship continue in the successors of Peter.

Christ was with his followers one day in northern Palestine, near the city of Caesarea Philippi. The distinguishing feature of the area was the temple of Augustus, which sat on a majestic rock and towered over the city. They were in sight of this rock when Jesus, aware that there had been much discussion about who He was among the people of the countryside, said to the Apostles: "And you, who do you say that I am?" Peter spoke up: "You are the Messiah, the Son of the living God!" Christ turned to Peter and addressed himself to him alone: "Blest are you, Simon, son of John! No mere man has revealed this to you, but my heavenly Father. I for my part declare to you, you are 'Rock,' and on this rock I will build my Church, and the jaws of death shall not prevail against it. I will entrust to you the keys of the kingdom of heaven. Whatever you declare bound on earth shall be bound in heaven; whatever you declare loosed on earth shall be loosed in heaven" (Mt. 16:15-20).

In this address of Christ to Peter there is no doubt that Peter was made supreme head of Christ's Church. There is, first of all, no doubt that it was Peter who was addressed. The account (by a very reliable eyewitness) says that it was. Christ leaves no doubt when He calls him Simon, son of John. Christ gives Peter's full name.

In the sentence "you are 'Rock,' and on this rock I will build my Church," strange as it may seem to us, there is a pun involved. In Aramaic, which was the language used, the word "peter" means "rock." This, incidentally, marked a change of name for Peter. Up to now he had been called Simon. In Biblical usage a change of name usually indicates a significant event; and so we might expect something of significance here. Actually that is the case.

"You are 'Rock' (Peter), and on this rock I will build my Church." Christ, standing before the foundation rock of the temple, promised to build his Church on Peter. Peter will be the foundation of his society.

Look at the next sentence: "I will entrust to you the keys of the kingdom of heaven." These words mean in our language: "I will give you supreme authority over my Church." "Kingdom of heaven" simply means Church here. We know this because often Christ referred to his Church as the "kingdom of heaven." It may seem to us like a roundabout way of saying things, but to the oriental mind there is no difficulty; it was easily understood. To give one "the keys" to a house or a city has always symbolized the granting of authority. Thus, a man is presented with the keys of a city. If a proprietor of a house, when leaving for the summer, says to a friend, "Here are the keys of my house," this would really mean, "You have full charge of my house. You may invite or exclude whom you wish. Until I come back, you take my place." In the time of Christ, particularly among the Hebrew people with whom we are dealing, keys were definitely an emblem of jurisdiction. To say that a man had received the keys of a city was equivalent to saying that he was placed in charge of the city. In the Bible, whenever the expression is used, it means just that. Therefore the meaning is: "I will give you complete authority over my Church."

What about the sentence "Whatever you declare bound on earth shall be bound in heaven..."? Peter is promised the supreme power to bind his subjects by laws and precepts, and to free their souls from spiritual ties such as sins or censures. True, the power of binding and loosing was given to the other Apostles, but it is here promised to Peter individually to show that Peter possesses it in a special way. Peter's precepts and prohibitions (for that is the meaning in common language of binding and loosing) are to be laws divinely sanctioned. In view of the previous two sentences we have seen, there is no doubt that Peter alone was to have the supreme authority in Christ's Church.

In light of all we have said, the address to Peter in our modern everyday language would run something like this:

"You are a rock, a foundation stone, Peter, and upon this foundation I will build my Church... I will give you supreme authority over my Church, and your precepts and prohibitions I myself will back up."

In reading the passage slowly and thoughtfully, there is no doubt that the supreme authority of Christ's Church is in Peter's hands. It is noteworthy that many modern Protestant theologians frankly admit the same interpretation, as do Catholic theologians.

There is another event in which we can see also that Peter is given the supreme authority in Christ's organization. To understand this incident, it will be well to glance for a moment at the background of the setting and at the kind of people involved. The event has to do with Christ, Peter, and some of the other followers of Christ. All lived in Palestine, most of which was rural territory, and sheep-raising was one of the main occupations. Much of the Middle East is the same to a great extent even today. In that land sheep can often be seen scattered over the bare hills, and at night the shepherd gathers them into enclosures, opening the door in the morning to let them out. At night he even sleeps with them in a hut or cave in the mountain. If one strays, he brings it back. Day and night the shepherd takes care of all the needs of the sheep; he feeds them and knows them all; he alone is their master. It is his duty to govern his flock, watch over it and protect it, and punish the obstinate sheep.

With all this in mind we can better appreciate this incident of

CHRIST ESTABLISHED HIS CHURCH

for all men / for all times

Christ gave supreme authority to Peter, the first Pope

| "Feed my lambs, feed my sheep." (Jn. 21:15 ff.) | "Whatever you declare bound on earth shall be bound in heaven." (Mt. 16:19) | "You are 'Rock,' and on this rock I will build my Church." (Mt. 16:18) | "I will entrust to you the keys of the kingdom of heaven." (Mt. 16:19) |

The Popes, as Peter's successors exercise supreme spiritual authority

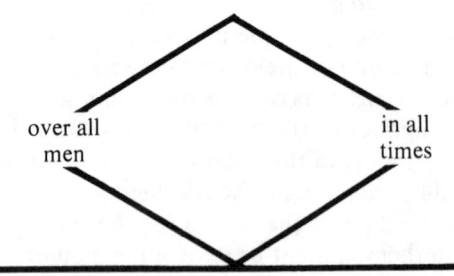

over all men / in all times

"WHERE PETER IS, THERE IS THE CHURCH"

Christ and Peter. It is by the Sea of Tiberias; there are seven of Christ's friends on the shore, and He comes to them, picks out Peter and asks him: "Simon, son of John, do you love Me more than these?" Peter answers that he does, and Christ says to him, "Feed my lambs." To the question again: "Simon . . . do you love Me?" Peter again replies in the affirmative, and Christ repeats, "Tend my sheep." Christ a third time asks the question of Peter (perhaps because Peter had denied Him three times): "Do you love Me?" and, after being answered by Peter, says to him: "Feed my sheep" (Jn. 21:15-17).

To us the incident seems to be hidden in strange language, but we must remember that it was a pastoral country; the shepherd and his sheep were a common sight. Remember, too, that Christ frequently made use of his surroundings in his conversation. He used this language before when He said He was the shepherd and his followers were his flock, his sheep. He was understood, for the image was from the people's everyday lives. Today in America we should rather understand a man telling his friend, "You are to be the head of this corporation." Put yourself in the country and time of Christ, and there the most natural thing would be to speak not of a "head of my concern" but a "shepherd of my flock."

The meaning, then, is that Peter is to do everything with reference to Christ's flock that a shepherd did for his sheep. In other words, he is a complete master, watches over it, protects it, rules it.

This picturesque way of expressing the meaning "to direct," "to rule," "to govern," by the expression "to be a shepherd over" is not strange, for it is often found not only in the New Testament but in secular literature of the time.

Peter was to be all this to Christ's lambs and sheep, Christ's flock. And we know that by Christ's "flock" is meant his followers, the members of his Church, for He often refers to his Church in this way.

Christ has before called himself the Good Shepherd, and He also referred to his followers, his Church, as his sheep or his flock. Now He says to Peter: "Feed my lambs, feed my sheep."

Peter is to do all for Christ's flock that a shepherd was known to do for his sheep. Peter is to take the place of Christ with reference to his flock. He is to be the head of Christ's spiritual flock, in a word, to be the Vicar of Christ. The figurative language was understood well: "You, Peter, are to be the supreme head of my organization."

The fact that Peter was to be head of Christ's Church is borne out when we read of his place in the early Church after he was given the position. The Acts of the Apostles is a book of the New Testament relating events of the early days of the Church. As we have seen, it is thoroughly reliable history. Here we see a picture of Peter acting as supreme head of the Church. In the question of choosing a successor to Judas, Peter alone speaks (Acts 1:15-26); Peter pronounces judgment on Ananias and Sapphira (Acts 5:1-10); and Peter presides over the Council of Jerusalem. The latter incident is significant because great dissension and controversy had arisen over whether Gentile Christians should be compelled to undergo the Mosaic practice of circumcision. After much debate, Peter took the floor and said: "Brothers, you know well enough that from the early days God selected me from your number to be the one from whose lips the Gentiles would hear the message of the gospel and believe." Having reminded his fellow Christians of his supreme authority, Peter said that it was not necessary for the Gentiles to undergo circumcision, and "at that the whole assembly fell silent" (Acts 15:1-12). Thus was Peter recognized as the supreme head of the early Church by his contemporaries.

The Church which Christ organized was to last to the end of time, as He himself said, and so certainly whatever is essential to it in teaching or organization must likewise last for all time.

The supreme headship of Peter was clearly an essential part of Christ's plan. This we see from the fact that Peter alone was the "foundation" of the Church, the "key-bearer," the supreme teacher, the one shepherd of the flock. Certainly the foundation is to last as long as the building; the key-bearer must last while there is a kingdom; a supreme teacher as long as there are people to be taught; a supreme shepherd as long as there is a flock. The mission which Christ gave to Peter and his fellow Apostles was concerned with all nations and all mankind. But Peter and his associates were to die; they were destined to pass away with their generation, while their mission was to continue. The only conclusion is that this office of supreme headship was to last as long as Christ's Church.

Christ promised and actually appointed a supreme head over his Church, and that position was to last to the end of time, that is, there were to be successors to this position.

What church today fulfills this requirement? Only one — the Catholic Church.

Down through the ages no person ever claimed to be the successor in Peter's office, nor was anyone ever acknowledged as the successor in Peter's office, except the Bishop of Rome, the head of the Catholic Church. As a matter of fact, today there is only one Church in the whole world which claims to have a successor in the function of Peter. That is the Catholic Church. The Pope alone claims this position.[1] No other religions claim it, nor did their founders. Men have claimed themselves prophets; some have claimed to be God. But no one claims the function of Peter's successor except the Pope. If the Pope is not in fact the successor to Peter's office, our only conclusion must be that there is no successor in the office of Peter. No one else even claims it. But this is impossible for, as we have seen, Christ determined that there should always be one supreme head in his Church, Peter and his successors.

To a sincere inquirer one conclusion presents itself: only the Catholic Church satisfies the requirements with respect to this essential characteristic of Christ's Church.

[1] Pope Paul VI stated this position very clearly when he told a meeting of the World Council of Churches in Geneva on June 10, 1969, that "our name is Peter." See the full text of the Pope's address in the *1970 Catholic Almanac*, p. 114.

Mass in catacombs — site of place of liturgical worship during persecutions and martyrdoms.

photo by Edward J. Hayes

Chapter 10

Where Is Christ's Church Today?

> In the Creed Christians confess their belief in the one, holy, catholic, and apostolic Church. These four marks simultaneously describe the Church and identify its mission. — *National Catechetical Directory, No. 72.*

In our everyday life, signs and symbols play a large part in our actions. For instance, a red traffic light. It does not *say* "stop," rather, it *means* "stop." When we observe some sign, the sensible thing, and, indeed, often the only safe thing to do, is to pay attention to it. What does this have to do with our subject? We are going to speak of a group of signs which are often overlooked; signs which are significant in our lives, yet which often go unheeded.

We know that Christ established a Church, and wants everyone to belong to it. Yet, look around your city and you will notice how many different religions there are. As a matter of fact, there are over two hundred kinds of religions in the United States alone. Christ wants you and me to belong to the one Church which He founded. You may say: "But how can I know which one is the Church Christ founded?" When Christ said that He wanted us to belong to his Church, He gave us some signs or marks by which we might know that Church. The police may be given a certain set of marks by which they can identify a criminal, for example, that he has blond hair, is six feet tall, two-hundred pounds, has a scar on his left cheek. These are marks of the man they are looking for, and if they come across a man they think may be the one they want, but upon closer examination they see that he does not have all the marks, they know that he is not the one they are seeking and that they must continue their search. It is the same in looking for Christ's Church. We can determine the characteristics of the Church He founded. Then we can compare churches today to see if they possess these marks. We are going to observe a set of marks or characteristics by which Christ indicated that we might identify his Church at any time. There are four such marks which we shall investigate: unity, holiness, universality and apostolicity.

The marks of the true Church of Christ are like the needles of so many compasses, all pointing without fail in the right direction.

UNITY

"We believe that the Church founded by Jesus Christ, and for which He prayed, is indefectibly one in faith, worship and the bond of hierarchical communion. — Pope Paul VI, *Credo of the People of God*.

Common sense alone convinces us that God planned unity for his Church. How could God, who is all truthful, assert to some that there is only one person in God, to others that there are three; to some that Christ is God, to others that He is only man; to some that hell exists, to others that it does not?

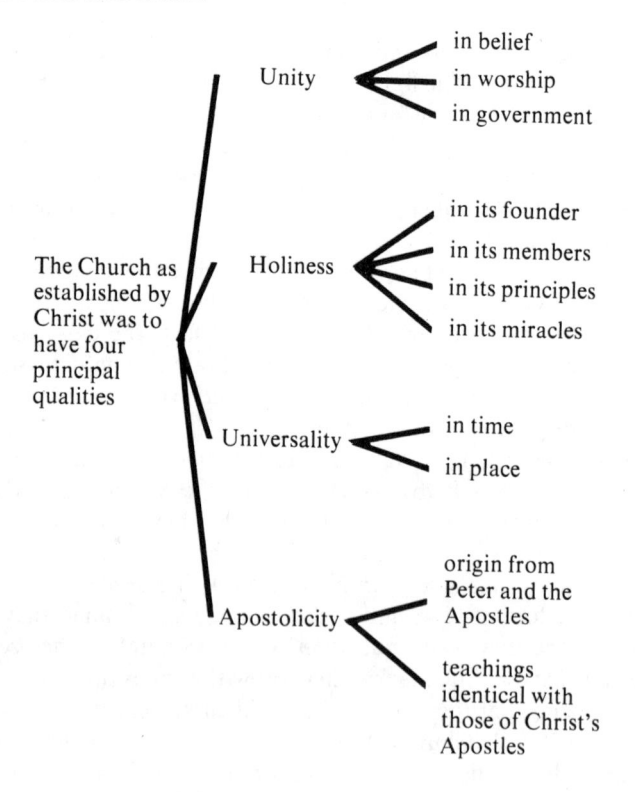

The Church as established by Christ was to have four principal qualities:

- Unity
  - in belief
  - in worship
  - in government
- Holiness
  - in its founder
  - in its members
  - in its principles
  - in its miracles
- Universality
  - in time
  - in place
- Apostolicity
  - origin from Peter and the Apostles
  - teachings identical with those of Christ's Apostles

There is perfect harmony in the laws which govern the physical world. There is a marvelous unity in our planetary system. Each planet moves in its own orbit with a precision far beyond that of any human instrument. Why should there not be harmony and unity in that spiritual world, the Church which God gave us through Christ?

In founding his Church, Christ determined that it should have unity of government, unity of belief, and unity of worship. Christ said, "There shall be one flock then, one shepherd" (Jn. 10:16).

In every place where Christ speaks for his organization, it is obvious that there is to be unity. For instance, He compares it to a seed planted, which will grow into a tree with its limbs spread everywhere. But there is always unity: one seed, one trunk, one tree.

Christ, looking down from on high upon the world today, would have all nations and all individuals united within the fold of the one Church He established in the world. Looking at the bigotry and friction existing all too often in our modern world, Christ seems to say once again: "How often have I yearned to gather your children, as a mother bird gathers her young under her wings, but you refused me?" (Mt. 23:37).

Christ came to earth, established his Church, and died with the concept of unity—"that all may be one" (Jn. 17:21) — as an underlying principle of his work on earth. ". . . Jesus would die for the nation — and not for this nation only, but to gather into *one* all the dispersed children of God" (Jn. 11:51-52).

There can be no doubt that Christ, in founding his Church, intended it to have unity. Indeed, on the very evening before He died Christ prayed: ". . . for those who will believe in Me through their word, that all may be *one* as You, Father, are in Me, and I in You" (Jn. 17:20-21). Christ, then, who was sent by God, was praying that the Church He established would have unity. Why? Christ gives the answer why He wants his Church to have unity: "I pray that they may be one in us, that the world may believe that You sent Me" (Jn. 17:21).

From the very organization which Christ set up we can see unity. All his "flock" were to be subjected to the one governing body of the Apostles under Peter. Thus, there was to be unity in the ruling and government of the organization.

There is the story told of a noted American scientist who was an outstanding intellectual, and whose specialty was the study of insects. He was a convert to the Catholic Church. On one occasion, when asked why he became a Catholic, he answered:

"Bugs!"

"Bugs!" his amazed inquirer asked, "Why bugs?"

"No matter how tiny the insect," the professor answered, "I have found that the God who made it provided one organism that controlled all parts and kept them working together. I believe that when

He was making so big a thing as the Church He would do as much for it. I know of only one Church with such a single controlling organism. That is why I became a Catholic."

From whatever approach, we come to the same conclusion: Christ, sent by God, established a Church which was to have the mark of unity. Certainly to the inquirer the Catholic Church does stand out in this characteristic.

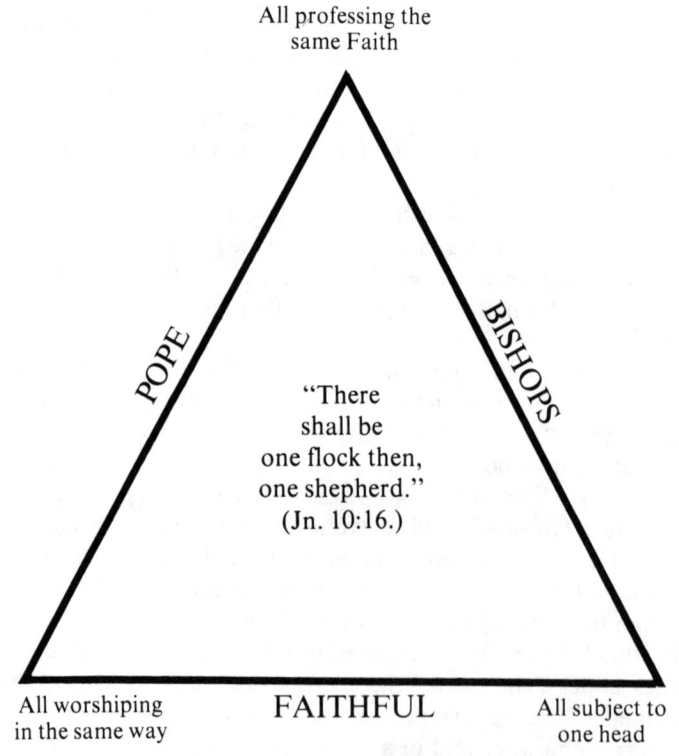

```
                    All professing the
                       same Faith

                           /\
                          /  \
                         /    \
                        /      \
                   POPE/        \BISHOPS
                      /          \
                     /  "There     \
                    /   shall be    \
                   / one flock then, \
                  /   one shepherd."  \
                 /      (Jn. 10:16.)    \
                /_____\
  All worshiping       FAITHFUL        All subject to
  in the same way                       one head
```

Wherever a Catholic goes in the whole world, whether he enters a church in Hong Kong or in Alaska, in New York or Cairo, the same doctrine will be preached, the same sacraments will be administered, the same Mass will be celebrated, and the Church will be subject to the same Holy Father at Rome.

The Catholic Church now numbers over six hundred million members, the largest single religious organization in the world today. Among her members there are those of every race and tongue, having different temperaments and diverse national traditions. But they are all bound together by the strong bond of a common faith. They believe the same doctrines, receive the same sacraments, and recognize the same spiritual head. The unity is not in name only but is a reality. A Catholic may attend Mass, receive the sacraments, and assist at the devotions in any Catholic church in the world, and, apart from the language difference, feel as much at home as if he were worshiping in his own parish church.

Every member is very closely united to the one spiritual head as the members of the human body are united to the head. The Catholics of each parish are subject to their immediate pastor; each pastor is subject to his bishop; and each bishop to the head of the Catholic Church, the Pope.

The facts are striking and inspiring: six hundred million Catholics, all believing in the same truths, all united under the same ruler, all with the same essential worship. Six hundred million Catholics all over the world recognizing the same Pope at Rome as the spiritual leader as their fellow Catholics through nineteen centuries.

Such a unity of doctrine, worship and government cannot be claimed by other churches today. There are countless sects, each differing fundamentally among themselves, and each denomination having splits within itself. Member differs from member in belief in the same religion; none has a supreme head. Non-Catholic sects have no unity in their government, for there is no supreme unified rule. New churches are constantly breaking away from each denomination. There is no unity in their worship, for this varies from place to place. Their belief shows no unity, for each may believe what he wants according to their principle of private interpretation.

In unity of belief, of worship, and of government the Catholic Church fulfills the standards set by Christ. This is one reason why a Catholic has a feeling of security in his Church.

The disunity which has resulted from the splits away from the Church of Christ down through the years is a source not of animosity but of concern and anxiety to any thinking Catholic. A Catholic has deep convictions that Christ established one Church in the world as a means of bringing spiritual life and, ultimately, eternal life to its members. The outlook of a sincere Catholic is not one of bitterness towards those who do not share this same conviction, but is reflected in the words of Christ himself: "I am the vine, you are the branches. He who lives in Me and I in him, will produce abundantly, for apart from Me you can do nothing" (Jn. 15:5). And a Catholic would welcome the day when all might harmoniously be reunited by the bond of unity in Faith, hoping and praying two thousand years after Saint Paul first uttered these words: "May God, the source of all patience and encouragement, enable you to live in perfect harmony with one another according to the spirit of Christ Jesus, so that with one heart and voice you may glorify God, the Father of our Lord Jesus Christ" (Rom. 15:5-6).

The same hope was in the minds of the bishops of Vatican II when they asserted that "promoting the restoration of unity among all Christians is one of the chief concerns of the Second Sacred Ecumenical Synod of the Vatican" *(Decree on Ecumenism,* No. 1). Pope Paul, too, made the position of the Catholic Church very clear:

"We want to give our assurance, once again, that we have an attentive, reverent interest in the spiritual movements connected with the problem of unity, which are stirring up vital and noble religious sentiments in various individuals, groups, and communities. With love and reverence we greet all these Christians, in the hope that we may promote together, even more effectively, the cause of Christ and the unity which He desired for his Church, in the dialogue of sincerity and love."[1]

HOLINESS

"The Church, whose mystery is being set forth by this Sacred Synod, is believed to be indefectibly holy. — Vatican II, *Dogmatic Constitution on the Church,* No. 39.

The Church which Jesus instituted was holy. Some may remark: "I can see how a person can be holy, but for a society to be holy, that is something which is not very tangible or concrete."

By saying that Christ's Church must be holy, we mean three things: holiness in its members, holiness in its principles, and miracles as a sign of holiness.

In order to see that the Church which is Christ's must be holy, we need not search far. If a society has a holy purpose it must be a holy organization. We judge whether an association is good or bad from its purpose. We judge a gang of thieves as bad, because their main purpose is to steal. We judge a group of policemen as good, for their main purpose is noble.

[1] Pope Paul VI, "Paths of the Church" *(Ecclesiam Suam),* August 6, 1964.

The nobler and better are the ends of any group or society, the nobler and better we adjudge the group itself. Should it be any different in the case of the society, the Church, which Christ founded? Its primary purpose is the noblest and holiest we can think of — the everlasting salvation of its members. The Church which Christ established must have truly holy principles, and so the members of it, as a general rule, will strive toward holiness.

Moreover, Christ's Church was to have miracles as signs of its holiness. Christ promised that there would be miracles in his Church at all times: "Signs like these will accompany those who have professed their faith: they will use my name to expel demons, they will speak entirely new languages, they will be able to handle serpents, they will be able to drink deadly poison without harm, and the sick upon whom they lay their hands will recover" (Mk. 16:17-18). The words of Christ put no limits on the time; miracles are promised throughout the existence of the Church. Any church whose faith is not accompanied by miracles cannot be the true Church of Christ.

God seems to say to those in his Church: "Be holy, for I, the Lord, your God, am holy" (Lv. 19:2).

We are invited to lead holy lives by the very fact that we bear the name of "Christian"; we can be proud of this title, but we must not forget that it carries with it a corresponding obligation. We ought to have something in common with Him whom we profess to follow. In our life we must reflect his character and virtues. The Church which He founded was to help us to do this.

To an impartial observer certainly the Catholic Church fulfills the requirements of holiness, demanded by Christ for his Church.

First of all, its founder Christ was eminently holy. That Christ founded the Catholic Church needs no proof. A glance at history is enough. No one denies it.

Second, the Church is holy in the lives of innumerable faithful and especially those heroic souls whom she has led to sanctity. Saints are saints because they conformed their lives so perfectly to Catholic teaching. Any open-minded inquirer will admit that, of those who follow not only the commandments but the counsels of Christ, who go all the way with Christ's standards, there are an amazing number of Catholics. There are thousands of men and women throughout the world who give up their lives to practice poverty, chastity, obedience and self-denial to serve God in the fold of the Catholic Church.

In the United States alone, for example, there are hundreds of Catholic religious institutions for men and women. There are tens of thousands of priests, to say nothing of brothers and sisters, in the United States who are now devoting their lives in the service of Christ.

Among her members the Church numbers those intrepid men and women who, abandoning homes and families, annually go forth to foreign lands to preach the Gospel. Their worldly possessions are often limited to a few books and clothes and not infrequently their lives are in danger. Small wonder that the bishops of Vatican II had such high praise for those "priests, religious, and laymen who are prepared to undertake mission work in their own countries or abroad, and who are endowed with the appropriate natural dispositions, character, and talents. These souls are marked with a special vocation. Sent by legitimate authority, they go out faithfully and obediently to those who are far from Christ. They are set apart for the work to which they have been called as ministers of the gospel. . . ." *(Decree on the Missionary Activity of the Church,* No. 23).

The Vatican Council might have been referring to men like Maryknoll Bishop James E. Walsh, who was a prisoner of the Red Chinese from 1958 to 1970. When a nun served him meat on his first day of freedom, the 79-year-old prelate reminded her that it was Friday. She told him that Catholics were no longer required to abstain from meat on Friday. "Meat wasn't often served," he said, referring to his long years in Communist captivity, "but if it was on a Friday I abstained."[2] What an extraordinary sacrifice for a man in his seventies to abstain from meat if one of those rare occasions on which it was served happened to fall on a Friday!

But Bishop Walsh is an extraordinary man. He once wrote from China, where he first went as a young priest in 1918:

"The task of a missioner is to go to a place where he is not wanted, to sell a pearl, whose value, although of great price, is not recognized, to people who are determined not to accept it even as a gift. . . .

"To accomplish this he need not be a saint but he must come close to passing for one. And in order to achieve this hoax he must do so many things that a saint does, that it becomes for him a serious question if the easiest way is not simply to be a saint in the first place and be done with it."[3]

---

[2] Germaine Swain, "From Bamboo Curtain . . . To Space Age," *The (Boston) Pilot,* July 18, 1970, p. 1.

[3] "Pilot Profile," *The (Boston) Pilot,* July 18, 1970, p. 3.

Look at the hundreds of extraordinary saints in the Church — men and women, boys and girls, religious and lay, from all walks of life. There has never been a century in which there were not outstanding saintly souls like St. Agnes, St. Augustine, St. Francis of Assisi, St. Catherine of Siena, St. Thomas More, St. Isaac Jogues, St. John Bosco, St. Teresa of Lisieux, St. Frances Xavier Cabrini, and St. Pius X. All of them fulfilled the requirements for sainthood: martyrdom or heroic practice of virtues and miracles brought about by prayers asking for their intercession with God.

In 1970, Pope Paul proclaimed sainthood for 40 English and Welsh men and women who were martyred for their faith during the Anglican Reformation, and for Maria Soledad Torres Acosta of Spain, founder of the Congregation of the Sisters Servants of Mary, who died in 1887 and was beatified in 1950. "In the case of Maria Soledad, her life can be summed up in two great words: humility and charity," the Pope said. "She appears to have been the first to have systematically conceived a congregation to bring assistance to the sick in their own homes."[4] Among those present at the two-hour ceremony in St. Peter's Basilica were five Spaniards who had been miraculously cured of various ailments after praying to the new saint.

Millions of martyrs have died for Christ in the Catholic Church. In many parts of the world the soil is soaked with the blood of Catholics, priests and people alike, who died for their Faith at the hands of Communist oppressors.[5]

Yes, we have in the Catholic Church modern martyrs for the Faith of Christ. Multiply the martyrs through the centuries and you have a picture of the Catholic Church. Remember Christ's prediction: "They will harry you as they harried me" (Jn. 15:20). Where else among the number of churches claiming to be Christ's is this so clearly fulfilled but in the Catholic Church?

Christ promised to his Church the gift of miracles: "Signs like these will accompany those who have professed their faith . . . the sick upon whom they lay their hands will recover" (Mk. 16:17-18). The gift of miracles has been with the Church at all times. We have already

[4] Barry James, United Press International, January 25, 1970.
[5] See, for example, such books as Albert Galter's *The Red Book of the Persecuted Church,* Fr. Walter Ciszek's *With God in Russia,* and Fr. Harold Rigney's *Four Years in a Red Hell.*

noted that incontestable miracles are required for sainthood. They are God's way of confirming that the potential saint is already in heaven with Him. Look at the accounts from such shrines as Lourdes, the French town in the Pyrenees where the Blessed Mother appeared to Bernadette eighteen times between February 11 and July 16, 1858. She told the young peasant girl to dig in the earth, and water came forth. It was only a trickle at first, but the spring now flows at the rate of 32,000 gallons a day.

The once tiny village now attracts more than three million visitors a year, over 40,000 of them sick and dying. Those in the last stages of some fatal disease are hoping and praying that God will bless them, as He has more than 5,000 others over the past century, by restoring them to health. The most impressive thing about Lourdes, apart from the cures, is the Medical Bureau. Established in 1882, the bureau is run by doctors for doctors. In the summer of 1969, over 2,000 doctors, specialists, and professors took part in the medical work at Lourdes. They were men of all religions and of no religion. This has been true from the outset and is of major significance because it rules out the argument that the study and medical confirmation of cures is under the domination of the Church.

The long, involved, and scrupulous procedure that leads to the certification of a cure is worth reviewing here. First, no sick person is accepted at Lourdes without a medical certificate from his own doctor, stating the nature and present condition of the disease. When an alleged cure takes place, the patient is immediately examined by the doctors who are registered at the Medical Bureau at that time. They are primarily interested in three things: (1) Did the disease really exist? (2) Can it be cured? (3) Is there a natural explanation for the cure?

If, after an exhaustive discussion of the case, it appears to have some validity, the doctors send the patient home, put him under observation of a physician in his area, and invite him to come back in a year. The second examination the following year is even more rigorous than the first. The patient's entire medical history is intensively scrutinized by doctors who will be risking their professional reputations when they either sign or refuse to sign the final report. But if after all this investigation the doctors believe that a supernatural cure has taken place, they send the complete record to the International Medical Commission on Lourdes for further study. This group, located in Paris, was set up to act as a check on the Medical Bureau at Lourdes. It conducts its own thorough evaluation of the case and then simply declares (or fails to declare): "We find no natural or scientific explanation of this cure."

If this commission can find no natural explanation for the cure, the case is forwarded to a canonical commission in the diocese of the person cured, where the strict standards for a miracle set down by Pope Benedict XIV must be met. The severity of these conditions should be evident from the fact that of thousands of cures recognized by the medical profession, only a tiny percentage have been declared miraculous by Church authorities. The conditions to be satisfied are: (1) The disease must have been serious and either impossible or nearly impossible to cure. (2) No medication could have been used, or if it had been, it had no effect on the disease. (3) The cure must have been instantaneous and perfect. (4) There must have been no crisis preceding the actual cure. (5) The disease must never appear again. Only when all of these criteria have been fulfilled can the bishop of the diocese pronounce the cure miraculous.

On May 18, 1955, Theodor Cardinal Innitzer of Vienna, Austria, decreed that "the sudden healing of Fraulein Edeltraud Fulda, at Lourdes on August 12, 1950, from severe Morbus Addison which for fully thirteen years had defied every medical remedy, is a miraculous cure, incapable of natural explanation, and that it must be attributed to an especial intervention of God, at the intercession of Our Blessed Lady of Lourdes."[6]

On May 21, 1965, Archbishop Marc Lallier of Marseilles, France, published a decree declaring that the recovery of a young woman from osteomyelitis was a miracle. For 12 years the woman, Juliette Tamburini, 29, had suffered from the disease and numerous treatments and operations had failed to arrest it. Her ailing leg was cured instantaneously, however, when it was treated with water at Lourdes in 1959.[7]

The remarkable events at Lourdes have been a source of fascination for more than a century. Some of the cures can only be described as spectacular, such as the instantaneous curing of paralysis, tubercular peritonitis, multiple sclerosis, and blindness. But the most stunning of all is a cancer cure. Ruth Cranston, in her book, *The Miracle of Lourdes,* from which much of the preceding information was obtained, explains why:

[6]Edeltraud Fulda, *And I Shall Be Healed,* New York: © Simon and Schuster, 1961, p. 307.
[7]"Lourdes Cure of Woman Called Miracle by Church," *New York Times,* May 22, 1965, p. 34.

"The instantaneous or even rapid cure of cancer by means of natural causes is impossible. For, as the doctors of the Medical Bureau point out, in this disease not merely the original cancerous organ is involved. The cancerous cells rapidly invade surrounding tissues, the disease gets into the blood and the lymphatic system, and swiftly penetrate the whole organism. It is thus *the entire body*, not merely the initial organ, which in a miraculous cure is instantly healed—an accomplishment medically and biologically impossible."[8]

A recent example of such an "impossible" cure involved a three-year-old Scottish girl who was brought to Lourdes in 1968. The child, Frances Burns, was suffering from a virulent abdominal cancer which had already taken one kidney and was causing rapid disintegration of the bones in her cheeks and skull. When she was conscious, her wasted little body was convulsed with excruciating pain. "The case had gone beyond surgery," according to her physician, Dr. Stuart Mann of the Royal Hospital for Sick Children in Glasgow, "and in this little girl there were all the signs of impending death."

Frances' mother, Deirdre Burns, was not expecting a cure when she took her daughter to Lourdes. In fact, after allowing her only one immersion in the waters, Mrs. Burns took Frances back home again "because I wanted her to die in Glasgow."

During the first two days back in the Royal Hospital, Frances' condition worsened and death was imminent. "And then suddenly one morning she was well. She sat up and began to eat. Her bones began to grow back and as far as anyone could tell, the cancer had vanished. Now Frances Burns is six and, says her mother, 'she doesn't even catch cold any more.' "[9]

In the Catholic Church there have always been numerous men and women whose extraordinary holiness of life is unquestionable, and God has testified to it by undeniable miracles. There have always been miracles in the Church just as there have always been saints in the Church.

In speaking of the holiness of the Catholic Church, we by no means intend to say that all Catholics are holy. We cannot close our eyes to the fact that many, far from living up to the standards set by the Church, are rather sources of scandal. Christ himself warned: "Scandals will inevitably arise, but woe to him through whom they

---

[8]Ruth Cranston, *The Miracle of Lourdes*, New York: © Popular Library, 1955, p. 140 fn.
[9]Edward Behr, "Lourdes: The Town Faith Built," *Boston Sunday Globe*. September 26, 1971, p. A-21.

come" (Lk. 17:1). The Church should be judged by those who live by her rules, not by those who refuse to conform. Such would be like making a judgment on a university by observing students who had failed.

It is true, too, that in the sixteenth century, there was a need for a reform in some quarters of the Church. But was it to be accomplished by a force inside or outside the Church? The proper way was to do it from within. Major reforms were in fact initiated at that time by the Council of Trent (1545-1563). In our own century, reforms have been implemented in accordance with directives issued by the Second Vatican Council (1962-1965). The Fathers of Vatican II saw clearly the need for reform:

"Christ summons the Church, as she goes her pilgrim way, to that continual reformation of which she always has need, insofar as she is an institution of men here on earth. Therefore, if the influence of events or of the times has led to deficiencies in conduct, in Church discipline, or even in the formulation of doctrine (which must be carefully distinguished from the deposit of faith itself), these should be appropriately rectified at the proper moment" (*Decree on Ecumenism,* No. 6).

The conclusion of an honest inquirer must be that the Catholic Church on several points fulfills the characteristics that Christ indicated would distinguish his Church.

The herald of everlasting good news to the whole world, to every nation and race, language and people. —Revelation 14:6

Chapter 11

Christ's Church—
Universal and Apostolic

UNIVERSALITY

This characteristic of universality which adorns the People of God is a gift from the Lord himself. By reason of it, the Catholic Church strives energetically and constantly to bring all humanity with all its riches back to Christ its Head in the unity of his Spirit. — Vatican II, *Dogmatic Constitution on the Church,* No. 13.

The true Church of Jesus Christ was to be universal *in time* and *in place.* Of course, Christ did not say in so many words: "My Church is going to be universal in time; my Church is going to exist in all places." But He did say just this in other words.

He announced that his Church was to be universal in time, that is, it would last for all time: "And know that I am with you always, until the end of the world!" (Mt. 28:20).

In simple language, Christ said that his Church would continue in the world right to the end. If Christ told us this, there can be no doubt that it is so. Many religions have come and gone since then, so that they cannot be the religion of Christ. Today, with so many different religions right around us, it may seem like an impossible endeavor to single out one from them all. But actually the task is not too difficult. We merely have to pick the one which existed all through the years from Christ down to the present day.

Christ said, too, that his Church was to be universal in place, that it would exist all over the world. He said that his Gospel would be "proclaimed throughout the world" (Mt. 24:14). Those are his words. He said to his followers: "Go into the whole world and proclaim the good news to all creation" (Mk. 16:15). Christ said simply that his Church was to be spread over all the earth.

When we find a church today with this stamp — universality in time and place — then we know that it is the real thing and not a counterfeit. Actually the only church that has this mark is the Catholic Church.

A look at history will show that it is universal in time. It was founded by Christ and has existed in every age from Christ's time right down to our own. A study will show that this fundamental characteristic of the Church of Christ is lacking in other churches.

All of them came into existence many hundreds of years after the time of Christ. They do not have the mark of Christ's Church — that they existed at all times from Christ's day to our own.

Christ's Church must be universal in place. The Catholic Church fulfills this requirement, because it embraces people of every nation. When we speak of Catholics, that means one out of every six people existing all over the earth. Europe, Australia, the Americas, Asia, and Africa — all the continents are represented in the Catholic Church.

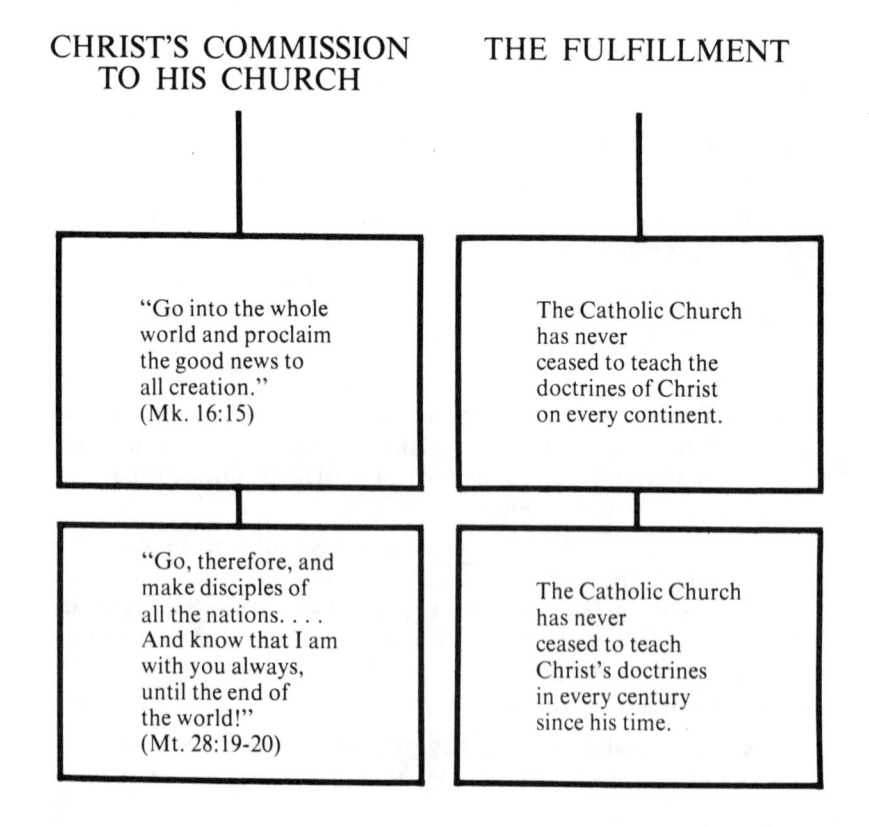

CHRIST'S COMMISSION TO HIS CHURCH	THE FULFILLMENT
"Go into the whole world and proclaim the good news to all creation." (Mk. 16:15)	The Catholic Church has never ceased to teach the doctrines of Christ on every continent.
"Go, therefore, and make disciples of all the nations. . . . And know that I am with you always, until the end of the world!" (Mt. 28:19-20)	The Catholic Church has never ceased to teach Christ's doctrines in every century since his time.

No one person has done more to emphasize this universality in place than Pope Paul VI, who, in the first eight years of his pontificate, travelled to all of these continents. By so doing, he became the first Pontiff to travel outside of Italy since Pius VII was forced to do so by Napoleon more than 150 years ago. The Holy Father's most spectacular journey, late in 1970, took him to eight Asian and Pacific countries in ten days. There were many memorable moments during the 30,000-mile trip as millions of Catholics turned out to greet their spiritual leader. But it was in Indonesia that Pope Paul proclaimed anew that the Catholic Church embraces all men regardless of race or nationality:

"The best reply that can be given to those who see in the Catholic Church a strictly European organization is this: the Church is catholic; that is to say, universal. In every land she gives the proof of it as you have here before your eyes."[1]

The significance of this papal mission was not lost on David Wilson, a columnist for the *Boston Globe,* who accompanied the Pope on his journey and then wrote a moving "personal journal, a recollection in tranquility by an American Episcopalian, in reverence and affection for the supreme pontiff of the Universal Church, of how it was to be with His Holiness on his greatest pilgrimage."[2] Mr. Wilson, who included in his article excerpts from the Gospels (Mt. 28:18-20 and Mk. 16:15), clearly recognized that the Holy Father was carrying out the command of Christ to preach the Gospel to all the world. His comments on the Pope's visit to Western Samoa, in the far reaches of the Pacific, are worthy of note:

The Nicene Creed in this setting, "I believe in one God . . ." has awesome significance for a Christian, so far from the rocky, spare and embattled land of Jerusalem and Bethlehem, and so firmly stated among the palm and pandanus, with the women and children sleeping in the long houses nearby and the pigs, dogs and chickens running about. The one, holy, Catholic and apostolic church in the person of Paul VI has indeed come a long way.[3]

No one non-Catholic church can claim the mark of universality. You will find some non-Catholic sect in every part of the world, but no single sect is everywhere. None of the Protestant churches is world-

---

[1] Barry James, "Moslem Indonesia Hails Pope," *Boston Herald Traveler,* Dec. 4, 1970, p. 16.
[2] David Wilson, "The Papal Journey: A Reporter's Diary," *Boston Sunday Globe,* February 21, 1971, p. 9.
[3] *Ibid.* p. 22.

wide as is the Catholic Church. Only the Catholic Church, then, of all the religions existing today, has the necessary twofold trademark: universality in time and in place.

Christ established his Church to bring his message through every century into each nation. Therefore, his Church must be found in every century since his time, teaching all nations. Only the Catholic Church fulfills this requirement.

It is now over 1,860 years since the death of a man who first used the phrase "Catholic Church." It was Saint Ignatius of Antioch who said, "Wheresoever the Bishop shall appear, there let the people be, even as where Jesus may be, there is the Catholic Church."[4]

There is only one Church that truly deserves the name "Catholic," implying its universality, embracing all races and nations, extending to all times and places since the day of Christ himself.

If the Catholic Church were not the Church of Christ, it would never have survived three centuries of brutal Roman persecution, or the invasions of the barbarians and the Moors, or the Reformation in Germany and England, the French Revolution, and the Communist bestiality. It withstood not only forces from without but also heresies and scandals from within. It is still about "its Father's business," says the Rev. Joseph E. Manton. "Not because it is physically powerful, not because it is financially wealthy, not because it is intellectually brilliant, not because it is incredibly lucky, but simply and solely because it was founded by Jesus Christ, the Son of God. The Son of God who once spread his arms in majestic benediction over the little band of Apostles and promised He would be with them all days, *even to the end of time.*"[5]

Saint Irenaeus, writing as early as the second century, proudly proclaimed the universality of the Catholic Church and the marvelous unity of the Church's teachings throughout the world. The words of Saint Irenaeus, relative to the Catholic Church centuries ago, give food for thought in our own day: "This faith and doctrine and tradition preached throughout the globe is as uniform as if the Church consisted of one family, possessing one soul and heart, and as if she had but one mouth. For, though the languages of the world are dissimilar, her doctrine is the same . . . as the sun gives the same light throughout

---

[4] Letter of Saint Ignatius of Antioch to the Smyrneans, about the year 110 A.D.
[5] Joseph E. Manton, C.SS.R., *Sanctity on the Sidewalk,* Boston, Massachusetts, 1969, p. 137.

the world, so does the light of faith shine everywhere the same and enlighten all men who wish to come to the knowledge of the truth."[6]

APOSTOLICITY

"This most sacred Synod, following in the footsteps of the First Vatican Council, teaches and declares with that Council that Jesus Christ, the eternal Shepherd, established his holy Church by sending forth the Apostles as He himself had been sent by the Father. He willed that their successors, namely the bishops, should be shepherds in his Church even to the consummation of the world." — Vatican II, *Dogmatic Constitution on the Church,* No. 18.

What do we mean when we say that the true Church of Christ must be apostolic? In brief, we mean that any church which is truly Christ's must go back to the Apostles for its origin, through an unbroken line; and that its teaching must be identical with that of the Apostles.

As for the first point, the Church of Christ must go back to the Apostles for its origin; this is clear because Christ established his society with the cooperation of the Apostles. Take up the New Testament and see that this society had its origin from the Apostles. Today, if a religion is the one of Christ, it must trace its origin back to this group.

A church may claim to be the Church of Christ, but if it can be shown that it does not go back to the Apostles, it is simply false.

There must be an unbroken line of successors from the Apostles, the founders. In the case of the English government one ruler has succeeded another. Suppose that a country on the continent gained enough control over England to put on the throne a king of its own appointing. The rule then would not be the rule of old; it would be *a* rule, but not the original one, for the succession was interrupted. The Church of Christ today is no different; if a church cannot point to an unbroken succession from the founders, the Apostles, it is *a* religion but not *the true* religion.

Second, the teaching of the Church of Christ today must be identical with the teaching of the Church of the Apostles. Let us take the example of the United States government. The purpose of the founders was to form a government in which certain fundamental rights would be guaranteed to its citizens. If the government today were to proclaim the principles of totalitarian dictatorship, that men have no

---

[6]Adv. Haereses, i. 1. cf. Most Reverend James Gibbons, *The Faith of Our Fathers,* Baltimore: John Murphy & Co., 1881, p. 52.

personal rights but are subjects of the state only, even if this government *claimed* to be that of the founding fathers of the United States, it would not truly be such because the teaching and doctrines had been radically changed. If a church today claims to be the Church of Christ, yet in fact is teaching something different from what the founders taught, it cannot be the true Church.

Consequently, no church can claim to be the true Church whose doctrines differ from those of the Apostles, or whose ministers are unable to trace, by an unbroken line, their authority to an apostolic source. Just as the United States Minister to England can exercise no authority in that country unless he is duly commissioned by the United States government and represents its views, so no minister of religion today may authoritatively preach Christianity unless commissioned by Christ's successors and authentically representing his doctrines.

The test of apostolicity is a matter of history. Christ organized his Church with Peter as its head, and said that his Church was to last through all ages. That means that there will have to be successors to Peter in all ages.

As we noted earlier, only the Catholic Church has even claimed to have Peter's successors. Pope Paul reiterated this claim in 1969 when he told the World Council of Churches that "our name is Peter." The Pope's candor was appreciated by the Reverend Doctor Eugene Carson Blake, the general secretary of the Protestant and Orthodox council at the time. At a business meeting of the WCC Central Committee on August 13, 1969, Dr. Blake said: "I am very glad Pope Paul made his position clear and did not feel the necessity to disguise it with diplomatic glosses. In this he showed that he understood better than some others that the ecumenical movement requires honesty and truth from all if it is not to degenerate into a movement of mere politeness and tolerance."[7]

During his Asian trip in 1970, the Holy Father discussed at some length the apostolic nature of the Church. Addressing an assembly of the Catholic bishops of Asia in Manila on November 28, he called attention to "the characteristic marks of the Church: one, holy, catholic, and apostolic." The Pontiff then went on to say:

> This last mark, apostolicity, concerns us now in a particular way. Let us think about it for a moment. All of us meeting here

---

[7]"Ecumenism Helped by Pope's Visit,"*1970 Catholic Almanac,* Paterson, New Jersey: St. Anthony's Guild, 1970, p. 87.

are successors of the Apostles. We have received from Christ himself the mandate, the power, his Spirit to carry on and to spread his mission. We are the heirs of the Apostles. We are Christ working in history and the world. We are the ministers of his pastoral government of the Church. We are the institutional organ, entrusted with dispensing the mysteries of God. (Cf. 1. Cor. 4:1, *Lumen Gentium* 20).[8]

The Catholic Church's claim to have Peter's successors could not be more clearly stated. If a successor exists, he must be in the Catholic Church. And remember that Christ said that a successor would exist for all time.

Look at the list of the successors of Peter down to the present day. All the priests of the Catholic Church were ordained by bishops in active communion with the See of Rome. These bishops themselves received their commissions from the Bishop of Rome. The present Bishop of Rome succeeded to the throne of Peter just as did his predecessors. And thus we go back from century to century until we come to Peter, the first Bishop of Rome.

What of all the other Christian sects now in existence? If you were to select any one of them and trace it back to see if it received its charter from Christ, you would find a gap of at least 1,000 years between the founding of this sect and the founding of the Church of Christ in 30 A.D. You would also find that each of the Christian religions stemmed from the Church of Rome or from some group that had stemmed from that Roman Church.

For more than ten centuries the Catholic Church was the only Christian religion, except for the few heretical sects that cut themselves off from the Church and soon disappeared. The other major Christian religions were founded in the eleventh, sixteenth, seventeenth, and eighteenth centuries. Were the Catholic religion to be erased from the pages of history, we would have neither Christianity of any sort nor a Bible. Protestantism is based upon private interpretation of the Bible. Since the books of the Bible were determined by and preserved by the Catholic Church, without Catholicism there would be no Bible, no Protestantism, no Christianity. The Catholic Church stands as the cornerstone of Christendom.

Some people may insist: "The Protestant Church is not a new church. It is the church of Christ purified of error, and only this purified form dates from the sixteenth century." No, you must choose be-

[8] Documentary Service, NC News Service, Washington, D.C. 20005.

tween these people and Christ. Jesus said that his Church would never teach error. If these people are right, Christ is wrong; if Christ is right, these people are wrong. We must choose one or the other; we cannot say both are right.

If the Church fell into error, then Christ lied when He said of his Church: "The jaws of death shall not prevail against it" (Mt. 16:18); "When he comes, however, being the Spirit of truth, he will guide you to all truth" (Jn. 16:13); "And know that I am with you always, until the end of the world!" (Mt. 28:20).

If the Church has gone astray, and error has crept in, then the Holy Spirit, the Spirit of truth, has not been with it all days; the jaws of death have prevailed against it.

It is impossible that Christ lied. If the Catholic Church was not the Church of Christ, but was teaching error, where was the Church of Christ for fifteen hundred years?

IS YOUR CHURCH THE ONE FOUNDED BY CHRIST?
An Examination of Credentials

30 A.D.

Christ Founded His Church with Certain Fundamental Teachings

1. *Authority of the Church as well as the Bible:* "On this rock I will build my church" (Mt. 16:18). "He who hears you, hears Me" (Lk. 10:16). "Whatever you declare bound on earth shall be held bound in heaven, and whatever you declare loosed on earth shall be held loosed in heaven" (Mt. 18:18).

2. *Divorce forbidden:* "Whoever divorces his wife and marries another commits adultery against her" (Mk. 10:11). "To those now married, however, I give this command (though it is

TODAY

Christ's Church Today Must Present the Same Teachings to the World

1. Does your church acknowledge a living teaching authority as well as the Bible?

2. Is the blanket approval of divorce a part of your belief?

not mine; it is the Lord's): a wife must not separate from her husband. If she does separate, she must either remain single or become reconciled to him again. Similarly, a husband must not divorce his wife" (I Cor. 7:10-11).

3. *Necessity of penance and fasting:* "When you fast, see to it that you groom your hair and wash your face. In that way no one can see you are fasting but your Father who is hidden; and your Father who sees what is hidden will repay you" (Mt. 6:17-18).

3. Does your church traditionally urge mortification and fasting?

4. *Necessity of faith and good works:* "My brothers, what good is it to profess faith without practicing it?" (Jas. 2:14). "Obey the commands I give you" (Jn. 14:15). "But whoever does not believe is already condemned" (Jn. 3:18).

4. Does your church teach the necessity of faith and good works?

5. *St. Peter and his successors as head of the Church:* "You are 'Rock,' and on this rock I will build my church" (Mt. 16:18). "And know that I am with you always, until the end of the world!" (Mt. 28:20).

5. What church today acknowledges Peter's supremacy and his successors as head of the church?

6. *Anointing of the Sick:* "Is there anyone sick among you? He should ask for the presbyters of the church. They in turn are to pray over him, anointing him with oil in the Name of the Lord" (Jas. 5:14).

6. Does your church have the sacrament of Anointing of the Sick?

7. *Confession:* "If you forgive men's sins, they are forgiven them; if you hold them bound, they are held bound" (Jn. 20:23).

7. Does your church claim the power to forgive sin?

8. *Real Presence in the Eucharist:* "If you do not eat the flesh of the Son of Man and drink his blood, you have no life in you" (Jn. 6:53). "This is my body to be given for you" (Lk. 22:19).

8. Does your church teach the real presence of Christ in the Eucharist?

9. *Purgatory:* "For if he were not expecting the fallen to rise again, it would have been useless and foolish to pray for them in death. But if he did this with a view to the splendid reward that awaits those who had gone to rest in godliness, it was a holy and pious thought. Thus he made atonement for the dead that they might be freed from this sin" (2 Mc. 12:44-46).

9. Does your church enjoin prayers for the deceased?

10. *Divinity of Christ:* " 'Are you the Messiah, the Son of the Blessed One?' Then Jesus answered: 'I am' " (Mk. 14:61-62). " 'If you really are the Messiah, tell us so in plain words.' Jesus answered: 'I did tell you, but you do not believe' " (Jn. 10:24-25).

10. Does your church unequivocally teach the divinity of Christ?

A non-Catholic may not logically say: "Though our public history dates from the Reformation, we can trace our origin back to the Apostles; we existed as an invisible church." This concealment then was so complete that no man can tell to this day where such a religion lay hidden for sixteen centuries. If any such religion did exist, it could not claim to be the Church of Christ, for our Lord predicted that his Church should ever be as a city placed upon the mountaintop, that all might see it, and that its ministers should preach the truths of salvation as from the watchtowers, that all might hear them.

Remember, too, that the founders of these churches had no right to establish *new churches* even if discipline and morality did need reforming. As individuals the reformers took matters into their own hands. Anyone who separated himself from the line of succession of the true Church ceases to have apostolic succession.

The doctrine of the Catholic Church is apostolic; the same fundamental truths are being taught today as were taught by the Apostles. Anyone seeking confirmation of this has only to compare the truths contained in the Apostles' Creed, drawn up in the first century, the Nicene Creed, compiled in the fourth century, and Pope Paul's Credo of the People of God, promulgated in 1968. If you deny this, then you must show where or when the change came. This no one has successfully done.

The Church of Christ will be the one which in all respects teaches doctrines identical with those of the first teachers.

Feed my lambs. . . . Tend my sheep.—John 21:15-16

Modern day shepherd in Holy Land.

photo by Paul J. Hayes

Chapter 12

The Authority of the Church

> This infallibility with which the divine Redeemer willed his Church to be endowed in defining a doctrine of faith and morals extends as far as extends the deposit of divine revelation, which must be religiously guarded and faithfully expounded. This is the infallibility which the Roman Pontiff, the head of the college of bishops, enjoys in virtue of his office, when, as the supreme shepherd and teacher of all the faithful, who confirms his brethren in their faith, he proclaims by a definitive act some doctrine of faith or morals. — Vatican II, *Dogmatic Constitution on the Church,* No. 25.

Perhaps the one thing which is most misunderstood, and which is the occasion for the most opposition is the authority of the Church. The idea that there should be an infallible teaching body is rarely accepted by those outside the Catholic Church. However, it is usually the case that what they really are opposed to is not the teaching of infallibility as held by the Church but a distorted caricature of this teaching.

In presenting our arguments for the truthfulness of infallibility and its reasonableness we shall appeal to the words of the founder of the true religion, Jesus Christ, and to our own common sense.

It might be well to begin by giving a few notions of what the Catholic teaching of infallibility *does not* mean:

It does not mean that the Pope is impeccable, that is, in any way incapable of moral wrong. There is often heard a line of argument such as this: "There was one Pope who was guilty of a serious sin. That proves that he was not infallible." The argument does not hold. We are speaking in two different spheres; infallibility does not mean freedom from moral guilt. As a matter of fact, we might point out that the Popes have been, with few exceptions, men of amazingly virtuous lives. The first thirty-two pontiffs died martyrs for the Faith. Over 260 men have sat in the throne of Peter, and yet only four or five have even been charged by enemies with serious moral lapses. Even if we admit the truth of all accusations, the proportion is strikingly small, especially when we recall that one out of the twelve chosen by Christ himself was a Judas Iscariot.

A judge is given certain legal authority in court. If, in his private life, he were guilty of sin, this would in no way affect the validity of his decisions. His authority in court is not dependent upon the character of his private life; it is conferred on him by virtue of his office. So it is with the Pope; his infallibility exists, not for his own sake, but for ours. It does not, therefore, make the salvation of his soul any easier. It is simply a way in which God uses him for the preservation of truth. And, as it does not affect his character, so it does not arise from it. If, by chance, a questionable man should become Pope, it is just as necessary for us that he should be prevented from teaching error, and just as easy for God to prevent him!

Remember, the Holy Father confesses his sins. At the beginning of Mass he says, "I confess to Almighty God . . . that I have sinned through my own fault in my thoughts and in my words, in what I have done, and in what I have failed to do." At the washing of the hands he prays, "Lord, wash away my iniquity; cleanse me from my sin." In the light of this, then, it is clear that infallibility by no means implies freedom from sin.

Nor does infallibility mean that the Pope is infallible in discussing matters not involving revealed truths, such as science; nor in political matters, as some would have us believe. Infallibility does not mean that a pontiff is free from error in any field at all when speaking as a private individual.

What, then, does infallibility mean?

When the Pope, in his official capacity, with the fullness of his authority as successor of Saint Peter and Head of the Church on earth, proclaims a doctrine on faith or morals binding on the whole Church, he is preserved from error.

There are four conditions that the Pope must fulfill in order to teach infallibly: (1) He must speak on a matter involving faith and morals. (2) He must speak in his official capacity as Peter's successor and the Supreme Shepherd of the Church on earth. (3) He must clearly indicate that he is making a solemn, definitive, and final pronouncement on the doctrine at issue. (4) He must declare his intention to bind all members of the Catholic Church to accept the new teaching.

Let us examine one of the Church's rare infallible pronouncements and see if all of these conditions are fulfilled. On November 1, 1950, Pope Pius XII proclaimed the dogma of the Assumption:

> Wherefore, having offered to God constant prayers of supplication and invoked the light of the Spirit of truth, to the glory

of Almighty God who has lavished on the Virgin Mary his especial favor; to the honor of his Son, the immortal king of the ages and the victor over sin and death; to the increased glory of the same august Mother; and to the joy and exultation of the universal Church; by the authority of our Lord Jesus Christ, of the Blessed Apostles Peter and Paul, and by our own authority, we pronounce, declare, and define it to be a dogma divinely revealed: that the immaculate Mother of God, Mary ever virgin, on the completion of her earthly life, was taken up to heavenly glory both in body and soul. Wherefore if anyone presume (which God forbid) willfully to deny or call into doubt what has been defined by us, let him know that he has fallen away entirely from the divine and Catholic faith.

Note: (1) The Holy Father is speaking on a matter of faith: the bodily assumption of the Blessed Mother into heaven. (2) He is speaking in his official capacity: "by the authority of our Lord Jesus Christ, of the Blessed Apostles Peter and Paul, and by our own authority." (3) He is indicating by the use of such words as "pronounce, declare, and define" that he is handing down an irrevocable decision, settling the question of the Assumption for all time. You will not find such authoritative language in any other papal pronouncements. (4) He is binding all Catholics to accept his decision or fall away "entirely from the divine and Catholic faith."

Considering the solemn, unchanging, and permanent nature of an infallible decree, and the fact that a Catholic who denies or questions it jeopardizes his eternal salvation, it is obvious that the Pope must be preserved from delivering an erroneous judgment.

In a word, the Pope is to the Church, though in a more eminent degree, what the Supreme Court is to the United States. The people of the United States have an instrument called the Constitution which is the charter of their civil rights and liberties. If a controversy arises regarding a constitutional clause, the question is referred to the Supreme Court in Washington. The Chief Justice of the United States, with his associate judges, examines the case and then pronounces judgment upon it.

If there were no such court to settle constitutional questions, the Constitution itself would soon become a dead letter. Every litigant would conscientiously decide the dispute in his own favor. Anarchy and civil war would soon follow. But, by means of the Supreme Court, constitutional questions can be resolved and domestic tranquillity preserved.

The revealed Word of God is the constitution of the Church. It is the Magna Charta of our Christian liberties. The Pope is the official guardian of our religious constitution, just as the Supreme Court is the guardian of the United States Constitution.

One may protest, "In the case of the Supreme Court it is not infallible. It may be wrong. But Catholics hold that the decision of the Pope is not only binding but infallible."

The decisions of the Supreme Court are final. Why is it not infallible? Simply because the founding fathers who conferred its powers *could not* give it actual inerrancy. Suppose the founding fathers had it in their power to keep the Supreme Court from errors in its decisions. We would say that they were poor Americans if they had the power and yet did not confer it on the Court. And therein lies the difference. *God has the power* to protect his Church from error. Should we not expect that He would grant it to his Church just as the founding fathers would have granted it to the Supreme Court if they could?

Americans have set up the Supreme Court of the United States to tell them finally what is the law. If an American had the power to prevent the Court from making mistakes, would he not use that power? He would, indeed. Not to use it would be a grave wrong to every one of his fellow citizens. So with the Church. Christ set up an organization, which we know as the Church, to carry on his teaching. Has he the power to prevent the Church from misleading us? He has, of course. Does He use that power? Most certainly He does.

Indeed, we must say that the only possible course was to grant this power to his Church.

Let us now see if the conclusion of our reason and common sense is supported by history. Is the conferring of inerrancy a historical fact? Did Christ grant it to Peter, the first Pontiff?

A study of the New Testament reveals several pertinent passages spoken to Peter:

1. "I for my part declare to you, you are 'Rock,' and on this rock I will build my church, and the jaws of death shall not prevail against it" (Mt. 16:18). This was addressed exclusively to Peter. In effect Christ says, "I will establish a Church which will last until the end of time. I will lay the foundation of this Church so deep and strong on the rock of truth that the winds and storms of error shall not prevail against it."

2. Also spoken to Peter, the first Pontiff, directly: "Whatever you declare bound on earth shall be bound in heaven; whatever you de-

clare loosed on earth shall be loosed in heaven" (Mt. 16:19). "The decisions which you make," says Christ in effect, "will be ratified in heaven." Surely God is incapable of sanctioning an untruthful judgment.

3. "Simon, Simon! Remember that Satan has asked for you, to sift you all like wheat. But I have prayed for you that your faith may never fail. You in turn must strengthen your brothers" (Lk, 22:31-32). It is worthy of note that Jesus prays only for Peter. And why for Peter in particular? Because on his shoulders was to rest the burden of the Church. Our Lord prays that the faith of Peter and of his successors might not fail. Christ utters a prayer and then says, "With the faith I have gained for you, shield the faith of your brothers from the assaults of Satan."

4. "Feed my lambs . . . Feed my sheep" (Jn. 21:15-17). Peter is appointed by our Lord the universal shepherd of his flock. The Pope must feed the flock not with the poison of error but with the healthy food of sound doctrine; for he is not a hireling, who administers questionable food to his flock, but, rather, a good shepherd.

"Yes," comes the remark, "I can see that the evidence is clear enough for the fact that Christ guaranteed to Peter a guidance that would safeguard him from error. But there is quite a gap from Peter to the Church of the twentieth century."

Remember that the mission which Christ gave to Peter and the Apostles was to cover all nations and all mankind. But Peter and his associates were mortal men, destined to pass away with their generation while their mission was to continue. The guidance of Christ was, therefore, to continue with their successors. That is clearly disclosed by the words of Christ: "And know that I am with you always, until the end of the world!" (Mt. 28:20). Since the Apostles were not to live until the end of the world, Christ promised to be with them in the person of their successors until the end of time.

The logic of this conclusion can be denied only by those who believe that Christ was interested in saving only the souls of those who lived in his day, and was totally indifferent about all posterity.

In connection with this subject we hear at times a remark such as, "For my part I have an infallible Bible, and this is the only infallibility that I require." While this may seem plausible at first view, it does not stand the test of further investigation. Either such a person is infallibly certain that his particular interpretation of the Bible is the correct one, or he is not. If he maintains that he is infallibly certain, then he claims for himself a personal infallibility. Furthermore, he cannot logically deny his personal infallibility to every other reader of the Bible. He denies it only to the Pope. We claim it only for the Pope. According to this view, each of the hundreds of millions of readers of the Bible becomes a pope while the only one who is not a pope is the Pope himself. You avoid admitting the infallibility of one man by multiplying infallibility by the number of readers of the Bible. If one who holds this theory does not claim to be infallibly certain that his interpretation of the whole Bible is correct, then of what value is it to have an infallible Bible without an infallible interpreter? In either case the statement crumbles. The plain fact is that an infallible Bible without an infallible living interpreter is largely futile.

If a church is not infallible, it is liable to err; for there is no medium between infallibility and liability to error. If a church and her ministers are fallible in their doctrinal teaching, as they admit, they may be preaching falsehood to you instead of truth. If so, you are in doubt whether you are listening to truth or falsehood. If you are in doubt, you can have no faith, for faith excludes doubt, and in that state you displease God, for "without faith, it is impossible to please him" (Heb. 11:6). Faith and infallibility go hand in hand.

You admit infallible certainty in the physical sciences, such as an astronomer's prediction of an eclipse; that certain insects have 8,000 eyes; that a drop of water sometimes contains more atomic bodies than there are inhabitants on our planet. If we accept these and countless other inconceivable statements as correct, it is evident that the vast majority of us do so on faith, depending solely on the assertions of a very few individuals, most of whom we have never seen. We are all disciples of someone, and many of us accept the declarations of the "popes of science" quite as submissively as Catholics receive an *ex cathedra* utterance of the Holy See.

It has been said, too, that the Catholic Church in the course of ages ceased to teach the pure truths of Christ, introduced error, and so today cannot be regarded as the true Church.

Remember these words spoken by Christ of his Church:

a) "I for my part declare to you, you are 'Rock,' and on this rock I will build my Church, and the jaws of death shall not prevail against it" (Mt. 16:18).

b) "I will ask the Father and He will give you another Paraclete — to be with you always: the Spirit of truth" (Jn. 14:16-17).

c) "And know that I am with you always, until the end of the world!" (Mt. 28:20).

So spoke Christ of his Church. Either the Catholic Church never was the true Church; or it once was the true Church and went into error; or it was and still is the true Church. There is no other choice.

As for the first possibility (it never was the true Church), where was Christ's Church for 1,600 years?

THE CATHOLIC CHURCH

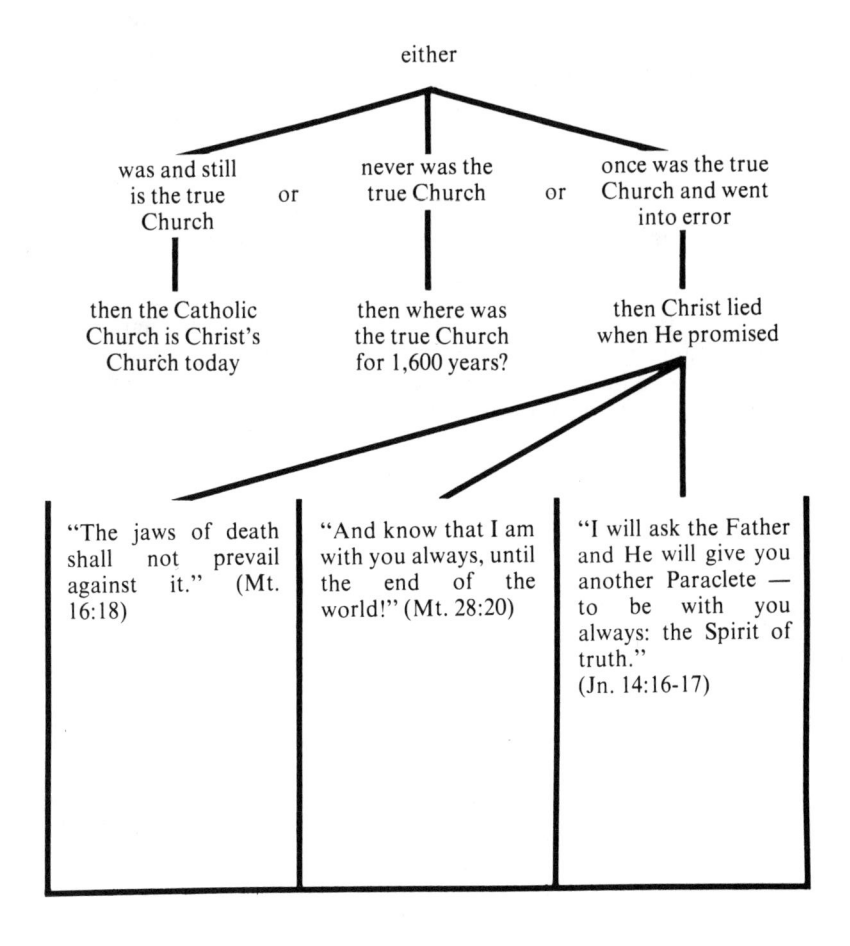

either

- **was and still is the true Church**
  - then the Catholic Church is Christ's Church today
  - "The jaws of death shall not prevail against it." (Mt. 16:18)

or

- **never was the true Church**
  - then where was the true Church for 1,600 years?
  - "And know that I am with you always, until the end of the world!" (Mt. 28:20)

or

- **once was the true Church and went into error**
  - then Christ lied when He promised
  - "I will ask the Father and He will give you another Paraclete — to be with you always: the Spirit of truth." (Jn. 14:16-17)

As for the second point, if it were the true Church and went into error, then Christ lied when He said the jaws of death would not prevail against it, and that the Spirit of truth would always be with it, and that He would be with it to the end of the world; for if it fell into error, then the Holy Spirit, the Spirit of truth, has not been with it all days.

The only conclusion is the third possibility: the Catholic Church was, and still is, the Church of Christ.

It is a marvelous fact, worthy of record, that in the entire history of the Church, from the first century to the twentieth, no example can be produced to show that any Pope or general council ever revoked a decree of faith or morals enacted by any preceding Pontiff or council.[1] Her record of the past nineteen centuries ought to be an assurance that there will be no change in the future. Pope John XXIII affirmed this fact on October 11, 1962, in his speech opening the Second Vatican Council:

> The Twenty-first Ecumenical Council, which will draw upon the effective and important wealth of juridical, liturgical, apostolic, and administrative experiences, wishes to transmit the doctrine, pure and integral, without any attenuation or distortion, which throughout twenty centuries, notwithstanding difficulties and contrasts, has become the common patrimony of men. It is a patrimony not well received by all, but always a rich treasure available to men of good will. Our duty is not only to guard this precious treasure, as if we were concerned only with antiquity, but to dedicate ourselves with an earnest will and without fear to that work which our era demands of us, pursuing thus the path which the Church has followed for twenty centuries.[2]

The infallibility which Christ promised to his Church, it should be noted, "resides also in the body of bishops when that body exercises supreme teaching authority with the successor of Peter," said the Fathers of Vatican II. This is true, they explained, only when the bishops are "gathered together in an ecumenical council," or "when they are dispersed around the world, provided that while maintaining the bond

---

[1] Non-Catholics ordinarily mention four Popes as having erred, viz., Paul V and Urban VIII, who condemned Galileo; and Liberius and Honorius, who are said to have fallen into heresy. The conditions required for an infallible decision were not present in any of these cases. For further discussion, cf. Most Rev. M. Sheehan, *Apologetics and Catholic Doctrine*, Dublin: M. H. Gill and Son, Ltd., 1944, pp. 191ff.

[2] Pope John's Opening Speech to the Council, *The Documents of Vatican II*, ed. Walter M. Abbott, S.J., New York: The America Press, 1966, p. 715.

THE HOLY LAND AT THE TIME OF CHRIST

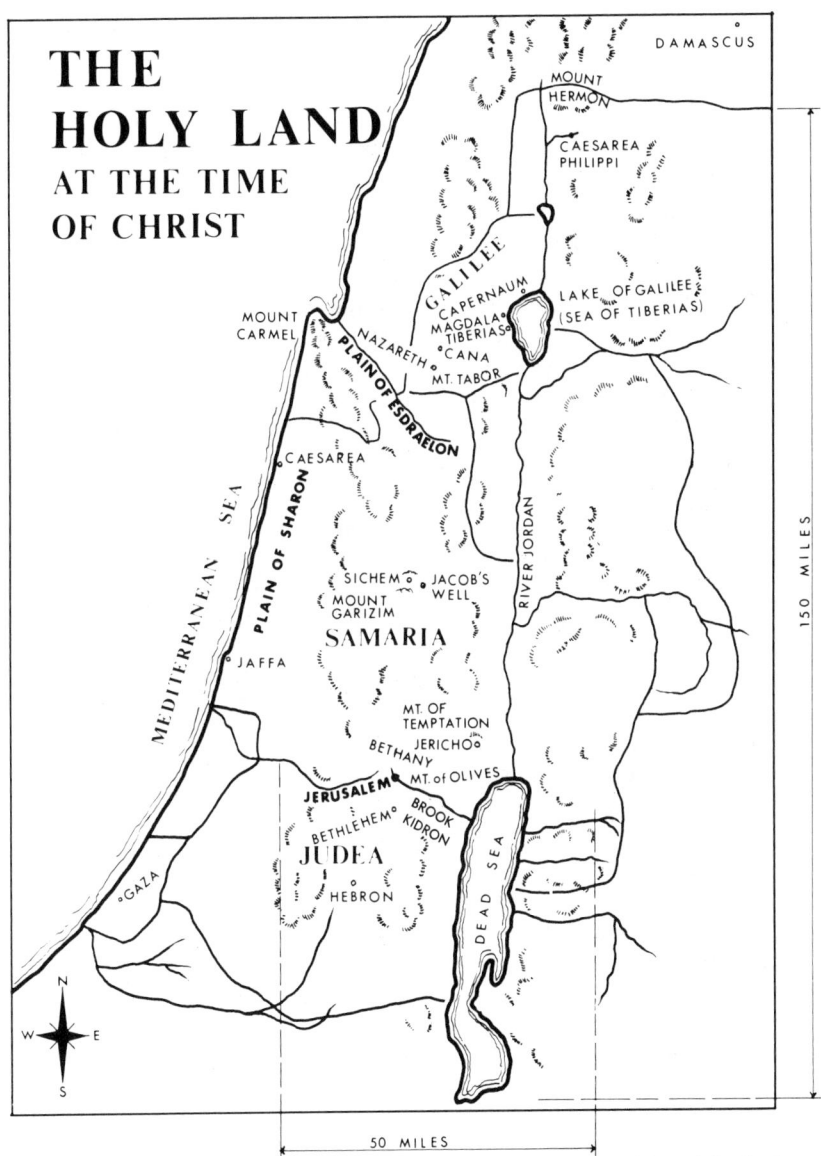

This map identifies the principal towns and cities associated with the life and death of Christ. In the events and happenings of his life the Church finds the roots for the authority she claims today. From this small area with a small beginning the Church has spread over the entire world.

of unity among themselves and with Peter's successor, and while teaching authentically on a matter of faith or morals, they concur in a single viewpoint as the one which must be held conclusively" *(Dogmatic Constitution on the Church,* No. 25). In both cases, the bishops must act in conjunction with the Pope. In other words, the successor of Peter must be involved in any infallible pronouncement. He does not need the approval of the bishops to teach infallibly, but they cannot do so without his approval.

We should not leave this question of papal authority and infallibility without saying something about the duty of Catholics to give positive assent to the Pope's non-infallible teachings, such as the encyclicals which are frequently issued by the Pontiffs. There are three good reasons why Catholics should accept these authentic, but not infallible, pronouncements: (1) They can be considered informed because the Pope seeks the advice of experts on the religious or moral issue to be treated. (2) They can be considered important because the Holy Father and his advisers are unlikely to use the power of the Papacy to influence the times in which they live needlessly or unwisely. (3) They can be considered reliable because the Pope still receives assistance from the Holy Spirit, even when he is not speaking *ex cathedra.*

The Second Vatican Council emphasized the importance of the non-infallible teaching of the Vicar of Christ when it declared that "religious submission of will and of mind must be shown in a special way to the authentic teaching authority of the Roman Pontiff, even when he is not speaking *ex cathedra.* That is, it must be shown in such a way that his supreme magisterium is acknowledged with reverence, the judgments made by him are sincerely adhered to, according to his manifest mind and will. His mind and will in the matter may be known chiefly either from the character of the documents, from his frequent repetition of the same doctrine, or from his manner of speaking" *(Dogmatic Constitution on the Church,* No. 25).

The concepts of authority and infallibility are not only reasonable, but are necessary safeguards for the transmission of God's truths to men.

Chapter 13

The Church and the Bible

> Holy Mother Church, relying on the belief of the Apostles, holds that the books of both the Old and New Testament in their entirety, with all their parts, are sacred and canonical because, having been written under the inspiration of the Holy Spirit they have God as their author and have been handed on as such to the Church herself. . . . Therefore, since everything asserted by the inspired authors or sacred writers must be held to be asserted by the Holy Spirit, it follows that the books of Scripture must be acknowledged as teaching firmly, faithfully, and without error that truth which God wanted put into the sacred writings for the sake of our salvation. — Vatican II, *Dogmatic Constitution on Divine Revelation,* No. 11.

The Bible is a collection of seventy-three books, forty-six belonging to the Old Testament and twenty-seven to the New. These books were not written at the same time. From the writing of the first book, Genesis, to the last one, the Revelation, there elapsed a period of more than 1,000 years. Even the books of the New Testament did not all appear together, but at intervals covering about half a century.

It was the Catholic Church that gathered these books into one volume and gave the world what is known today as the Bible.

Jesus himself never wrote a line of Scripture. He did not commission his Apostles to write, or even to circulate the Scriptures then existing. He sent them forth to "teach" all nations. As a matter of fact, of the twelve Apostles, seventy-two disciples, and early followers of Christ, only eight have left us any sacred writings. The Apostles were never reported to have circulated a single volume of the Holy Scriptures, but they "went forth and preached everywhere" (Mk. 16:20).

From the earliest days, then, the people were guided by a living authority, and not by a private reading of the Scriptures.

Indeed, until the religious revolution of the sixteenth century, it was a thing unheard of from the beginning of the world that people should be governed by the dead letter of the law either in civil or ecclesiastical affairs. How are civil affairs regulated? Certainly not in accordance with individual interpretation of the laws of the land, but rather in accordance with decisions which are rendered by properly constituted judges. What the civil code is to the citizen, the Scriptures are to the Christian. The Word of God, as well as the civil law, must have an interpreter by whose decision we are obliged to abide.

The theory that Christ simply enunciated certain truths and failed to provide any responsible agency for the transmission of these teachings to all mankind is not only uncomplimentary to the wisdom of Jesus and to his solicitude for the salvation of all mankind, but it also finds no warrant in Holy Scripture. To place upon each individual who is to be born into the world the task of seeking out for himself the precise teachings of Jesus, and the equally difficult task of interpreting them with unerring accuracy, would be an unreasonable demand of Christ.

A competent guide for the Christian religion must have three characteristics: it must be within the reach of everyone; it must be clear and intelligible to all; and it must present all truths of the Christian religion.

The Bible could not in any period have been within the reach of all. It could not have been accessible to the first Christians, for it was not completed until some time after the establishment of Christianity. The Christian religion was founded in the year 30 A.D. The first Gospel did not appear until some years later. The rest of the New Testament was not in existence until some time later still. The first Christians lived and died and went on into eternity before the most important parts of the New Testament were written. And what would have become of them if the Bible alone had been their guide? How about the good thief and all the martyrs and Christians who died confident in their acceptance of the teaching of Christ before the first Bible was gathered together between the covers of one book?

Printing was not invented until the fifteenth century. How utterly impossible it was to supply everyone with a copy of the Scriptures from the fourth to the fifteenth century! During that period books had to be copied by hand, and there were but a relatively few Bibles in the Christian world. There were no printing presses in the early days. A Bible was a treasure. Men worked for at least a year copying it. It was a sacred book, bound in stout leather set with precious stones in a fitting manner. If Christ had intended the Bible to be the only guide for salvation, He must have come to lead only the wealthy to heaven.

"In his gracious goodness, God has seen to it that what He had revealed for the salvation of all nations would abide perpetually in its full integrity and be handed on to all generations."
— Vatican II, *Dogmatic Constitution on Divine Revelation*, No. 7.

Even at the present day, with all the aid of printing, with numerous Bible associations in various parts of the world supported at enormous expense, it taxes all our energies to supply every missionary country with Bibles printed in the languages of the tribes and peoples for whom they are intended. Even if the Bible were at all times accessible to everyone, how many millions exist in every age and country to whom the Bible is not accessible because they are incapable of reading? Hence the doctrine of the Bible as the sole rule of faith and that of private interpretation would render many men's salvation not only difficult but impossible.

A competent guide to the Christian religion must be clear and intelligible to all. Is the Bible intelligible to all? Far from it. It is full of difficulties and obscurities, not only for the illiterate, but even for the learned. Scholars who have spent their whole lives in the study of the Scriptures are unanimous in pronouncing the Bible a book full of difficulties.

The Bible does not contain all the teachings of the Christian religion. If you belong to a religion which claims that the Bible is the sole rule of faith, then:

1. Why do you not observe Saturday instead of Sunday? Read the Bible from Genesis to Revelation, and you will not find a line authorizing the sanctification of Sunday.

2. Why do you not believe in the absolute necessity of baptism for salvation?

3. Why pray to the Holy Spirit, a practice which is not found in the Bible?

4. How can you hold that the Catholic Church fell into error against the plain promises of Christ to protect it from error? (Mt. 28:20; Mt. 16:18; Jn. 14:16-17; Jn. 16:13; 1 Tm. 3:15).

5. What did Christ mean by the words "refer it to the Church"? (Mt. 18:17).

We must therefore conclude that the Scriptures *alone* cannot be a sufficient guide and rule of faith, because they cannot at any time be within the reach of every inquirer; because they are not always of themselves clear and intelligible, even in matters of highest importance; and because they do not contain all the truths of the Christian religion.

The Christian religion demands a living interpreter. In the words of Vatican II: "The task of authentically interpreting the word of God, whether written or handed on, has been entrusted exclusively to the living teaching office of the Church, whose authority is exercised in the name of Jesus Christ. This teaching office is not above the word of God, but serves it, teaching only what has been handed on, listening to it devoutly, guarding it scrupulously, and explaining it faithfully by divine commission and with the help of the Holy Spirit; it draws from this one deposit of faith everything which it presents for belief as divinely revealed" *(Dogmatic Constitution on Divine Revelation,* No. 10).

The Catholic Church has been the preserver and custodian of the Bible through the centuries. What has become of the thousands of once-famous books written in past ages? They have nearly all perished. But the Bible has survived the wars and revolutions and the invasions of nineteen centuries. Who preserved it from destruction? The Catholic Church.

The remark that the Catholic Church in the past suppressed the Bible and today does not use the Bible is entirely false. The people who make such a statement have never stopped to inquire into the origin of the Bible, nor into the institution which determined its books and preserved it for all the centuries previous to the existence of any other Christian religion.

Far from being hostile to the Bible, the Catholic Church is its staunch champion. She determined which are the true books of Holy Scripture, and cast aside the spurious writings circulated as inspired during the early days. The Church assembled all the inspired writings within the covers of a single book, shielded it from destruction, and translated it into many languages long before Protestantism saw the light of day. If she regarded the Bible as her enemy, she had plenty of opportunity to destroy it centuries before Protestantism came into existence.

The laity who lived before printing was invented and when manuscripts were rare and costly learned much Scripture from the Church's sculpture, paintings, frescoes, and mosaics, many remains of which we can still see today. Yes, the Church through the ages has used every means to further the knowledge of Scripture.

"Is it not true that the Church in the Middle Ages chained the Bibles in the churches to keep them from the people?" Yes, Bibles were chained in churches. Why? To prevent theft and to render them accessible to the greatest number of people. The telephone directory is often chained to a public booth, not to keep it from the people, but to keep it for the people!

The widely quoted statement attributed to Martin Luther, that before his time "the Bible lay under the bench forgotten in the dust," has contributed to the impression that the Bible was practically unknown in the Middle Ages. The truth is that this assertion is contradicted by the facts as reported by innumerable non-Catholic historians.

When printing became a reality, the Bible was spread rapidly. There were over nine German editions of the Bible printed before 1483, the year Luther was born, while eighteen other editions of the Bible are known to have been printed before the one Luther published. Before Luther's translation of the New Testament was published in 1534, Catholics had already published over 200 editions in Latin, German, Italian, French, Hebrew, Bohemian, Flemish, and Russian.

Do non-Catholics believe the Bible to be the Word of God? Most denominations do. How can they prove that, except by the authority of the Catholic Church? The Bible remained for several centuries in scattered fragments, spread over different parts of Christendom. Meanwhile, many spurious books were circulated among the faithful, under the name of Scripture. There was, for instance, the spurious gospel of Saint Peter; there were also the gospels of Saint James and of Saint Matthias. The Catholic Church separated the chaff from the wheat and declared which books were canonical, and which are apocryphal.[1]

The Catholic Church was either infallible when she said so, or she was not. If she were not, she might have been mistaken, and in such case the Protestants do not know whether the books they accept are the Word of God or not.

If the Bible and only the Bible is to be your guide, then a series of questions remains unanswered. Why did not Christ say so? Why did Christ himself not write it? Why did not Christ tell his disciples to write, but rather instructed them to *teach?* And why did the Apostles then go out and *preach* everywhere? History tells us that the Bible was not compiled until some three hundred years after Christ; what about the people before this time? Why did the Apostles not teach that the Bible is the sole rule of faith? Did, then, Christ's promise of assistance fail? Out of twelve Apostles, seventy-two disciples, and innumerable other followers of Christ, why did only eight write? If they thought they were writing a book which was to be the sole rule of faith, why did

---

[1] A. Weikerhauser, *Einleitung in das Neue Testament,* Freiburg: B. Herder Book Co., 1953, p. 15.

30 A.D.	The Catholic Church established by Christ	The Catholic Church was preaching Christ's teachings for years before a word of the New Testament was written
50 A.D. to 100 A.D.	The Gospels written	
1450 A.D.	Printing press invented; first Catholic Bible printed	The Catholic Church was preaching and teaching throughout the world and preserved the Bible for over 13 centuries before it was first printed and widely distributed
1483 A.D.	Birth of Martin Luther	Nine editions of the Bible in German alone were published before Luther's birth
1552 A.D.	Luther's translation of the Bible published	Over 600 Catholic editions were published in all languages
1611 A.D.	King James (Protestant) version of the Bible published	

they not state that purpose clearly? When the Apostles prepared successors to take their place, why did they insist on faithful *teaching* and say nothing of their writings? How explain the words with which Saint John closes his Gospel: "There are still many other things that Jesus did, yet if they were written about in detail, I doubt there would be room enough in the entire world to hold the books to record them"? (Jn. 21:25).

Is private interpretation reasonable? If the Holy Spirit, the Spirit of truth, who cannot deceive, inspires the readers of the Bible with the result that there are over two hundred interpretations of the simple sentence, "This is my Body," there is something wrong some place. Before the Reformation the words were understood only in one sense. With the reformers of the sixteenth century there were given no less than eighty different meanings to the four simple words. The number of interpretations has been increasing ever since. Where is the difficulty? With the Holy Spirit? Or with the supposition that the Holy Spirit will inspire men so that they will interpret the Bible correctly?

Whence does the information come that the Holy Spirit has promised this? It is not in the Bible.

How can the Holy Spirit inspire one to say that there are seven sacraments: another that there are none at all: another that there are three? How can one tell when he is being inspired in this private reading? For those who say that the writings themselves bear upon their face the marks of their inspired character, read some passages from the Old Testament which at first glance bear no semblance of being God's work; then note that the Koran of the Mohammedans contains many inspiring and edifying passages. What standard are we to use?

Do you see now why the Catholic stand on the Bible is entirely reasonable?

The Church has always been, and today continues to be, the protector of the Bible. A brief consideration will reveal the constant and devout use of the Sacred Scriptures by Catholics. Countless Catholic doctrines are based on it; the Catholic Church year is Bible history reviewed; Scripture is an important part of the Catholic Mass and breviary; Catholic prayers are based on it; many Catholic customs are based on it. Catholic priests read each day the "Divine Office" which is largely composed of sections of the Bible.

The Bible forms an integral part of Catholic life.

There is another source of divine truth available to Catholics known as tradition.

Divine Tradition is the unwritten word of God — that is, truths revealed by God, though not written in the Bible, and given to the Church through word of mouth by Jesus Christ or by the Apostles under the inspiration of the Holy Spirit. Divine Tradition has been committed to writing especially by saintly writers called Fathers, who lived in the early centuries but were not inspired, as were those who wrote the Bible. Divine Tradition has the same force as the Bible since it too contains God's revelations to men.

Tradition is closely linked with the Bible, said the bishops of Vatican II, "for both of them, flowing from the same divine wellspring, in a certain way merge into a unity and tend toward the same end.... Therefore both sacred tradition and sacred Scripture are to be accepted and venerated with the same sense of devotion and reverence" (*Dogmatic Constitution on Divine Revelation,* No. 9).

Just as the Bible must have an authentic, living interpreter, so, too, must Divine Tradition. The teaching office of the Church, as we noted earlier, has exclusive jurisdiction over both. "It is clear, therefore, that sacred Tradition, sacred Scripture, and the teaching authority of the Church, in accord with God's most wise design, are so linked and joined together that one cannot stand without the others, and that all together and each in its own way under the action of the one Holy Spirit contribute effectively to the salvation of souls" *(Dogmatic Constitution on Divine Revelation,* No. 10).

"To speak of Tradition and Scripture as the source of catechesis," Pope John Paul II has said, "Is to draw attention to the fact that catechesis must be impregnated and penetrated by the thought, the spirit, and the outlook of the Bible and the Gospels through assiduous contact with the texts themselves; but it is also a reminder that catechesis will be all the richer and more effective for reading the texts with the intelligence and the heart of the Church and for drawing inspiration from the 2,000 years of the Church's reflection and life" *(On Catechesis in Our Time, No. 27).*

The Church does not see herself as one more human institution in a world of many institutions. She does not view herself as an organization of social service at a time when there are so many such services available to us. The Church is a sacred religious, charismatic, incarnational reality. The Church is the complement of the Redeemer, while Christ, in a sense, attains through the Church a fullness in all things.

—Pastoral Letter of the U.S. Bishops, "The Church in Our Day," January 11, 1968

photo by Paul J. Hayes

Chapter 14

The Church and Ecumenism

> Today, in many parts of the world, under the inspiring grace of the Holy Spirit, multiple efforts are being expended through prayer, word, and action to attain that fullness of unity which Jesus Christ desires. This sacred Synod, therefore, exhorts all the Catholic faithful to recognize the signs of the times and to participate skillfully in the work of ecumenism. — Vatican II, *Decree on Ecumenism,* No. 4.

One of the most obvious facts of the day is the tragic lack of unity among the various religions and especially among the followers of Jesus Christ. Pope Paul has described this situation as "one of the gravest problems of Christianity and we might say, of humanity."[1] It was to promote restoration of this unity that the Second Vatican Council was called. Pope John, in his opening speech to the Council in 1962, stated that the aim of the Synod was to prepare and consolidate "the path toward that unity of mankind which is required as a necessary foundation, in order that the earthly city may be brought to the resemblance of that heavenly city where truth reigns, charity is the law, and whose extent is eternity."[2]

It is the purpose of this chapter to define and explain the concept of ecumenism, as the Church has circumscribed it, so that Catholics may participate intelligently in efforts to hasten the day when there will be one flock and one shepherd.

Because many people have an erroneous idea of what ecumenism means, it may be instructive at this point to show what ecumenism *does not* mean:

Ecumenism does not mean ignoring or watering-down fundamental truths, for "nothing is so foreign to the spirit of ecumenism as a false conciliatory approach which harms the purity of Catholic doctrine and obscures its assured genuine meaning. . . . Catholic belief needs to be explained more profoundly and precisely, in ways and in terminology which our separated brethren too can really understand"

[1] Address, January 20, 1971.
[2] Pope John's Opening Speech to the Council, *The Documents of Vatican II,* ed. Walter M. Abbott, S.J., New York: The America Press. 1966, p. 718.

(Decree on Ecumenism, No. 11). A superficial and pragmatic approach toward unity, Pope Paul has said, "would produce only illusions and confusion; only a ghost of our Catholicism would remain, not its real life, not the living Christ whom it bears within itself."[3]

Ecumenism does not mean substituting charity for truth. Charity, of course, is indispensable in any ecumenical gathering. But is it charitable to deceive non-Catholics by not acquainting them with the truth? Can genuine charity exist where truth is concealed? Pope Paul demonstrated the virtue of charity when he candidly told the World Council of Churches that "our name is Peter," thus prompting Eugene Carson Blake to say that "the ecumenical movement requires honesty and truth from all if it is not to degenerate into a movement of mere politeness and tolerance."[4]

Nor does ecumenism mean making converts to the Catholic Church, although the two are not mutually exclusive. "It is evident that the work of preparing and reconciling those individuals who wish for full Catholic communion is of its nature distinct from ecumenical action. But there is no opposition between the two, since both proceed from the wondrous providence of God"*(Decree on Ecumenism,*No. 4).

What, then, does ecumenism mean?

"The 'ecumenical movement' means those activities and enterprises which, according to various needs of the Church and opportune occasions, are started and organized for the fostering of unity among Christians. These are: first, every effort to eliminate words, judgments, and actions which do not respond to the condition of separated brethren with truth and fairness and so make mutual relations between them more difficult; then, 'dialogue' between competent experts from different Churches and Communities" *(Decree on Ecumenism,* No. 4).

Simply stated, the specific aim of ecumenism is to overcome the obstacles that stand in the way of Christian unity. This objective is to be accomplished through dialogue based on truth, honesty, and love. According to Pope Paul, dialogue must have the following characteristics:

> 1.) Clearness above all; the dialogue supposes and demands comprehensibility. . . . This fundamental requirement is enough to enlist our apostolic care to review every angle of our language to

---
[3]Address, January 20, 1971
[4]"Ecumenism Helped by Pope's Visit," *1970 Catholic Almanac,* Paterson, New Jersey: St. Anthony's Guild, 1970, p. 87.

guarantee that it be understandable, acceptable, and well-chosen.
2.) A second characteristic of the dialogue is its meekness, the virtue which Christ sets before us to be learned from Him: "Learn of Me, because I am meek and humble of heart" (Mt. 11:29). The dialogue is not proud, it is not bitter, it is not offensive.
3.) Trust, not only in the power of one's words, but also in an attitude of welcoming the trust of the interlocutor. Trust promotes confidence and friendship. It binds hearts in mutual adherence to the good which excludes all self-seeking.
4.) Finally, pedagogical prudence, which esteems highly the psychological and moral circumstances of the listener, whether he be a child, uneducated, unprepared, diffident, hostile. Prudence strives to learn the sensitivities of the hearer and requires that we adapt ourselves and the manner of our presentation in a reasonable way lest we be displeasing and incomprehensible to him.
In the dialogue, conducted in this manner, the union of truth and charity, of understanding and love, is achieved.[5]

Another condition for fruitful dialogue is that Catholics "understand the outlook of our separated brethren. Study is absolutely required for this, and should be pursued with fidelity to truth and in a spirit of good will. When they are properly prepared for this study, Catholics need to acquire a more adequate understanding of the distinctive doctrines of our separated brethren, as well as of their own history, spiritual and liturgical life, their religious psychology and cultural background. Of great value for this purpose are meetings between the two sides, especially for discussion of theological problems, where each can deal with the other on an equal footing. Such meetings require that those who take part in them under authoritative guidance be truly competent. From dialogue of this sort will emerge still more clearly what the true posture of the Catholic Church is. In this way, too, we will better understand the attitude of our separated brethren and more aptly present our own belief" (*Decree on Ecumenism,* No. 9).

Clear thinking on the subject of ecumenism is imperative, especially among Catholics. Failure to grasp its true essence will only place still another obstacle in the road toward Christian unity.

In setting forth the principles which were to govern ecumenical activities, the Second Vatican Council would have been remiss if it had not also stated plainly the unique place of the Catholic Church in the plan of salvation. The Council, heeding its own admonition against adopting a "false conciliatory approach" in the presentation of reli-

---
[5] Pope Paul VI, "Paths of the Church" *(Ecclesiam Suam),* August 6, 1964.

gious truths, unequivocally asserted the Catholic claim to be the only Church founded by Jesus Christ.

In the *Declaration on Religious Freedom,* for example, the Fathers of Vatican II professed their belief that "God himself has made known to mankind the way in which men are to serve Him, and thus be saved in Christ and come to blessedness. We believe that this one true religion subsists in the Catholic and Apostolic Church, to which the Lord Jesus committed the duty of spreading it abroad among all men" (No. 1). In the *Decree on Ecumenism,* they proclaimed that "it is through Christ's Catholic Church alone, which is the all-embracing means of salvation, that the fullness of the means of salvation can be obtained" (No. 3). And in the *Dogmatic Constitution on the Church,* the bishops declared that "the Church, now sojourning on earth as an exile, is necessary for salvation. For Christ, made present to us in his Body, which is the Church, is the one Mediator and the unique way of salvation. In explicit terms He himself affirmed the necessity of faith and baptism and thereby affirmed also the necessity of the Church, for through baptism as through a door men enter the Church" (No. 14).

So fundamental is this teaching, in fact, that the bishops specifically declared: "Whosoever, therefore, knowing that the Catholic Church was made necessary by God through Jesus Christ, would refuse to enter her or to remain in her could not be saved" *(Dogmatic Constitution on the Church,* No. 14). They also warned Catholics in the same article that mere membership in the Church is not enough. To be fully incorporated in the Church and to be saved means that one must possess the "Spirit of Christ," accept the "entire system and all the means of salvation" given to the Church, and "persevere in charity."

Does this mean that only Catholics can be saved? No, it does not. The plan of salvation also includes other Christians and non-Christians. Again, we turn to the documents of Vatican II for the Church's position on this matter.

With regard to other Christians, members of the Protestant and Orthodox communities, the Council has said that "the Catholic Church accepts them with respect and affection as brothers. For men who believe in Christ and have been properly baptized are brought into a certain, though imperfect, communion with the Catholic Church. Undoubtedly, the differences that exist in varying degrees between them and the Catholic Church — whether in doctrine and sometimes in discipline, or concerning the structure of the Church — do indeed create many and sometimes serious obstacles to full ecclesiastical communion. These the ecumenical movement is striving to overcome" (*Decree on Ecumenism,* No. 3).

The same document goes on to note that many significant elements of truth and sanctification found in the Catholic Church — "the written word of God; the life of grace; faith, hope, and charity, along with other interior gifts of the Holy Spirit and visible elements" — can also be found in other Christian religions. These elements, as well as "many of the sacred actions" carried out by other Christians, the Council said, "can truly engender a life of grace, and can be rightly described as capable of providing access to the community of salvation. It follows that these separated Churches and Communities, though we believe they suffer from defects already mentioned, have by no means been deprived of significance and importance in the mystery of salvation. For the Spirit of Christ has not refrained from using them as means of salvation which derive their efficacy from the very fullness of grace and truth entrusted to the Catholic Church" (*Decree on Ecumenism,* No. 3).

Speaking of non-Christian religions, including Hinduism, Buddhism, and Islam, the Council said that God's "saving designs extend to all men," and it called for dialogue and collaboration with the followers of these religions in order to "acknowledge, preserve, and promote the spiritual and moral goods found among these men, as well as the values in their society and culture" (*Declaration on the Relationship of the Church to Non-Christian Religions,* Nos. 1, 2).

In discussing Judaism at some length, "since the spiritual patrimony common to Christians and Jews is . . . so great," the Council Fathers looked forward to "that day, known to God alone, on which all peoples will address the Lord in a single voice and 'serve him with one accord.' " To that end, they recommended "that mutual understanding and respect which is the fruit above all of biblical and theological studies, and of brotherly dialogues" (*Declaration on the Relationship of the Church to Non-Christian Religions,* No. 4). The same article also repudiated the notion that all Jews living at the time of Christ, and even those living today, can be collectively blamed for the crucifixion:

> "True, authorities of the Jews and those who followed their lead pressed for the death of Christ; still, what happened in his passion cannot be blamed upon all the Jews then living, without distinction, nor upon the Jews of today. Although the Church is the new people of God, the Jews should not be presented as repu-

diated or cursed by God, as if such views followed from the Holy Scriptures. All should take pains, then, lest in catechetical instruction and in the preaching of God's Word they teach anything out of harmony with the truth of the gospel and the spirit of Christ."

Finally, the Council said that "those also can attain to everlasting salvation who through no fault of their own do not know the gospel of Christ or his Church, yet sincerely seek God and, moved by grace, strive by their deeds to do his will as it is known to them through the dictates of conscience. Nor does divine Providence deny the help necessary for salvation to those who, without blame on their part, have not yet arrived at an explicit knowledge of God, but who strive to live a good life, thanks to his grace. Whatever goodness or truth is found among them is looked upon by the Church as a preparation for the gospel. She regards such qualities as given by Him who enlightens all men so that they may finally have life" (*Dogmatic Constitution on the Church*, No. 16).

All Catholics have a solemn responsibility to work and pray for the restoration of religious unity, especially among their fellow Christians. They have been reminded, however, that "there can be no ecumenism worthy of the name without a change of heart. ... This change of heart and holiness of life, along with public and private prayer for the unity of Christians, should be regarded as the soul of the whole ecumenical movement, and can rightly be called 'spiritual ecumenism'" (*Decree on Ecumenism,* Nos. 7, 8). "Every Catholic must therefore aim at Christian perfection and, each according to his station, play his part so that the Church, which bears in her own body the humility and dying of Jesus, may daily be more purified and renewed, against the day when Christ will present her to himself in all her glory, without spot or wrinkle" (*Decree on Ecumenism,* No. 4).

The road of ecumenism is long and difficult, but with the help of God, all obstructions can be removed. If the Catholic faithful and their spiritual shepherds manifest their truthfulness, honesty, and brotherly love, "the result will be that, little by little, as the obstacles to perfect ecclesiastical communion are overcome, all Christians will be gathered, in a common celebration of the Eucharist, into that unity of the one and only Church which Christ bestowed on his Church from the beginning. This unity, we believe, dwells in the Catholic Church as something she can never lose, and we hope that it will continue to increase until the end of time" (*Decree on Ecumenism,* No. 4).

THE CHAIN OF FAITH

(The following steps represent a thumbnail sketch of the line of reasoning expanded in the first fourteen chapters of this book.)

A. God exists. Evidence of his existence can be found in history, philosophy, and the design and order in the universe.

B. Man has a relationship with God which we call religion. Religion is part of man's nature and is necessary for the human race.

C. Hundreds of religions exist in the world today. Because there are profound differences between them — what some religions hold to be true, others believe to be false — one religion cannot be as good as another. We must investigate the various religions to determine if there is one which possesses all of the truth.

D. We will start with Christianity because of its tremendous influence in the world. If that is found to be the true religion, we need look no further; if not, we may begin investigating other religions.

E. The New Testament is the historical source book dealing with Christianity. Studies over the centuries by biblical scholars, historians, scientists, archaeologists, etc., have shown the New Testament to be a reliable history book.

F. The founder of Christianity, Jesus Christ, said that He was God. From a study of the Gospels, we know that He was not a liar, nor was He mentally unbalanced. His contemporaries, even his enemies, agreed that He was a superb preacher, a brilliant teacher, a skilled debater, and a Man of outstanding character.

G. Jesus proved that He was God by the prophecies He fulfilled, by the prophecies He made, and by the many miracles He performed. Hundreds and thousands of people witnessed his extraordinary wonders.

H. The greatest miracle of all and the clearest proof of his divinity was Jesus' resurrection from the dead. He had predicted that He would suffer and die and raise himself from the dead on the third day. There is abundant historical evidence to support the fact of the resurrection.

I. Jesus founded an organization, a Church, to carry on his work in the world and chose Peter to head his Church. We can find this Church today by looking for certain characteristics or marks which are essential elements of the Church founded by Christ.

    1.) His Church must have unity:
        a. of government;
        b. of worship;

c. of doctrine.
2.) His Church must be holy:
   a. in its purpose;
   b. in its membership;
   c. in its miracles.
3.) His Church must be universal:
   a. in time;
   b. in place.
4.) His Church must be apostolic:
   a. in doctrine;
   b. in its succession of rulers.

J. Of all the Christian Churches, only the Roman Catholic Church today measures up to these standards. No other Church has the necessary marks.

K. If, then, the Catholic Church is the true Church of Jesus Christ, we have no choice but to follow its norms and its teachings. We may feel safe in doing so because of the authority and infallibility which Christ guaranteed to his Church.

L. The two sources of divine truth in the Catholic Church are the Bible and Tradition, both of which are interpreted by the living teaching office of the Church.

M. While the Catholic Church believes that it is the Church of Christ, it urges its members to show charity toward those of all religions and to work and pray for the day when there will be one flock and one shepherd.

Chapter 15

Getting to Know God

> God, the beginning and end of all things, can be known with certainty from created reality by the light of human reason.— Vatican II, *Dogmatic Constitution on Divine Revelation,* No. 6

It is impossible for a man to be serious about trying to know the important things about himself or the world around him, unless he first knows something about God. The fact that man in the twentieth century is anxious to know about himself is evident from the growing interest in psychiatry. That he is interested in knowing about the world is obvious from the great interest in the advancement of science. But for the complete answer to the one big question "why?", whether that be in psychiatry or science or medicine or religion, there must be some place in the picture for the one word "God," if we are to have our findings lead us in the right direction.

At the Harvard Club in Boston in a room set apart for the medical students there, a visitor once observed with interest a plaque above the fireplace with the inscription: "We dress the wound, God heals it." That motto is an indication of God's part in our whole life, not just at church once a week.

If we take an average life span of seventy years, it would be divided something like this:

3 years would be spent in education
8 years in amusement
6 years in eating
24 years in sleeping.

And if you went to church every Sunday, and each day spent five minutes in prayer in the morning and evening, there would be but five months given to God! That is a general picture of what part God and religion now play in the daily life of an average American.

One of the world's most prominent psychiatrists once said that of all the patients over thirty-five who came to be treated by him, there was not one whose problem ultimately was not solved by a regaining of a religious outlook on life which he had lost.

The key to happiness and peace in the last analysis is God. That is why He created us. It was not to add anything to his happiness, but rather to share that happiness with us. And the key to the gaining of that is given in the simple yet profound sentence: "In order to gain happiness — true happiness and not merely a passing pleasure — we must *know, love,* and *serve* God in this world."

In point of fact we will not serve someone we do not love. True, we may give "eye-service," do things for them that will help us, but there will never be any true serving of a person, unless there is love. Or to put the matter in another way: Some people, once you know them, you cannot help liking. Once we know God, we will love Him, and one whom we love we will serve. Those three things cannot be separated. To know God then is the first step.

In the twentieth century United States, men are training their imaginations and talents to make life easier. There are countless drive-in theaters; we are hearing more about drive-in banks, restaurants, grocery stores — all so that as much as possible can be accomplished without even getting out of the family car. Not too long ago, there was added to that list the first drive-in church, where several hundred members of a congregation could take care of their obligation to God without budging from their automobile. But God's part in our life must become more than driving in to pay our respects for an hour a week. God's part in our life is an all-week task, a task of serving Him in all we do. Perhaps the reason why God is so little served or loved as one who is very close to us is because He is not sufficiently known.

GOD AND HIS QUALITIES

That God exists we know. There are times and events in the life of every one which seem to make us feel as if we are face to face with God. Sometimes his presence is so felt that we speak to Him and expect to hear his voice. But at other times — and perhaps most of the time — his place in our life is one of a somewhat distant and indefinable God. And when events in our life hit a low ebb, God even seems so clouded and obscure as to almost disappear. But if we only look around, the marks of God's presence and power are all around us. The trouble is, our vision of Him is obscured by so many anxieties of twentieth century life.

What is God like? We cannot see Him, but we must in some way get to know Him or else we will not love Him, for we cannot love what we do not know. Man left to himself would really be at a loss to know

*Praise him with the blast of the trumpet,
praise him with lyre and harp,
Praise him with timbrel and dance,
praise him with strings and pipe.
Praise him with sounding cymbals,
praise him with clanging cymbals.
Let everything that has breath
praise the Lord! Alleluia.*

—Psalm 150: 3-6

photo by John Connolly

about God. But actually, God himself came to man's aid, and spoke through revelation. It is in this way that we know about God. In other words, besides knowing about God, by our own natural reason, we can learn of God by supernatural revelation — from tradition and from truths found in the Bible. We know that the Bible is the word of God and through it God tells us many of the things He wants us to know.

A fable of the Brahmans in India illustrates somewhat our position in learning about God. There was a village, the story has it, where only a group of blind people lived. It happened one day that an elephant wandered into the village and the report spread about. No one was able to picture the animal to himself and so the crowd surrounded the elephant and began to touch it curiously. One caught hold of the trunk and remarked: "Strange, an elephant is just like a snake." Another felt the animal's ear and concluded: "No, an elephant is like a big fan." A third, touching the elephant's legs, disagreed, saying that the animal was most like a pillar.

We are in somewhat the same position with regard to God. We perceive one or other of his qualities but our human mind cannot apprehend his entire greatness. As Saint Augustine remarked several hundred years ago: "God would not be God were He not greater than your power of comprehension."

It is not surprising then, that man, relying on his own reason, came to erroneous conclusions on God — He is just too big for our mind. That is why the Persians thought God was fire, for He is indeed light. That is why the Chaldeans thought He was a beautiful star, for it is true He is beautiful. That is why so many today as in the past think of God as matter or force, for God is the Creator of them. Such ideas are warped ideas of God, as the blind people got warped ideas of the elephant because they only came to know a small part of him.

How much can we get to know about God? About as much as we would get to know of Saint Patrick's Cathedral in New York by walking around it some dark night with merely matches to light our way. Perhaps we would see the altar but we could not make out the surroundings; here we would see a pillar but only a few feet of it and the rest lost in darkness. After walking about inside, we would have to piece together in our mind all we had seen and try to form a picture of the Cathedral as a whole. We are in the same position with reference to God — we can look at several of his qualities, his attributes, and from them form our idea of Him. In brief, here are the main qualities we may look at to get to know God in some way: infinity, eternity, omnipresence, immutability, perfect knowledge and wisdom, omnipotence, goodness and mercy, holiness, justice. That is a formidable list, but we are familiar with most of those qualities in our everyday life, if not the words. What we must do is apply them to God.

1. — Infinity, means simply without limit, and this applies to all God's perfections. It is an idea difficult for us to grasp. Think of the unlimited power of the wind, the lightning, the ocean, the planets traveling at unspeakable speeds. God produced them. Think of the wisdom manifested in the minute order of all the movements of the universe; the knowledge and genius of men through the ages. God created them. Think of all the power, wisdom, beauty, love multiplied countless times and centered in one being — it is still only a shadow of the reality.

2. — Eternity. There never was a time when God did not exist. He existed before the world, as a watchmaker must exist before the watch he makes. He can never cease to exist. If someone were to carry away a grain of sand from the seashore every thousand years the time would come some day when there would be none left. But that tremendous period of time is not even a dent in the eternity of God's existence.

3. — Omnipresence. God is present everywhere. Before the time of Christ, Solomon declared to God at the dedication of the Temple: "If the heavens and the highest heavens cannot contain you, how much less this temple which I have built!" (I Kings 8:27). There is no place where God is not, and as He himself reminds us in the inspired words of the Bible: "The eyes of the Lord are in every place, keeping watch on the evil and the good" (Prv. 15:3). Man is filled with shame when detected in some sin by his fellow men, and yet many do not hesitate to sin in the presence of God. If we could but realize that God is always present with us, we would in our lives stay closer to Him. A certain railroad was concerned with having trustworthy officials and in order to assure this they employed a special corps of detectives. On one occasion an employee asked for a leave of absence because of the death of a relative. When he returned after a week or so his superior showed him a photograph in which he was pictured not at a funeral but enjoying himself at a social gathering. Detectives had photographed him. If that man had known that his every step was observed and photographed, he would have acted very differently. God's eyes are on us at all times. Our least deed is visible to Him. If this is so then our standard ought to be never to do anything or say anything or

even think anything that we would not want God to see or hear.

4. — Immutability. God never changes. He does not change when He punishes the sinner or rewards the good. If a man looks into a mirror when he is angry he will see a very different reflection from when he is cheerful and looks into the same mirror. It is not the mirror that changed, but the man. So with God, our position with reference to Him may change, but He always remains the same.

5. — God's knowledge. Every snowflake, the speck of dust that clogs a clock, the secrets in the heart of every man — all these things are fully known to God. God's knowledge and ours have very little in common. We come to know things one after another very slowly, somewhat as a child learns to speak his language word by word. But God knows all things in one glance. He sees all men who have ever lived, every tree and plant, every thought of men, and all this in one instant. Scholars work a lifetime to gain a knowledge of one subject. God knows all instantaneously and completely. He knows our needs better than we do ourselves and will take care of them if we will but leave it to Him. Christ assured us of this: "Stop worrying, then, over questions like, 'What are we to eat, or what are we to drink, or what are we to wear?' The unbelievers are always running after these things. Your heavenly Father knows all that you need" (Mt. 6:31-32). "Look at the birds in the sky. They do not sow or reap, they gather nothing into barns; yet your heavenly Father feeds them. Are not you more important than they?" (Mt. 6:26). We have the assurance of Christ that God knows our needs and will take care of them if we only do our part and leave the rest to Him. This loving care of God for us is called Divine Providence.

6. — God is all powerful. He can do all things and this by a mere act of his will. As the inspired writer of one of the psalms says: "For he commanded and they were created" (Ps. 148:5). God has shown his power in a thousand different ways. Remember all the miracles performed by Christ — the raising of Lazarus, the changing of water into wine, the healing of a blind man. But He has not stopped there. Even today the wonders worked at shrines such as Lourdes give us ample testimony of God's power in the world today. With all this do we not have every reason to rely on God's help rather than in our own strength? Because God can do all things we call Him Almighty.

7. — God is all good and merciful and holy. Our Lord gives us a concrete picture of his love for us and mercy in the story of the prodigal son. Christ indicates in some measure his own mercy in the story of

the young boy who had come of age and asked his father for his share of the inheritance. With that the reckless youth went on his way in the world aimlessly to have a "good time and enjoy life" unhampered by family ties or God's law. He, as so many since his time, found that the throwing off of God's law to enjoy life is not what it seemed to be in anticipation. "He squandered his money on dissolute living" (Lk. 15:13). And within a short time, destitution and ill fortune brought him to his knees in repentance. Returning in sorrow, he acknowledged his evil and ungrateful life — "I have sinned against God and against you" (Lk. 15:18). Would his father then at least take him back as a servant? He was received with open arms into his father's house. It is in this story that the mercy of Christ is reflected. But unlike that father, Christ in his mercy goes a step further. He does not wait for the sinner to return, but with his grace pursues him, trying to draw him back to his friendship so that Christ, as the father of the prodigal son, might rejoice at the return of one who "was dead and has come back to life" (Lk. 15:32). That is our position with reference to God. Though we have sinned, we will be received with open arms by Him who is all good and merciful.

8. — God is all just. God rewards all good and punishes all evil deeds. Sometimes He may partly reward or punish men on earth, but this is chiefly taken care of after death. Sometimes the question comes up in our mind why some person who is not good, far from being punished seems to be blessed with good fortune, while a person who is trying to do the right thing has many sufferings and misfortunes. God never promised that the good would receive their reward in this life; He did say that the good would receive eternal happiness in heaven and the evil would be punished. Remember no matter how good a person is, he is still not faultless and no matter how bad a person is, he has some little good in him. Perhaps at times the good receive their punishment in this life and the bad their little reward here. At any rate, one thing we can be perfectly sure of: God is absolutely just in his dealings with us. He rewards the least good action and punishes the smallest sin. On February 25, 1758, Voltaire, one of the most violent foes of the Catholic Church, exclaimed to a friend: "Twenty years hence the good God will be doomed." It was just twenty years later, 1778, that his doctor broke the news to Voltaire that his condition was beyond medical help. It was at this critical point that Voltaire asked for a Catholic priest. But his anti-Catholic friends would not allow it. The dying man begged in despair to go to Confession. We can see examples of God's

justice. But very often it is not shown in so striking a way. God's final justice, reward of good and punishment of evil, is usually left until after death. Of this we may be sure: without fail, sinners will be punished, and the good will be rewarded.

We have seen several of God's qualities. Put them all together and we get some idea of what God is like. We can learn a good deal about God by our own natural reason — by looking at the world around us. Think of all the good in the world. God created it all, and so must be infinitely good. Think of all the beauty. God is responsible for it and must be more beautiful than we can imagine. He created the whole world — how powerful He must be! The whole world and man himself are the work of the Divine Artist. If the masterpiece is beyond our comprehension, what must be the Artist himself?

We have been talking of the various aspects of God. By building up a picture in that way, we can get some idea of God but not a deep appreciation. A girl might describe the young man she hopes to marry some day by speaking of the color of his hair, his eyes, the way he walks, the things he says, but she knows that only a deep acquaintance, a real friendship and a solid love can bring a true knowledge and appreciation of him. So it is with ourselves in relation to God. We may speak of his mercy, infinite knowledge and beauty, but only close friendship and true love can give us the appreciation of the God we are seeking.

THE BLESSED TRINITY

Shortly after the birth of a Catholic child, the new-born is presented to the church. There his godparents and parents see the child baptized. "In the name of the Father and of the Son and of the Holy Spirit."

One of the first steps in the religious training of any Catholic child is the day his mother takes his hand in hers and tracing the sign of the cross on him — from forehead to heart and from left shoulder to right — they say together "In the name of the Father and of the Son and of the Holy Spirit. Amen." The first prayer of the child is a calling upon the Blessed Trinity.

Years after, the child will kneel beside the priest to receive Christ's forgiveness in Confession through words spoken in the name of Christ by the priest: "I absolve you from your sins in the name of the Father and of the Son and of the Holy Spirit."

Every time a Catholic assists at Mass, he hears the priest begin by calling on the three Persons in God. As he has his spiritual needs filled by Christ's sacraments, he hears constant reference to the Trinity. And in his last hour, he will hear the words addressed by the priest in the Last Blessing: "I . . . grant you a plenary indulgence and remission of all your sins. In the name of the Father and of the Son and of the Holy Spirit." All through the life of a Catholic, spiritual truths and holy things are associated with the Blessed Trinity, the three Divine Persons in One God.

At times we may hear a person express the question: "Why does God have 'mysteries' in his religion? Why do we have truths that we must believe but cannot understand?"

First of all, why aim that question at the field of religion and not history or science? There are still, for instance, mysteries in science which may not ever be fathomed and yet scientists do not question their truth. We can prove that many facts are true and yet not be able to go the step further to understand them. No science can exhaust the subject matter with which it deals. There are always the questions: "Why?" "How?" But we still accept even these truths which we cannot fully see. If there are mysteries in the sciences, why should not we expect things that we cannot understand in the science of religion?

Secondly, it is certainly a fruitful thing for us to be able to make an act of faith in God. If we could reason out for ourselves all the truths we are to believe, we would be putting our own mind before God's word. We readily believe the word of a friend, the truth of whose statement we cannot and do not have the least desire to verify. And should we question God's word? We accept without hesitation truths a chemist or historian or a scientist tells us, truths we cannot see through but accept because they tell us and are authorities in that field. It would be interesting but perhaps hectic to attempt to go through a day without taking another's word for anything that we could not prove or see for ourselves. Our daily life is a series of acts of faith in others. We might expect then that there will be something similar in our relations to God.

A mystery is not something which contradicts our reason, but rather something that is beyond our grasp. When a Catholic is face to face with sublime religious truths which he cannot understand, he simply says "I believe these . . . because you have revealed them who can neither deceive nor be deceived." God asks of us not that we understand all, but that we trust Him.

The Blessed Trinity is one of the truths which God has asked us to accept on His word. It is a supernatural mystery. Here the seven-year-old Catholic pupil repeating the truth to the sister in the classroom and the most learned scholar are on the same plane — both can state and believe the truth; neither can understand it.

The mystery of the Holy Trinity is not a riddle or a game of deception. It is a simple but sublime statement of one of the mysteries of God's life. It is not a truth about which we cannot know anything. It, as the other mysteries, is a fact about which we cannot know all.

A supernatural mystery is a truth which we cannot fully understand but which we believe because we have God's word for it. We are unable to comprehend how there are three Persons in God, yet only one God. We can learn something about God, through the work of his hand, the world about us. But God has gone a step further, by directly telling us things of himself. In the Blessed Trinity He has told us something about his personality. He has told us that there are three Persons — not three Gods; not three Persons in one Person since that is an impossibility. Rather He has said that God's being consists of three *Persons* but one *Nature*.

In discussing this topic at times the only comment may be a yawn, or a prompt nod of agreement and then hastening to change the subject to the score of the latest ball game. But if God thought the truth of the Trinity important enough to tell us about it, we ought to consider it important enough to spend a little energy on.

It is said that Saint Patrick made use of the shamrock to illustrate the mystery of the Trinity to the Irish. The picture of three leaves springing from one stem may help in gaining some idea of this mystery, though it will not bring us much closer to an understanding of it, for we cannot picture the Blessed Trinity. However, any picture that throws even the slightest light on this mystery of Faith is better than no picture at all. Saint Patrick holding a shamrock before his listeners could present some idea of the threeness and oneness in God. Not that three are equal to one. Rather there are three Persons and one Nature, as in the shamrock there are three leaves but one stem.

We might well ask then "what is the difference between a nature and a person?" The distinction is not something for which we need years of study, but a thing with which we are very familiar, though not in such terms. If we are driving along on a dark evening and see a figure on the sidewalk but cannot make out whether it is a fire hydrant, a sack of potatoes or a small child, we ask the question: *"What* is that?" That question is equal to saying "Of what nature is that subject —

inanimate nature, animal nature or rational nature?" If however we are driving along at dusk some evening and see a child on the sidewalk but do not know his name, we ask the person with us, *"Who* is that?" We know it is a human being but we do not know which person it is.

We have something in common with others; that is our nature. We have something distinct from others, and that is our person. When a person signs a check, says "excuse me," or accuses himself of wrongdoing — that is his own *person* he is referring to. The fact that we have a body and soul, that we talk or eat, that we are social — that is our *nature*. The ways in which we are different from others are our person. The question "What?" corresponds to nature; the question "Who?" corresponds to person. In God, if we might reduce it to the prosaic in its simplest form, there are three "Who's" and one "What" — distinct Persons (the Father, Son and Holy Spirit); one Divine Nature.

We may use various comparisons and illustrations, as Saint Patrick is said to have done, to gain some understanding of how this can be, but when we are finished it still will remain one of God's mysteries. If we take three lighted candles and hold them close together in our hand the three flames fuse into one, and yet the candles remain distinct — three sources of light but one flame.

Scientists tell us that white light is composed of the three primary colors of the spectrum — red, yellow and blue. Though one light appears to us when we look at a white electric bulb, it is composed of three colors in point of fact. One light can be divided into red, yellow and blue rays, but put all three colors together in equal amounts, and one white light is the result.

All these comparisons are but weak and we must fall back on God's own word for some idea of his existence and personality.

It was at the end of Christ's earthly life. Christ was surrounded by his first eleven Apostles. They heard from his lips the commission to go out and convert the world, bringing all to his feet in the name of the three Divine Persons: "Go, therefore, and make disciples of all the nations. Baptize them in the name of the Father, and of the Son, and of the Holy Spirit" (Mt. 28:19). Note Christ said "in the name" not "names" — one God.

And at the Baptism of Christ, there was a voice heard, "This is my beloved Son" (Mt. 3:17), and Saint Matthew tells us in his gospel, "He saw the Spirit of God descend like a dove. . . ." (Mt. 3:16). There was a reference to this mystery — the Father speaking, the Son being baptized and the Holy Spirit appearing in visible form.

Here is one of God's secrets which He has not revealed to us fully. He has chosen to tell us the *fact* without telling us *how*.

In God there is a Person who gives us all we look for in fatherhood. He cares for the birds of the air, and more for us. "Look at the birds in the sky. They do not sow or reap, they gather nothing into barns; yet your heavenly Father feeds them. Are not you more important than they?" (Mt. 6:26). He is a Father of loving providence and protection, of justice, a Provider. He is our ideal of Fatherhood. He is the Creator of the world.

In God there is a third Person, identical with the Father and Son in power and perfection and yet distinct from them — the Holy Spirit. He is the Person who distributes to the world the spiritual fruits gained by the Son.

Christ told us the fact of the mystery of the Trinity and that is enough for us. The Catholic Church taught it from the day Christ left this earth. Men have even died rather than deny it.

It was in the year 304 in Sicily that Euplius, a deacon, one of the helpers of the priests, was seized for being a Catholic and summoned before the official, Calvisianus. The young man was told to renounce the truths of his faith. He refused and was handed over to the torturers to be stretched on the rack. In suffering he spoke the words: "I adore Christ . . . do what you will. I am a Christian." The official urged him to deny his God and he would be set free. To that Euplius mustering his last bit of strength replied:

"I worship the Father and the Son and the Holy Spirit. I adore the Holy Trinity."

On the dying lips of this martyr, there is re-echoed Christian belief in the mystery of the Blessed Trinity.

Christ has told us that the answer to lasting happiness rests in serving God. We will not serve one whom we do not love and we cannot love one we do not know. That is why energy spent in getting to know more of God is not wasted. We may grow in this knowledge through visible creation (as we get to know something of an artist through his pictures); or we may gain some knowledge of God through things He has chosen to reveal to us. There is beauty in the world; God produced it all. The world itself points to his infinite power. Our very life reveals his goodness. The love between a mother and her child is only a spark of the divine love. The visible things of creation were not meant to be as a pair of dark glasses to cut down our vision, but as a set of glasses to aid us to get a better vision of God, by looking beyond this world to the One who created the world and ourselves and all the good and beauty therein.

When we have done our utmost, we still will know very little of God. But though we cannot comprehend the divine mysteries in this life, there is an emptiness in our life which can be filled by God alone. We may wait to learn by experience what our faith will tell us now, that our hearts were made for God and will not rest until they rest in Him.

God, his qualities and the mysteries of the Blessed Trinity are like the sun which blinds the eye looking at it. Our position in viewing the existence of God is like the child standing on the shore looking out over the "endless" ocean. We in point of fact know so little of this world, of the constitution of human life, of the vast achievements of the human mind — how can we expect to begin to grasp the existence of the One responsible for all? The very angels, the highest of God's creation, with immeasurably higher powers than ourselves, cannot perceive the secret of God's infinite existence. And men, living a lowly existence, studying years to gain even some small knowledge of the world, blinded by pride and sensuality, surrounded by material things, do not hesitate to criticize or call into doubt the most sublime mysteries of God!

And after our study of God and his mysteries, we must only say with Saint Paul nineteen centuries ago in his words recalled in the Mass on the feast of the Blessed Trinity each year:

"How deep are the riches and the wisdom and the knowledge of God! How inscrutable his judgments, how unsearchable his ways!" (Rom. 11:33).

Just as the whole of creation is ordained to its Creator, so spiritual beings should of their own accord orientate their lives to God.
— Pope Paul VI, Encyclical "On the Development of Peoples," March 26, 1967

Chapter 16

In the Beginning . . .

> *I do not hesitate to proclaim before you and before the world that all human life — from the moment of conception and through all subsequent stages — is sacred because human life is created in the image and likeness of God.* — Pope John Paul II.

One of the great milestones in the exploration of outer space was man's first approach to the moon. The voyage was the culmination of the combined efforts of a great number of scientific minds. Three astronauts were carefully selected. They were intelligent, well educated, scientific, practical, realistic, well disciplined men. As they made their near approach to the moon, the people of the earth listened breathlessly to hear what they would say. From space come the message — old, old words, now thrillingly new: "In the beginning, God created heaven and earth."

To this profound thought, man must ever address himself. What happened in the beginning?

"In the beginning, when God created the heavens and the earth . . ." (Gn. 1:1).

That is perhaps the best known line in the Bible, but a line upon which we might spend some time in discussing.

"In the beginning," means at the very beginning of time, when nothing else but God existed.

When we say that God created heaven and earth, we mean that things — those which we can see and those which we cannot — were made through the almighty power of God. We can make a thing if we have materials and the tools; we can build a chair if we have the wood. But it was God who brought the material into existence. Man must employ materials and labor to produce anything. God spoke and the universe came into existence.

When the Bible says that God created heaven, the author did not mean the stars and moon, but rather the invisible world, the dwelling place of the angels and saints. The reference to heaven in the very first line of the Bible is a reminder to men of the place to which they are destined. And when the author speaks of God's having created the earth, he means everything we can see, man himself included.

Why did God create the world and man? Certainly not because He needed the world or us. It was because of his goodness, for He wanted to share his happiness with others. A father might pick an old album of photographs from a shelf, and go over them with his sons and daughters to share his happiness and pleasant memories with them. God has put before us his works as a means of sharing his happiness with us and as a means of drawing us to love Him. God created all earthly things for you and me in some way — animals, for instance, are necessary as food; some things are for our instruction, others for our enjoyment; and God allows other things to serve as a trial to us so that we might turn more completely to Him (so, e.g. sickness, suffering). God had no need of the world. He created it to show men the glory of God. He created us to recognize that glory, and share his unending happiness.

"The heavens and the earth and all their array were completed. . . . He rested on the seventh day" (Gn. 2:1-2).

The story of God's production of the visible world is related in the Bible as taking six days. Actually God did not confine himself to a week in the work of creating the world. Rather, that is the author's method of telling us that God was responsible for everything as it successively came into existence and took form. It may have taken many thousands of years. All the world was meant for man, that he might see it and give glory to God. Man could see the countless stars and planets and their precise movements, and realize the majesty and power of God. Man could see the beauty of the world and be led to realize the beauty of God. These words of Saint Augustine were spoken many hundreds of years ago and we might make them our own today: "All things that I see upon the earth, proclaim that you have made them for love of me, and call upon me to love you."

The crown and glory of God's creative act were angels and men. Angels were created before the world and man. They are pure spirits without bodies. We are composed of body and soul, but the angels are superior to us in that they do not have bodies. They, by their nature, had higher dignity than ourselves. They were brought into existence with a greater knowledge and power and holiness than we. After their creation, they were given a period of trial by God. The ones who remained faithful would be given happiness without end; those who were not, would be punished. The great number of angels who remained faithful now enjoy eternal happiness in heaven, constantly seeing, loving, and adoring God. God uses these angels to help and protect men.

But not all the angels remained faithful in their period of trial. Many sinned through pride and were cast into hell forever — "Did God spare even the angels who sinned? He did not! He held them captive in Tartarus — consigned them to pits of darkness" (II Pet. 2:4). It is these who are now our invisible enemies and envy us aiming toward heaven; they seek to lead us to sin and away from God to the state in which they themselves are. They can do nothing against God and so they use their energies against men who bear the image of God. When the angels fell, they were cast into hell, but they are not confined to any one place; they are permitted to wander about the earth tempting men. The devil then is an angel — a bad angel it is true, but with the qualities of an angel just the same. Yes, we Catholics believe in the devil, just as firmly as we believe in God. He is not a character out of a story book. Many a joke has been told about him, but, however men take him, of his existence we have no doubt.

One of the strongest warnings about the devil and his evil influence in the world was delivered by Pope Paul VI on November 15, 1972. At a general audience, the Holy Father described the devil as "a living, spiritual being, perverted and perverting. A terrible reality. Mysterious and frightening.... He is the enemy number one, the tempter par excellence. So we know that this dark and disturbing spirit really exists, and that he still acts with treacherous cunning; he is the secret enemy that sows errors and misfortunes in human history." Noting that the influence of the devil on people, places, and events "is given little attention today," the Pope urged that this "very important chapter of Catholic doctrine" be studied anew.

With God's help and our own efforts we need fear no power against us. But we must do our part. There is an old saying well worth reflecting on: "He who wishes to play with the devil, cannot rejoice with Christ."

"LET US MAKE MAN..."

"Let us make man in our image, after our likeness" (Gn. 1:26).

We have discussed the creation and existence of the angels, good and bad. The seas and plants and stars and animals had been brought into existence by God's power. "God looked at everything He had made, and He found it very good" (Gn. 1:31). And then God spoke the words: "Let us make man in our image, after our likeness" (Gn. 1:26).

How does man resemble God? Man is composed of body and soul. It is chiefly in the soul that man resembles God in some way, for man's soul is endowed with the ability to reason, and with the gift of free will; and it will live forever. Everything that a person makes reflects something of himself: his mind thought of it; his labor produced it; it bears his imprint. A thing cannot help but reflect some of the qualities of the person responsible for it. But there is a much greater similarity when a person sets out to create a likeness of himself. All the paintings of Rembrandt reflect many characteristics of the artist, but Rembrandt's self-portrait is a likeness of himself. When we say that man is created in the image and likeness of God, we mean that God set out to make man in some way like himself and this resemblance is principally in his soul. Man's soul is a spirit, having understanding and free will. The body is the dwelling place of the soul. "The Lord God formed man out of the clay of the ground and blew into his nostrils the breath of life" (Gn. 2:7).

"But I've never seen a soul, and I've operated on many a patient." So said a young atheist doctor in a group in which a priest was present. The priest took up the challenge: "Perhaps you have cut into many a brain too, and you have never seen an idea. You've never seen the force of gravity, but you believe it exists."

Yes, there are many very real things we have never seen or weighed or felt. One of them is the soul. Our ability to think and to choose to act or not to act indicates something beyond our body. Since we were children back in school many years ago we have changed a lot. As a matter of fact, scientists tell us that blood and bone and flesh have changed many times since then and yet we are still the same person. Doctors may continue to cut into human bodies and will never see a soul. And yet it is our soul which will last forever, even after the body has returned to dust from which it was created. It is the soul which bears the likeness to God.

"The Lord God planted a garden in Eden, in the east, and He placed there the man whom He had formed" (Gn. 2:8).

The story of Adam and Eve, created by God and placed in the garden of paradise, is not a fable or pious myth. The story given in the Bible is a history of mankind. They are called our "first parents" because from them came the whole human race. Men receive their body through descent from Adam; the soul of each person is directly created by God.

Adam and Eve were created in a state of happiness almost equal to the angels, and they had many special gifts. Of old, the Jewish people used to sing a hymn, which is now in our Bible, containing these words: "You have made him little less than the angels, and crowned him with glory and honor" (Ps. 8:6).

1. Adam and Eve were created with sanctifying grace, a gift making them pleasing to God and giving them a right to heaven.
2. They had a knowledge far superior to ours.
3. The passions were completely under control of their reason. There were no sensual desires. The lower appetite of man was entirely under control of his higher faculties. They were not drawn to evil by their nature; felt not the slightest inclination to sin.
4. Adam and Eve were not subject to death or suffering. Just as the angels were given a period of trial, and those who were faithful were to be given unending happiness, and those who sinned were punished, so Adam and Eve were put on probation by God. They too were to go through a period of trial. God gave them one commandment. He forbade them to eat of the fruit of one tree which stood in the midst of Paradise. It was by their act of obedience to this precept that God willed our first parents to merit eternal life. But the devil tempted them, and both disobeyed, giving way to pride. This act of disobedience had disastrous consequences. The privileges granted them were lost. They became subject to death and suffering; they had no longer a right to heaven; they now had a strong inclination to evil.

Just as all of Adam's descendants would have inherited his gifts, had he come through the period of trial faithfully, so they have inherited Adam's punishments and shortcomings. We receive our human nature from Adam and Eve, and we receive it just as they had it to hand down, that is without sanctifying grace, with no right to heaven, with an inclination to evil. This state in which we are born is called the state of Original Sin since we inherit it through our origin from Adam. Therefore:

1. We are subject to death and suffering, since that is the human nature that Adam had after the fall. If he had remained faithful, we should not have to suffer in this life.
2. When we enter this life, we are without sanctifying grace, with no right to heaven. God, however, has not abandoned us in this state. To remedy our plight, Christ, the Son of God, gave us Baptism, which restores our right to eternal happiness. Had Adam not sinned, there would be no need for Baptism.
3. We have in our very nature, all through life, an inclination to

evil. That is the kind of human nature that Adam had to give us, after his sin. That is why the modern theory of self-expression — "let the child develop" — can never work.

Just as a stream polluted at its source carries that polluted water along its shore for its whole length, so the original sin of Adam and Eve is carried through all the human race.

We have been done no injustice by God. In creating us, He did not deprive us of anything to which we had any right. If a wealthy man in his will leaves $10,000 to a servant if he remains a faithful servant, and the servant is unfaithful, he will not receive the money. If he had remained faithful, not only would he benefit by the sum of money, but his wife and children would share it also. Since the servant was unfaithful and did not receive the money, the family will not share the pleasure of it either. But the employer has done no injustice to the family. So with the human race. We are born in the state of original sin, not through any fault of our own, but because we receive the human nature which Adam and Eve had to give us.

Only one human being was preserved from this original sin. Mary, the mother of Christ, was from the very moment of her existence free from the shortcoming of human nature. This privilege we call her Immaculate Conception.

Vatican Council II puts it this way: "Although he was made by God in a state of holiness, from the very dawn of history man abused his liberty, at the urging of personified evil. Man set himself against God and sought to find fulfillment apart from God. Although he knew God, he did not glorify Him as God, but his senseless mind was darkened and he served the creature rather than the Creator" *(Pastoral Constitution on the Church in the Modern World,* No. 13).

And again the Second Vatican Council declares: "In the course of history, temporal things have been foully abused by serious vices. Affected by original sin, men have frequently fallen into multiple errors concerning the true God, the nature of man, and the principles of the moral law. The result has been the corruption of morals and human institutions and not rarely contempt for the human person himself. In our own time, moreover, those many who have trusted excessively in the advances of the natural sciences and of technology have fallen into an idolatry of temporal things and have become their slaves rather than their masters" (*Decree on the Apostolate of the Laity,* No. 7).

Concerned with the modern confusion about original sin, our first parents and the repercussions of their sin on the human race, Pope

Paul declared: "The fact and the universality of original sin are clearly taught, as well as the intimate nature of the state from which mankind fell through Adam's guilt: 'The eternal Father, by a free and hidden plan of his own wisdom and goodness, created the whole world. His plan was to raise men to a participation of the divine life. God the Father did not leave men, fallen in Adam, to themselves, but ceaselessly offered helps to salvation in view of Christ, the Redeemer,' (Cf. Col. 1:15; Vatican Council II: *Dogmatic Constitution on the Church,* Ch. 1, n. 2). . . . The doctrine of original sin regarding both its existence and universality, its character as true sin even in the descendants of Adam and its sad consequences for soul and body, is a truth revealed by God in various passages of the Old and of the New Testament. . . . It is therefore evident that the explanations of original sin given by some modern authors will seem to you irreconcilable with the true Catholic doctrine . . . the sin from which so many cesspools of evil have come to mankind was first of all the disobedience of Adam, 'first man,' figure of the man to come . . . the sin of the first man is transmitted to all his descendants not through imitation but through propagation, 'in each one as his own' and is 'the death of the soul,' that is privation and not simple lack of holiness and of justice even in newborn babies" (Pope Paul VI, Address to the members of the Symposium on Original Sin, July 11, 1966).

Pope Paul VI, in the midst of pinpointing the drastic consequences of original sin for the human race, strikes an optimistic note: "What is the aim of the Church's pastoral action if not the redemption of human nature which, being admirably created by the all-powerful God in Adam and in him wretchedly fallen, was even more admirably re-created and regenerated by the merciful God through the grace of the only mediator Jesus Christ?" (Address to members of the Symposium on Original Sin)

The story of original sin and its part in the life of every human being born into the world offers the key to the answering of many problems facing us in the twentieth century as well as at the dawn of civilization. Why sickness and suffering? Why cannot we just let children "express themselves" and grow up "naturally"? Why do men have to fight against sin and temptation instead of "coasting along" through life?

The answer to all those questions will not be difficult to fathom if we realize the teaching of the Catholic Church on original sin.

Anyone who has accepted Christianity possesses a precise awareness of sin.
—Pope Paul VI, Address on Ash Wednesday, 1968

photo by Don Smith

Chapter 17

The World's Greatest Evil

> People no longer talk of sin because this very sad and very real condition of sinning man implies the idea of God. It implies the idea of the offense perpetrated against God. It implies realization of having broken the real, life-bringing relationship with Him; it implies awareness of an intolerable disorder in delinquent man; it implies the absolute need of salvation, nay of a Savior. — Pope Paul VI, March 17, 1971.

One of the former officials of Nazi Germany, Hans Frank, shortly after World War II, was on trial at Nuremberg, with several other "war criminals." He had become a Catholic while in prison and was now found guilty of several crimes during the war and given the penalty of death. In his final statement to the Catholic chaplain before he died, he said: "We did not imagine at the start of our road that turning away from God could have such destructive and deadly consequences."

When man turns his back on God there will be, without fail, deadly consequences, very often in this life and certainly in the next. Man turns his back on God by sin, by violating God's law for man.

We are hearing more and more today in "modern" circles about self-expression, about the fact that repressing the desires of a child (or an adult for that matter) is bad. "People must not suppress their desires or a bad case of nerves will result." A book could be written on that statement, but one of the main difficulties with people who apply it to their lives today is that the term "self-expression" is much misunderstood. Every being ought to express itself in accordance with its nature, not against that nature. The fact that an automobile was meant to drive on a road and not through peoples' backyards does not mean that the use of the automobile is being suppressed. When steam finds itself repressed by being confined to a boiler and exerts its pressure, blowing up the boiler, it finds that that is not self-expression but rather results in destruction. So too, when man comes to the conclusion that the law of God involves repression of his nature and desires, and throws off all restraint, he will find that that kind of self-expression will bring about harm (here or hereafter).

There are two kinds of sin: First, original sin is that sin which our first parents committed and which every man born into this world inherits because of his origin from Adam and Eve. That is wiped away through Baptism. Second, actual sin which we commit ourselves. Sin is the only enemy that can bring eternal ruin to man. Many other things might cause him difficulty: a mistake may mean a loss of friends, or money; sickness might mean the loss of health; the devil can make living up to God's law more difficult. But only sin can ruin man spiritually and eternally.

From our point of view, sin on the surface looks attractive and after all every one of us is looking for happiness. Many seek that happiness in money — and as so many who have attained it will tell you, that is not the solution to happiness; honor and worldly pleasures are not what they were "cracked up to be." So too, sin always looks better beforehand. The Catholic Church never said that sin would not give some pleasure, but it is momentary and much less than contemplated, while man's heart still seeks lasting happiness. We cannot stop a child from eating sugar by telling him that it is bitter. As soon as he tastes it, he knows you are wrong. Give him something sweeter, honey; so too, with worldly pleasures. They are pleasures or else people would not seek them. But men must see that the only happiness lies in keeping God's law, and that in violating it the passing pleasure is more than paid for, not infrequently here and certainly hereafter.

SIN — A VIOLATION OF GOD'S LAW FOR ALL MEN

How can it be that a person who knows God would ever commit a mortal sin? The answer to that question must be found in man's own nature and in his present relationship to God. First of all, God has left man free; it is up to him to say "yes" or "no" in the face of a temptation. God, who has created man with his will, has decreed that He will not save him without his will. Sin is in the will, and no one can force our will. Sin in the last analysis is simply willfully turning our back on God.

The chief happiness in heaven will consist in seeing God face to face, and that very fact excludes any possibility of sin. The sight of the Divine Goodness will put out of the question any substitute. Then we will see things in their true light, and there will be no question of seeking happiness elsewhere.

However, to come back to earth and our present state — we do not now see God or experience the complete happiness which only that can give. We know God by the use of our powers of reason and faith. "Now we see indistinctly, as in a mirror; then we shall see face to face" (I Cor. 13:12). That is the way Saint Paul described the situation.

God could have created us with that sight of himself in this life, and then there would be no question of sin. Rather He has chosen to hide himself from our view for the present so that we might have the privilege of meriting our final reward. The situation might be compared to the young millionaire, hiding his wealth from the girl he hopes to marry so that she might choose him for what he is, not for what he can give her. God has given us the power to reject Him. Every day of our lives we can choose either God or something in preference to Him. The choice of the former may mean sacrifice and giving up our own wishes but it also brings with it the promise of complete happiness; the choice of the latter is sin which might bring some pleasure for a time but will be punished by eternal banishment from the sight of God.

The person who murders, steals, commits adultery, hates a neighbor, is envious, may protest that he does not want to give up God. But the fact of the matter is, that was his choice. You cannot eat your cake and have it too. You cannot choose both God and sin.

Usually a sinner finds that the true character of sin and the lack of the power to give happiness is revealed after the sin is committed. The picture of sin has an entirely different aspect before and after. Sometimes the sinner tries to pacify his conscience, building up a case to justify his actions — "this isn't really too wrong" or "after all human nature is human nature and everybody does it"; or he simply tries to drown out any thought on the matter by filling his mind with so many things that there is no conscience to reproach him: movies, reading, talking, the radio, television, and the host of other distractions and attempts to smother one's conscience. The sinner has taken the first step back to God when he stops, looks at himself and honestly admits that he is wrong in trying to fool himself.

It takes real humility and character to admit when we are wrong. It is not easy at times for a sinner to return to God. A well known scholar in the United States some time ago returned to the Church after being out of the Faith for thirty years. He was asked on one occasion why he left the Church and what took him so long to come back. He replied that in all the years outside the Faith and among all those with whom he came in contact, he never met one who left because of intellectual conviction that the Catholic Church was wrong, but because the Church is a reproach to their own conscience; because they wanted to sin; and once a person has begun to lead a life in violation of God's law, it is not easy to conquer his pride even though he be completely unhappy in his sin, and come to the loving arms of Christ.

God's law is violated willfully by having thoughts and desires against it, by saying or doing something forbidden by it, or by not doing what is commanded by it.

There is no evil which comes even close to being as great an evil as sin — no disease or pain, no death or destruction, earthquake or famine. For sin is the rebellion of a creature against his Creator.

The tragedy of our day is not so much that there is sin in the world, for this is the history of man. But it lies in the fact that in our day men have lost their sense of sin. On March 17, 1971, Pope Paul during his general audience spoke of a secularized world that tries to forget the existence of sin and declared that Christians must remind themselves that "sin and redemption are interwoven in a way that we can never forget." For this reason, the Pope said, we must develop "the wholesome sense of good and evil." It was on Ash Wednesday, 1968, that the same Holy Father declared: "We must renew in ourselves a sense of true Christian conscience, which accuses us of guilt and gives us no peace until we have found a remedy to our erring nature."

The saying: "A saint is a sinner who kept on trying" gives a balanced picture of what our attitude should be.

THE DRASTIC CONSEQUENCES OF SIN

The thought of the drastic consequences of sin will help us to realize in some measure what an evil sin really is.

In the beginning thousands of angels worshiped God in happiness. They had much stronger intellects and wills and were much more gifted and happy than ourselves. God left them free and with the obligation to worship Him. And yet, in spite of their great perfections, they sinned through pride — Lucifer and his followers exclaiming: "We will not serve." And because of this one serious sin, hell was created and Lucifer and his cohorts were cast into it forever. From overwhelming joy to everlasting pain, that was the punishment for the first mortal sin.

The meaning of sin is brought even closer to us by the thought of the one sin of our first parents. Adam and Eve were intensely happy with great perfections of mind and body. But being creatures, they owed God reverence and obedience. In return for all God's gifts to them, He asked one simple expression of obedience. Pride entered their hearts, and they disobeyed that one command. By that one sin they were cast from Paradise; they and all after them were now subject to death, sickness, suffering. One sin caused all that. What an awful thing one sin must be!

As a Catholic kneels at a crucifix, he realizes that Christ died because of man's sin. Our sins were responsible for the nails in Christ's hands, for the crown of thorns on his head. What an evil sin must be in God's sight!

When a man violates one of God's laws, he says with the fallen angels: "I will not serve." What drastic consequences those words can have for man!

There are two kinds of sin that a person may commit. Mortal sin is a serious offense against God. Venial sin is a light offense against God.

Sanctifying grace is spiritual life and health. Anything which takes away life is deadly or mortal (a mortal wound). Mortal sin deals a death blow to the soul; it takes away sanctifying grace and spiritual life; it makes man an enemy of God; it takes away his right to heaven; it makes him worthy of punishment forever in hell; it deprives man of all the reward for his good actions. We can well understand why Queen Blanche told her son Louis, the future king and later a saint: "My son, I would prefer to see you dead than ever guilty of a mortal sin."

Venial sin is a sin which is not as serious as mortal sin. Some diseases are so serious that they destroy life. Others only weaken the health and strength of the body. Venial sins weaken our power to resist mortal sin. They make us deserving not of punishment forever in hell, but punishment for a time in purgatory or in this life. Though there is a vast difference between mortal and venial sin, a venial sin is still the worst evil in the world, mortal sin alone excepted. By mortal sin we turn our back on God. Venial sin will impede our progress toward Him. One venial sin is a greater calamity than the destruction of heaven and earth. By mortal sin a stroke of the axe cuts off the root of a tree and its nourishment from the soil; venial sin is an axe's stroke at the bark; it may hinder its growth but not destroy it.

Since there is such a vast difference between mortal and venial sin and their consequences for us, the question of how to distinguish the two is tremendously important.

There are three questions — all of which must be answered with the word "yes" for a mortal sin to be committed:

1. Was the thought, desire, word, deed or omission seriously wrong; was it a serious violation of God's law? For instance, murder, stealing a large sum of money, adultery.

2. Did the person know it was a serious violation of God's law or the Church's law? If a person commits a mortal sin but at the time, through no fault of his own, sincerely thinks it is venial, he is not guilty of mortal sin.

3. Did the person fully consent to it; did he fully want to do it? For instance, a man in the hospital under the influence of drugs does some act against the commandments. He has not committed a mortal sin. If a person is forced to do something against his will, he has not committed a mortal sin. If the answer to any one of those questions is "no" then there was no mortal sin. If the answer to all of them is "yes" then a mortal sin was committed.

We ought to do all in our power to avoid all sin, mortal or venial. One day Saint Frances Chantal was nursing a leper. Someone standing by remarked that she might in that work contract the disease. "I fear no leprosy, but the leprosy of sin," was her reply.

It is God himself in the Bible who reminds us: "Those habitually guilty of sin are their own worst enemies" (Tb. 12:10).

TEMPTATIONS

There is a vast difference between sin and a temptation to sin. A temptation puts before a person some evil, painting it as good and pleasurable, and drawing the will to say "yes." Eve would not have sinned unless she had first been tempted. But temptations no matter how strong they are or how long they last are not sinful. There are three sources of temptation:

First, the world — e.g. bad companions, shows, immoral literature.

Second, the flesh — human nature's leaning toward evil. Since the fall of our first parents man no longer finds it easy to do the right thing at all times. There is a downward pull. To keep God's law requires a fight and effort. "Is not man's life on earth a drudgery?" (Jb. 7:1).

Third, the devil — who goes about "prowling like a roaring lion looking for someone to devour" (I Pt. 5:8). Satan is a very real being.

His attempts to draw us away from God are constant and persistent.

In 1885, Pope Leo XIII, a voluntary prisoner in the Vatican, ordered prayers to be recited after Mass. They were to be offered for the peaceful settlement of the "Roman Question" and the restoration of the Sovereign Pontiff's independence. Forty-four years were to pass before the matter was finally and amicably settled by the Lateran Treaty of February 11, 1929.

Then Pius XI, the Pope of the Lateran Treaty, looked to Russia writhing under atheistic communism, and directed that those same prayers be offered for the restoration of religion and religious freedom in Russia. Years have passed since. The prayers are no longer recited after Mass. Today, religion is still suppressed in many parts of the world.

It may take many more years, just as it did for the settlement of the "Roman Question." It may require a long period of still bloodier persecution. But in God's own good time the prophetic words of Pius XI must at length be fulfilled, that "Christ, the Redeemer of mankind, will at last restore peace and free possession of their religion to the faithful people persecuted in Russia."

The following is the prayer that was said after Mass for some seventy-five years to implore God's help against the attacks of Satan in the modern world:

"Saint Michael, the archangel, defend us in battle, be our protection against the malice and snares of the devil. We humbly beseech God to restrain him, and you O prince of the heavenly host, by the divine power, thrust into hell Satan and the other evil spirits who roam through the world seeking the ruin of souls. Amen."

A near occasion of sin is anything which can easily lead us to sin. We must avoid any person, place or thing which could easily lead us to fall into a sin.

God allows temptation, so that in overcoming it we may earn eternal life. Every temptation overcome renders a person that much stronger.

There are seven chief sources of sin. They are called *Capital Sins*, not because they are the seven greatest sins, but because they are the main things leading men to sin. Pride, covetousness, lust, anger, gluttony, envy, and sloth. Pride, of course, is at the root of all sins. It was the reason Lucifer and the fallen angels sinned, for they wanted to be equal to God; it is the reason Adam and Eve sinned — for they were too proud to obey the one command God gave them; it is the reason we sin, for in every sin we say in effect to God, as Lucifer did: "I will not serve."

Before any sin there is a temptation. And man always has the strength to say "no" in any temptation. It may require an effort, but no person ever committed a sin against his will. "In whatever you do, remember your last days, and you will never sin" (Sir. 7:36). A temptation begins first in the mind, and that is the time to conquer it. A fire just begun is not too difficult to extinguish, but give it ten minutes and it becomes much more difficult. A disease in its first stages may be warded off before it does too much harm.

It requires little effort to swim with the tide, in fact we can just float along with it. But when we have done that it takes strong swimming and effort to get back to the shore. It is easy to break the moral law, but when that is done it takes an extra effort to get back to God.

It does not pay to aim at merely avoiding mortal sins. Small sins may have more serious consequences than we suspect. A single spark may set off a keg of gun powder. It does not take a bullet to cause death. A pin wound when neglected has been known to fester and cause an infection, doing harm far beyond what the person thought a mere pin could do.

God has left man with free will to face sin, to say "yes" or "no" in the face of temptation. He has created us without our will, but will not save us without our will. God has chosen to decline to be a dictator in order to abolish sin.

A cataract in a person's eye if not removed will darken and gradually remove the sight. Sin will darken the intellect and wear down the will. Every time one gives in to sin, the next becomes easier, conscience is dulled, doing the right thing becomes harder. It is as leprosy, working slowly, breaking down tissues and health for a time without much visible effect. By the time it develops, a cure becomes more difficult.

However deeply a man has cast himself into sin, God is ready to stretch out a helping hand to get back into his grace. And to one who has returned from sin, Christ says once again: "Let us eat and celebrate, because this son of mine was dead and has come back to life. He was lost and is found" (Lk. 15:23-24). The return of a sinner to God brings peace and happiness not only to him but to the very angels of heaven: "There will . . . be more joy in heaven over one repentant sinner than over ninety-nine righteous people who have no need to repent" (Lk. 15:7).

It is a strange thing about sin. The more you experience it — commit it — the less you know about it. Saints, who seldom or never commit a serious sin, know more about it than sinners. A person swimming with the current in a river does not realize its strength. Christ and Mary never committed sin, yet they knew the power of temptation and sin better than anyone else. They are willing to help us in our struggle if we will stretch out our hand for their aid.

Man fears failure. His job in life is to live, pray, and work following the rules laid down for him by God. If he follows God's rules, he will attain some measure of happiness here, higher than he could attain in any other way; and will attain the highest eternal happiness of heaven. If man attains that he is a success. If he does not, he is an utter failure, no matter what his other accomplishments may be. There is only one thing that can make for that failure — not sickness or loss of money or honor or friends. Sin is the only thing that can make man a failure. To be successful in our struggle against sin is the most important thing in man's life, and man must spare no effort to attain this success.

Interior of Franciscan church on the site of Shepherd's Field outside of Bethlehem

photo by Paul J. Hayes

Chapter 18

Jesus Christ — God and Man

> Only in the mystery of the incarnate Word does the mystery of man take on light. —Vatican II, *Pastoral Constitution on the Church in the Modern World,* No. 22.

A young virgin-mother 1900 years ago laid her newborn infant in a manger inside a cave used as a stable for animals; angels brought the joyful news to a few simple men on a hillside; shepherds without flourish entered the cave in Bethlehem to adore their King.

Who is this Baby? The world had been looking forward to this event for centuries. At the time of the birth of Christ the whole world was at peace. Augustus had reached the peak of his glory as emperor. The people proclaimed him as almost divine. He was their "savior"; he was referred to as "the star rising over the world." Among all the glorious titles, there is one which down through history has not been associated with any worldly ruler — Prince of Peace. But 700 years earlier a Hebrew prophet did use this title, referring to the future Messiah, to Christ who would come to fulfill his prophecy centuries after it was spoken.

"For a child is born to us, a son is given us; upon his shoulder dominion rests. They name him Wonder-Counselor, God-Hero, Father-Forever, Prince of Peace" (Is. 9:5).

And 700 years after these words were spoken, a Child was born. His birth was announced to the shepherds by angels with words that this obscure birth brought with it glory and peace.

It is rare that a man has a biography written about him; rarer yet is it that a man's life be written before he dies. Christ was unique in that He had the details of his life set down in writing before his birth.

The Messiah was to be born in Bethlehem. In the eighth century before Christ, Micah wrote: "But you, Bethlehem-Ephrathah, too small to be among the clans of Judah, from you shall come forth for me one who is to be ruler in Israel" (Mi. 5:1). Bethlehem at the time of Christ's birth was a small village of perhaps no more than one thousand people. Practically all were peasants or shepherds. And today in the hills of Bethlehem there can still be seen small caves used by the shepherds to shelter their flocks. It was in such a cave used as a stable for animals that Christ was born. It was in the obscure town which the Jewish prophet speaking of the birth of Christ referred to as "little," that the Savior of the world was born.

The Messiah was to be born from the descendants of David, wrote one of the prophets 650 years before Christ's birth. Mary was of the line of David.

And seven centuries before the Christian era, Isaiah, painting many of the details of Christ's life spoke the words: "The virgin shall be with child, and bear a son, and shall name him Immanuel" (Is. 7:14). Here was a picture painted many centuries before it took on reality in a cave at Bethlehem where "she gave birth to her first-born Son and wrapped Him in swaddling clothes and laid Him in a manger" (Lk. 2:7).

When some incident of widespread importance happens, newspaper reporters grasp the opportunity to put it in headlines; the radio and television re-echo it every hour on the hour from coast to coast; commentators strain their vocabularies to paint a graphic description; column after column is written about it. But when we come to the most important event in history, it is related in one simple paragraph. The story of Christ's Incarnation, the story of God becoming man, of God taking on human nature, as told by Saint Luke would be rejected by a newspaper editor today as being too simple, without color.

"In those days, Caesar Augustus published a decree ordering a census of the whole world. This first census took place while Quirinius was governor of Syria. Everyone went to register, each to his own town. And so Joseph went from the town of Nazareth in Galilee to Judea, to David's town of Bethlehem — because he was of the house and lineage of David — to register with Mary, his espoused wife, who was with Child. While they were there the days of her confinement were completed. She gave birth to her first-born Son and wrapped Him in swaddling clothes and laid Him in a manger, because there was no room for them in the place where travelers lodged" (Lk. 2:1-7).

The complete story is there in one paragraph. The very simplicity of it, leads us to see that it deals with something sublime, something beyond the human.

WHY CHRIST SHARED OUR LIFE

The reason for all this goes back to the dawn of mankind. Our first parents, Adam and Eve, were given a period of trial. If they remained faithful they would gain eternal happiness; if not, they would lose their right to heaven. Our first parents sinned, and since every offense is measured by the dignity of the one offended — a child, e.g. who strikes his mother has committed a much more serious act than if he struck a fellow playmate — and since God is of infinite dignity, the offense of mankind against God was infinite. And so no mere man could make up for it. God, the second Person of the Blessed Trinity, took on our human nature at Bethlehem. That fact we call the Incarnation.

As God, Christ could make *infinite* satisfaction for the offense; as man, He could make up for an offense committed by men. Jesus Christ became man without ceasing to be God. Christ then is both God and Man. He has a *divine* nature and a *human* nature, but in Christ there is only *one Person.*

There is no contradiction in that if we remember the difference between a nature and a person. If we can see an object, but cannot distinguish it, we ask *"What* is that?" — of what nature is it? If we see a person but cannot make out which person, we say *"Who* is that?" In Christ there are two natures — two "what's," the divine and human; there is only one Person. For every man we can ask "What is he" and "Who is he." For every one of man's actions his nature and person have a part. It is that man who is speaking — that person; but he is speaking because he is a man. He cannot fly because he does not have the nature of a bird. My nature determines what I can do, but it is the person who does it. When Christ acted, his actions were those not only of man but of God.

Suppose a great king with noble ideals were to leave his throne and the comfort of his palace, and take on the rags of a beggar, live with the poorest of the poor, share their inferior homes and their trials, so that he might get to know their life first hand. That king, though becoming a beggar, did not cease to be a king. We could still say that what that beggar suffered had value as the acts of a king. That King was Jesus Christ. It was out of love for us that God, the Creator of heaven and earth, took on a human nature in a cave at Bethlehem.

God so loved men that He became one himself.

We can scarcely appreciate what a lowering this was for Christ to become one of us. Perhaps a comparison will help us to appreciate it. Would you by your own will become a worm, crawling on the earth? This would never do — it is far below us. God is infinitely further above us, than we are above worms. What a degradation for the Son of God to become one of us!

Christ is true God and true man. Any being gets its nature from where it takes its origin. A child, for instance, gets his human nature through his origin from his parents. Christ is the Son of God and so has a divine nature. By being born of Mary, He derives from her his human nature.

Christ became man, was born of Mary in a miraculous way on the first Christmas. This unique mystery is called the virgin-birth. Christ was in the words of the Apostles Creed: "born of the Virgin Mary."

This Man, Christ, who lived on earth in the country of Palestine and died in the year 30 A.D. claimed before the world to be God.

CHRIST OUR REDEEMER

Why did God take on our human nature with all its infirmities and choose for himself a life of suffering?

In the sin of our first parents, God was offended by man. The result was that man's right to heaven was taken away. After the fall of our first parents, they no longer had any rights to supernatural happiness. No mere man or even the most perfect angel could make up for that infinite offense.

To redeem man, to make up for the offense against God, God himself became man.

If a valuable portrait becomes damaged greatly beyond recognition, the person whose picture it was will have to sit again before the artist so that the picture or likeness can be re-painted and restored. So God came down to earth to restore man's likeness to God. This we call the Redemption. Jesus Christ as the Redeemer of the human race, offered his life, sufferings and death to God in satisfaction for the sins of men, and regained for them the right to heaven.

Christ's whole life from birth to death was offered to make up for the sins of men. The climax of that life was his last hours on earth, his bloody sweat, the scourging, the crowning with thorns, and his crucifixion and death on the cross on Good Friday.

THE REDEMPTION IN THE TWENTIETH CENTURY

There is a hotel in North Carolina, which has as its motto on the letterhead, a Latin inscription meaning "Salvation through the Cross." It is a strange motto for a hotel, but expresses one of the foundation stones of Catholic belief.

Christ once said: "I — once I am lifted up from earth — will draw all men to myself" (Jn. 12:32). Perhaps the meaning of those words was not fathomed by the Apostles on the day they were spoken. Christ was lifted up on the hill of Calvary on a cross. And for two thousand years this symbol of our salvation has acted as a magnet — drawing all men of all ages toward the Man on that cross.

Christ died on the cross on that first Good Friday, but only to rise again more gloriously.

Immediately after Christ's death, his soul went down in triumph to the place where the good who died before Christ were detained. When we say: "He descended into hell," we mean his soul descended to the place of rest called limbo, which is distinct from purgatory or hell as we ordinarily use the word today. The good who died before Christ could not go to heaven, for the redemption of Christ was not accomplished yet; they were not deserving of hell. And so they were detained in a state of rest called limbo. It was to this place that Christ went after his death, to announce the joyful news of man's Redemption. While his soul was there, Christ's body was in the holy sepulchre where it was placed after his death.

It was on the third day, the first Easter Sunday, that Christ's body and soul were re-united and He rose from the dead. This fact was final proof if any more were needed that Christ was really God.

Just as Christ arose from the dead, so at the end of time all men will rise and those who have been faithful to Christ shall share his glory.

Forty days after Christ arose from the dead, after appearing to his Mother, and the Apostles, and to large groups of people — to prove the fact of his resurrection, He ascended into heaven.

"Then He led them out near Bethany, and with hands upraised, blessed them. As He blessed, He left them, and was taken up to heaven" (Lk. 24:50-51).

In the Apostles' Creed we say of Christ that He "sits at the right hand of God the Father." To sit on the right hand is a mark of special honor. By the expression we mean that Christ is above all the angels and saints and is equal to God the Father. He is Christ the King, who will come at the end of the world to pronounce judgment of eternal reward or punishment on all peoples.

INCARNATION AND REDEMPTION — LOVE PAR EXCELLENCE

The Son of God was conceived and made man by the power of the Holy Spirit, born of Mary in a miraculous way. Christ had no human father, but Saint Joseph was the guardian and foster father of Christ. The fact that God in this way took on a human nature, that is, a body and soul like ours, is called the mystery of the Incarnation. And through becoming man and through his suffering and death, Christ redeemed us.

This central truth of Catholic teaching we celebrate on Christmas day. If Christ, the Eternal Son of God, thought so much of us, that He came into this world and suffered and died for us, we must mean a lot to Him. The question then is, what does He mean to us?

Suppose you knew that if you gave a certain person a Christmas present of a watch, he would five minutes later throw it to the ground and step on it. Would you give it to him anyway? Christ knew as He washed the feet of Judas, what Judas was going to do in a short time. Yet He washed his feet anyway. Christ knew when He lay in the stable at Bethlehem and when He hung on the cross that men would sin, and yet He redeemed us anyway.

An artist in Japan one day requested an audience with the emperor. He bore with him a life-size portrait of the emperor. What impressed the emperor was not so much the artistry of the picture but the fact that the artist had painted it with his own blood. For twelve years, day after day, he had drawn enough blood from his veins to add a few more strokes of his brush to his life's masterpiece. Christ shed every drop of his blood for us. He accomplished our redemption at a great price.

Chapter 19

Grace and the Virtues

> Who will separate us from the love of Christ. . . . I am certain that neither death, nor life, neither angels nor principalities, neither the present nor the future, nor powers, neither height nor depth nor any other creature, will be able to separate us from the love of God that comes to us in Christ Jesus, our Lord. — *Romans* 8:35, 38-39.

"The Catholic Church takes all the fun out of life." Have you heard that, or a similar statement? At times we hear the reproach that the Catholic religion is one of joylessness. But invariably it is the statement of one who does not know the full teaching of the Church. Actually no other religion has so steadfastly championed joy and happiness in the right way and not mistaken it for pleasure. The very foundation of the Catholic Church was based on a gospel characterized by a note of joy — "I come to proclaim good news to you — tidings of great joy to be shared by the whole people" (Lk. 2:10). Its Founder, Jesus Christ, time and time again assured his followers of peace of soul and abundant joy — joy far surpassing fleeting pleasures, a joy that would last forever if we follow his program and take advantage of his gifts to us. "Your hearts will rejoice with a joy no one can take from you" (Jn. 16:22). But Christ and the Catholic Church would have us make no mistake on how to attain the happiness we are destined for; we can never gain that until we realize the purpose of our existence and regulate our life accordingly.

Recently it was reported by news commentators that a young scientist had discovered a mathematical formula involving the force of gravity and other laws of nature which would give the answer to many mysteries up to this time in the field of science. One commentator hastened to add that certain scientists were of the opinion that the formula would in time solve the mystery of "life." It was an interesting sidelight, but interesting too is the fact that with all our scientific progress, no scientist has even come close to producing life by chemical elements or applying mathematical formulas.

If we look around us, we can observe three types of life: first, vegetative life (found in plants); second, sensitive life (found in animals); third, intellectual life, which includes the other two (found in ourselves).

In each of these kinds of life, there is a principle of life responsible for its kind of activities.

Plant life is characterized by such activities as growth; nourishing itself through soil and air. A rock cannot do these things because it is not alive.

Sensitive life (as found in animals) — is characterized by growth, nourishment (the same as plant life) and also by feeling, seeing, tasting, hearing. It can do all a plant can, plus something more.

Intellectual life has as its activities all that plants and animals have, plus the power to think and use free will.

Did you ever think that there is another kind of life — a "supernatural" life. Vegetative, sensitive, and intellectual lives are "natural." By the very fact that God created plants, animals and man, each has certain activities proper to itself "naturally." But God went a step further and created a fourth kind of life, a supernatural life — found in persons in "the state of grace." Anything we know about this fourth kind of life, does not come from our observation but from what God told us about it. This fourth kind of life enables a man to do things which he would not do otherwise — to do things that are meritorious for heaven.

When a man has this principle of "super-life" (we call it grace) he is different from a man not having it, just as a dog can do things that a turnip cannot, and a man can do things that a dog cannot.

All this ties up with the particular purpose that a thing has. If we want to get to know anything fully we have to know first what it is for. We really do not know how to use a thing or very much about it until we know its purpose. If a man never saw a thermometer before, and instead of asking what it was, went ahead and used it to stir a pot of boiling soup, it would not be long before the thermometer broke. Why? Because he is using it for a purpose for which it was never meant. Any man who uses anything without knowing its purpose is acting blindly and will probably do harm. The fact that he meant well does not change the situation.

Applying this principle to ourselves: We cannot act rightly until we know what we are for and what means we have to accomplish our purpose. The best way to find out the purpose of a thing is by asking the maker why he made it. We can find out the purpose of our own

I was hungry and you gave me food. I was thirsty and you gave me drink. I was a stranger and you welcomed me, naked and you clothed me. I was ill and you comforted me, in prison and you came to visit me. —Matthew 25:35-36

photo by Paul J. Hayes

existence from God and through religion. To act without such knowledge is a fine formula for chaos.

Man is meant for heaven. He has been given a soul with a threefold natural life (vegetative, sensitive, and intellectual). But God has gone a step further in helping him to get to heaven by giving him a supernatural life and supernatural aids. This help we call grace.

Grace is a supernatural gift of God bestowed on us through the merits of Christ for our salvation.

Let us take a little further look into this word "grace" so often heard in Catholic teaching.

No mere natural act on our part can make us worthy of heaven (which is our objective). Perhaps an illustration will help. A little boy standing under an apple tree, sees the fruit above him, but out of his reach; he stretches as far as he can, but the fruit is still out of his reach. So his father lifts the boy up, so that he can reach the fruit. The boy takes the fruit himself, but can only do this because his father lifted him up to do so. In a similar way, we cannot attain salvation by our own efforts naturally. We have to be aided, lifted up spiritually, by our Father, God. That supernatural aid we call grace.

THE PLAN OF SALVATION

God always existed and was infinitely happy from all eternity. He did not need anything or any one else to increase his happiness. But his love was so great that He wanted to share his happiness with others and so God created angels and men. But in order to share his happiness, they in some way had to share his nature. A dog, for instance, can enjoy himself but he could never enjoy anything above his nature, as a good joke or symphony — in order to do this he would have to become in some measure human, to partake of human nature. In our case, we could not enjoy divine happiness as God planned for us until our human nature was raised. In the beginning God created Adam and Eve with a human nature raised to a higher level. As a matter of fact they were "sharers of the divine nature," as Saint Peter (II Pt. 1:4) tells us. They and all who came after them were to maintain this state if they remained faithful. But they fell, lost sanctifying grace and the higher state in which they were. God in order to give man again a right to that state, to regain grace for him, became man and merited by his life and death on earth all the grace and supernatural helps we need to get to heaven. Grace then is given in virtue of the merits of Christ, for our salvation.

It is the Holy Spirit, and third Person of the Blessed Trinity, who distributes to men the graces won by Christ.

There are two kinds of grace: sanctifying grace and actual grace.

SANCTIFYING GRACE

Sanctifying grace is that grace which gives our souls a new life, a sharing in the life of God himself. It gives the ability of doing things which we could not do of ourselves. It enables us to do things beyond our own mere human nature, that is to perform acts able to bring us to eternal happiness. We cannot picture a cow sitting down enjoying a good cigar, listening to Toscanini — such things are beyond the nature of any animal. A cow would have to be raised to the level of human nature for such things. Similarly if we are to be capable of attaining the happiness of heaven, we have to be raised beyond our human nature. Grace does this.

Sanctifying grace may be compared to a passport to heaven. Death is our journey from this world into eternity. Just as we would not think of beginning a journey to a foreign country before getting all our papers in order and obtaining a passport from the Government so that we would be allowed across the borders of that country so we should be prepared for our entrance into eternity. Sanctifying grace is that passport. If our soul is in the state of sanctifying grace we have a right to enter heaven. Without this grace, we have no title to heaven.

Grace is our ticket to heaven. That ticket is first obtained when we are baptized. It may be lost through mortal sin. It is regained by contrition and Confession.

By this grace we are made children of God and heirs of heaven. As a child is pleasing to and loved by his father as his own, so by grace we are made pleasing in God's sight. And as an heir receives a title to the fortune, so we by grace receive a title to the eternal inheritance, if we do nothing to cancel that title by the commission of serious sin.

We get a fuller idea of sanctifying grace by comparing it to the physical health of our body. Grace is spiritual health of soul. Just as some people enjoy health, while others have some disease, so some have sanctifying grace—spiritual health, while others are in the state of spiritual disease, sin. And just as one person may be healthier and stronger than another, so one person may have more sanctifying grace than another. After sanctifying grace comes into a person's soul by receiving the Sacrament of Baptism, he ought never to do anything to lose this grace by committing a single mortal sin. But just as a person may lose his health and have to go to a doctor to have it restored, so one who loses sanctifying grace by a serious sin, must go to Confession to have his spiritual health restored. And so too, as physical health may be built up by exercise and good food, so sanctifying grace may be increased by prayer and especially by the sacraments.

Grace is an invisible quality in our soul. We cannot see it (just as we cannot see the health of our body), but we know it is present whenever there are no mortal sins present.

By sanctifying grace, a man is made a friend of God. By it we are made temples of God, for in a very real way God dwells in a soul in the state of grace. "Are you not aware that you are the temple of God, and that the Spirit of God dwells in you?" (I Cor. 3:16). Through this grace a man is united to God as a vine to a branch. The whole world and all it contains is of less value in the eyes of God than the grace in a single soul.

Sanctifying grace is meant to bring a man heaven. One who has this grace is pleasing to God and is like a traveler making a journey during good weather and sunshine. One without this grace is traveling through life like a man forced to make a trip through storms and rain.

Weeds on a farm will prevent the sun and nourishment of the soil from bringing a good crop. Any farmer knows that the weeds must be rooted up. Sin prevents the action of grace in our soul. Sanctifying grace and mortal sin cannot exist together. We must banish the one, if we are to have the other.

ACTUAL GRACE

The second type of grace is actual grace. This is a special supernatural help of God which enlightens our mind and strengthens our will to do good and to avoid evil.

Actual grace is a passing influence on our mind or will — an extra "push" toward good, so to speak, on God's part. For instance a person is passing a church and gets the idea to go in to make a visit. He may actually go in or not; that is up to him. But the original idea was an actual grace. Actual graces are innumerable: an actual grace might be a sermon, a good book, a picture, a stimulus on our will to avoid an act which is wrong. At times a thing which seems to us to have happened by chance may be God's way of drawing us to Him by an actual grace. All these are channels by which God the Holy Spirit influences us.

In the southwestern part of our country, there was a man who (as he later admitted) had a great contempt and hatred for the Catholic Church. A few years ago, he turned on his radio. There was a sermon on, and the man related that if he knew it was a Catholic priest he would not have listened. Since it was a good sermon, he did not turn to another station but continued listening. He was impressed. At the end he found it had been a Catholic priest and he wrote to him. The outcome was that that man became a staunch Catholic. Such a sermon can be an actual grace working in an individual soul.

The number of actual graces we get each day is incalculable. But no matter how much supernatural help God gives us, we still are free to cooperate with it or reject it. God does not force us to accept it. Saint Paul accepted it; the rich young man in the gospel rejected such a grace. As Saint Augustine said many centuries ago: "God who created us without our cooperation, will not save us without our cooperation."

The greater graces we receive, naturally the more God will expect of us. Remember the words of the Bible itself: "When much has been given a man, much will be required of him. More will be asked of a man to whom more has been entrusted" (Lk. 12:48).

MORE HELP FROM GOD

When sanctifying grace becomes present in the soul, usually through Baptism or Penance, certain other supernatural powers come with it. Chief among these are the three theological virtues, the moral virtues and the seven gifts of the Holy Spirit.

THE THEOLOGICAL VIRTUES

The three theological virtues are faith, hope and charity.

Faith is a virtue leading us to believe firmly anything God has revealed, merely on his word, not necessarily because we understand it.

Hope is that virtue leading us to put all our trust in God, who can do all things and is all-good, knowing that He will do everything to help us toward heaven.

Charity is that virtue leading us to love God above all things, just because He is God, and to love our neighbors for the love of God.

THE GIFTS OF THE HOLY SPIRIT

The seven gifts of the Holy Spirit which come to us with sanctifying grace are: *wisdom,* helping us to see God as the all-important thing in life; *understanding,* helping us to distinguish the truths of our religion from error; *knowledge,* enabling us to grasp the teachings of God; *counsel,* helping us to see in our life what is God's will; *fortitude,* helping us to bear or do courageously whatever is necessary to carry out God's will; *piety,* helping us to honor God more and in the right way; *fear of the Lord,* leading us to fear giving offense to God as our Father.

MORAL VIRTUES

Besides the theological virtues, there are also moral virtues. They are called moral virtues because they lead us to good moral lives. There are four chief ones (called cardinal virtues):

Prudence helps us to make right judgments on what we should do or not do in particular circumstances of our everyday life.

Justice helps us to give everyone what belongs to him and not to take what does not belong to us.

Fortitude is an extra help to do the right thing even if it is hard or difficult.

Temperance helps us to control our desires and to use all things which please our senses, in the right way.

Besides these four cardinal or main moral virtues, there are several others; for instance, obedience, truthfulness, purity, patience, and all those other virtues regulating the leading of good moral daily lives.

All these virtues and gifts of God help us in doing our part toward getting to heaven.

In every human heart there is a desire for joy, for happiness. And that is God's plan for every one of us. But the actual accomplishment of that must be worked out through partnership. It will not become a reality if either partner falls down on his job. God is doing his part in giving abundant spiritual and material aids, especially the aid of grace. He has left the cooperation with those aids to each of us.

In view of grace and the virtues and gifts of God, as gained by Christ and applied to our life by the Catholic Church, our daily lives with all our activities take on a new meaning.

One way in which we can sanctify, elevate and give a new meaning to all our daily actions, is to recite each morning the brief prayer:

"O my God, I offer you all my prayers, works, joys and sufferings in union with the Sacred Heart of Jesus, for the intentions for which He pleads and offers himself in the Holy Sacrifice of the Mass, in thanksgiving for your favors, in reparation for my offenses, and in humble supplication for my temporal and eternal welfare, for the wants of our holy Mother the Church, for the conversion of sinners, and for the relief of the poor souls in purgatory. I wish to gain all the indulgences attached to the prayers I shall say and to the good works I shall perform this day."

No smallest action need be dull, uninteresting or just another cog in the round of tasks to be performed. Every act that is not a sin can be done in cooperation with God's grace and have a value for our eternal happiness.

It is not enough that we just exist from day to day. We have a job to do, a purpose to accomplish. God has given us the supernatural materials and the tools. We are the workmen. It is in our hands to work out our future.

photo by Richard Lowey

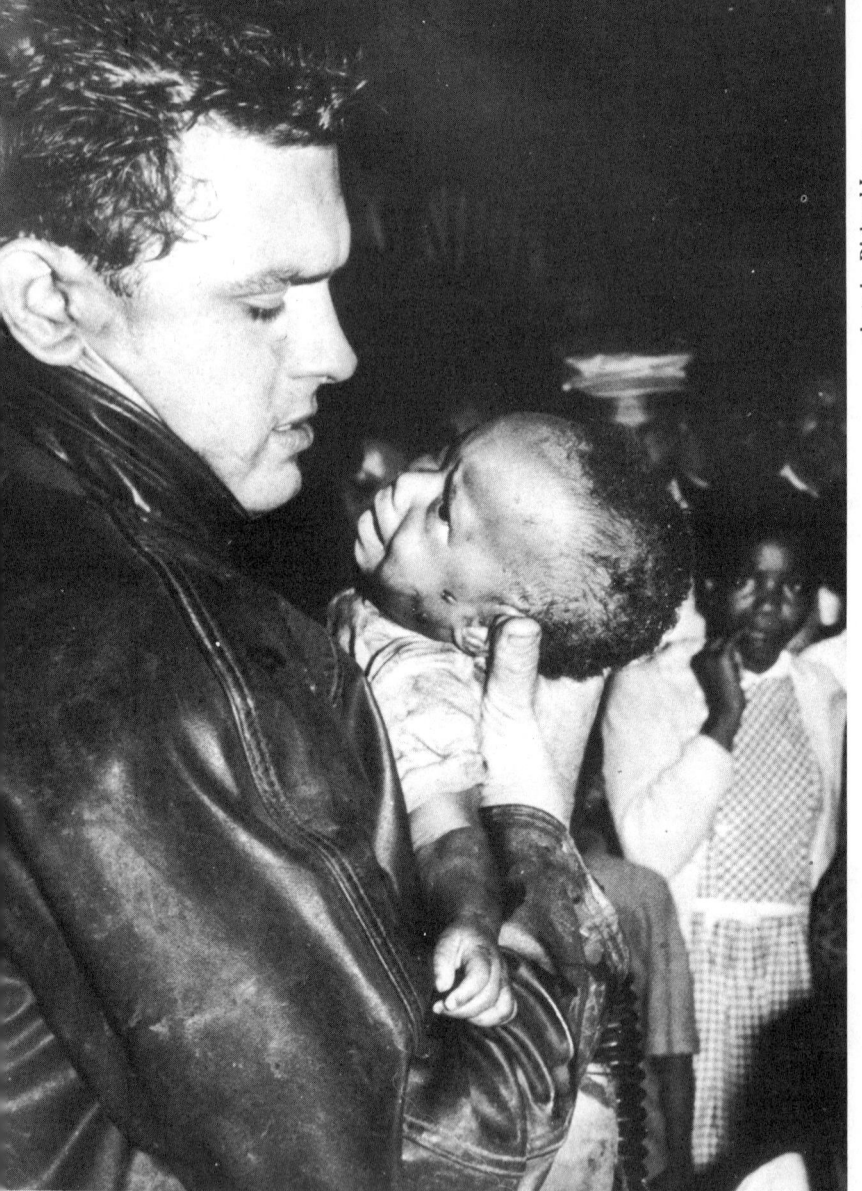

A man's relationship with God the Father and his relationship with his brother men are so linked together that Scripture says: "He who does not love does not know God" (I Jn. 4:8).
— Vatican II, *Declaration on the Relationship of the Church to Non-Christian Religions,* No. 5

Chapter 20

The Bridge to Eternity

> Men are more than brothers; each is a living part of all the others. . . . I am no longer my brother's keeper; I am one with my brother and somehow we are both Christ. — Pastoral Letter of the U.S. Bishops, *The Church in Our Day,* January 11, 1968.

Not too long ago a young boy from Cincinnati heard his father saying that his older brother needed a blood transfusion immediately. The youngster, though not quite sure entirely what these blood transfusions were, asked his father if he could give his brother the transfusion. The parents thought it over and within fifteen minutes the nurse had removed the half pint of blood that was needed. The young boy was tense, and then raising his eyes he asked his mother: "Mom, do I die now — like Jesus?" The mother only then realized that her young son thought a blood transfusion meant losing all his blood. It was not long before he found that one could give blood to help another and yet do no harm to himself. If one person needs blood, someone may supply for that deficiency by giving a blood transfusion.

The same principle holds with reference to spiritual blood transfusions among the members of Christ's Mystical Body, the Church. If one member is failing spiritually, another may aid him, help him toward spiritual health.

In the Mystical Body of Christ, there are many spiritually sick, anemic, dying, who need the daily help of the more healthy members. A spiritual blood transfusion, just as a physical one, is not a blood draining. Rather, through giving to others, we strengthen ourselves.

The good or evil done to another is good or evil done to Christ. The story of Saint Paul's persecution of the Church and his dramatic conversion is well known. Paul was one of the outstanding persecutors of the Church in the first days of its existence. Then one day while riding to Damascus he was struck to the ground and heard the voice of Christ: "Saul, Saul, why do you persecute Me?" (Acts 9:4). It was not Christ whom Paul was persecuting, but his followers — and yet those words rang in Paul's ears — "Why do you persecute Me?" And then

Paul recalled what Christ said about the last judgment. Jesus calling the just will say: "Come. You have my Father's blessing! Inherit the kingdom prepared for you from the creation of the world. For I was hungry and you gave me food. I was thirsty and you gave me drink. I was a stranger and you welcomed me . . . the just will ask him: 'Lord, when did we see you hungry and feed you or see you thirsty and give you drink?' . . . The king will answer them: 'I assure you, as often as you did it for one of my least brothers, you did it for me' " (Mt. 25:34-40).

Whatever we do to one, anyone of his followers, we do to Him.

The bond between all Christians in the Mystical Body of Christ is exemplified in a comparison with the human body. Christ is the Head, we the members. If a member is cut off from the head, it is useless. But if it remains in contact with the head, and healthy, it will work for its own good, and the good of the other members. So too, if a Catholic, a member of Christ's Mystical Body, remains in contact with Christ the Head, he will benefit himself and others. If the eye sees a stick sailing through the air aimed at the chest, the eye does not say "That is not going to hit me — I'll let my chest worry about that." Rather, it does all it can to prevent injury to the chest, for both are parts of one and the same body.

Catholics cannot be indifferent to the fate and well-being of any other members of the Body of which they are all members, with Christ as their one Head.

When the Church in Russia or Hungary or Poland or any part of the world suffers, we suffer, for those members are part of Christ's Mystical Body, just as our arm is part of our body. That is the unique bond which Christ set up among his followers.

What is true of sorrow and pain in the Mystical Body is true of its joy and spiritual well-being. In the human body if the ear hears a beautiful melody, the whole being shares it. In a similar way in Christ's Mystical Body, among the members of the Catholic Church, when there is a spiritual rejuvenation in France or Germany, we rejoice, and share in the spiritual benefit as members of the same Body.

The bishops of the United States formally reminded every individual of his relationship with his fellow man in these words:

"The Church, seen as the family of God but even more profoundly when seen as the Body of the Lord, is the doctrinal justification and the premise of the mandate for our social apostolate to the world. It insists that in a unity so intimate men are more than brothers; each is a living part of all the others. In such a community of life, beyond mere community of interest, I am no longer my brother's keeper; I am one with my brother, and somehow we are both Christ." (Pastoral Letter of the U.S. Bishops, *The Church in Our Day,* January 11, 1968).

We may compare the Church to a baseball team. If one player strikes out, it not only pulls down his average but hinders the team by just that much as well. If a member of the team hits a home run, it boosts his average, and helps the whole team as well.

The doctrine has many applications in our own personal life. In a family there are no foreigners; among brothers and sisters there are no strangers. Under Christ as the Head, we are all united as one Body. And Christ's norm is: Whatever you have done for the least of my brethren, you did it for Me.

And there is no such thing as an isolated Christian. Wherever a Catholic may be, he is not alone, for he is joined to the millions of Catholics all over the world. Just as a whole team benefits by the hit of one player, so all Catholics share in the spiritual riches of the Church. All share in the fruits of the Mass, wherever it may be said.

Through our own prayers and sacrifices, we not only help ourselves, but also give a spiritual blood transfusion to other members of the Church throughout the world.

The faithful on earth as members of the Mystical Body can help one another by practicing supernatural charity, by prayers, and the spiritual and corporal works of mercy.

The chief corporal works of mercy are seven:
1. To feed the hungry
2. To give drink to the thirsty
3. To clothe the naked
4. To visit the imprisoned
5. To shelter the homeless
6. To visit the sick
7. To bury the dead

The chief spiritual works of mercy are seven:
1. To admonish the sinner
2. To instruct the ignorant
3. To counsel the doubtful
4. To comfort the sorrowful
5. To bear wrongs patiently
6. To forgive all injuries
7. To pray for the living and the dead

But Christ has gone a step further. The Communion of Saints is not only a bond of unity between all Catholics on earth, but a union of those on earth, the blessed in heaven, and the souls in purgatory.

The Church is composed of three separate groups: *The Church Militant,* that is, those who are still on earth, fighting against the world, the flesh and the devil to attain their final goal; the *Church Triumphant,* those who have fought successfully and now are receiving the reward of their triumph; the *Church Suffering,* those who are still making up for their sins in purgatory, being purified for heaven.

The "Communion of Saints" is the union of these three groups and the mutual spiritual aid that can be given to each other. All members can share in the spiritual treasury of the Church, and aid one another by prayers and good works. Of course, those already in heaven have no need of our prayers but they can help us.

There is a similar relationship between the members of the human body. Strong, healthy lungs and a good heart may help the body to withstand what otherwise would have been a serious illness.

A man's debts may be taken care of by another person. So a man in need of spiritual aid may receive that needed help from the prayers of another. Our prayers may not only help ourselves but others as well. Saint James reminds us: "Pray for one another, that you may find healing" (Jas. 5:16). The prayers of Saint Monica helped to bring back her wayward son, Saint Augustine.

Catholics on earth can pray for each other and for the souls in purgatory. The souls in purgatory so aided will, we may be sure, when they reach heaven aid those on earth; those in heaven can intercede with God for those on earth and the souls in purgatory.

> Following in the footsteps of Christ, the Christian faithful have always endeavored to help one another on the path leading to the heavenly Father through prayer, the exchange of spiritual goods and penitential expiation. The more they have been immersed in the fervor of charity, the more they have imitated Christ in his sufferings, carrying their crosses in expiation for their own sins and those of others, certain that they could help their brothers to obtain salvation from God the Father of mercies. This is the very ancient dogma of the Communion of the Saints, whereby the life of each individual son of God in Christ and through Christ is joined by a wonderful link to the life of all his other Christian brothers. (Pope Paul VI, *Apostolic Constitution on Indulgences,* January 1, 1967, No. 4).

God wants us not only to pray for ourselves but for others. We can assist friends and anyone on earth or in purgatory by offering our prayers, works, penances for them. It is a consoling thought and a privilege to think that what we do may not only benefit us, but help others too.

And can we doubt that those in purgatory whose time we help to shorten, will intercede for us in heaven?

Saint Paul asked his converts and the Catholics of the early Church in the community of Thessalonica: "Brothers, pray for us" (I Thes. 5:25). We often ask friends to pray for us; why not ask friends who have left this world and are now in heaven to pray for us? Materialists who deny any after-life, scoff at such an idea, but why should so many people who believe in heaven forget or deny that those in heaven can help us? Yet, outside the Catholic Church, we seldom hear that truth emphasized or put into practice. Those in heaven do have an interest in us and know of our needs. It was Christ himself who assured us: "There will likewise be more joy in heaven over one repentant sinner than over ninety-nine righteous people who have no need to repent" (Lk. 15:7). How could that be true if those in heaven have no knowledge of or interest in us?

Does it seem true that Catholics, who while living on earth prayed for each other and for friends, would lose their interest in them when they come so close to God in heaven? When one reaches heaven and sees more clearly the needs of those on earth, he will as a saint use his powers of intercession with God all the more. Saint Jerome saw this clearly in the fourth century, and his words reflect the thorough belief of Catholics in the twentieth century. "If Apostles and martyrs while still in the flesh and still needing to care for themselves, can pray for others, how much more will they pray for others after they have won their crowns, their victories."

We, as Catholics, going through life with the final goal of heaven in view, know that only one thing can impede that goal, sin. And as Catholics, we are deeply convinced that Christ while on earth gave us a remedy for sin in Confession. For on earth Christ spoke the words to his first priests and to all who would succeed them in the priesthood: "If you forgive men's sins, they are forgiven them; if you hold them bound, they are held bound" (Jn. 20:23). That does not mean merely telling sins to God to obtain forgiveness, but obtaining forgiveness through the institution which Christ set up for the purpose, Confession.

Every sin causes a perturbation in the universal order established by God in his ineffable wisdom and infinite charity, and the destruction of immense values with respect to the sinner himself and to the human community. Christians throughout history have always regarded sin not only as a transgression of divine law but also — though not always in a direct and evident way — as contempt for or disregard of the friendship between God and man (Pope Paul VI, *Apostolic Constitution on Indulgences,* No. 2).

Those who approach the sacrament of Penance obtain pardon from the mercy of God for offenses committed against Him. They are at the same time reconciled with the Church, which they have wounded by their sins, and which by charity, example and prayer seeks their conversion (Vatican II, *Dogmatic Constitution on the Church,* No. 11).

Chapter 21

After Death — What?

> The importance of the individual judgment after death, of the refining and purifying passage through purgatory, of the dreadful possibility of the eternal death which is hell, of the last judgment — all should be understood in light of Christian hope. — *National Catechetical Directory, No. 109.*

Of two things all men may be certain: that all men will die, and that the exact time of death will remain unknown.

Death is one of the results of original sin. Our first parents as they were created, were not subject to death. "Through one man sin entered the world and with sin death, death thus coming to all men inasmuch as all sinned" (Rom. 5:12).

Our death is not something to be feared; nor is the death of a loved one something to cause feelings of hopelessness or helplessness. In the Catholic scheme of things, it is the all important moment of life. For the good, it is the beginning of reward. Saint John Chrysostom speaks of it as a change from a tumbledown shack to a beautiful mansion. In every Catholic Mass for a deceased person, we are reminded of the Christian view of death: "Life is not taken away, it is changed." That is why in the early Church the "dies natalis" or birthday of a saint was celebrated — and this was not the anniversary of his birth but of his death. We might well get back to that Christian outlook. Death for those who die in God's friendship is a real birthday.

At the death of Lazarus in the gospel, his sister expressed her belief that at the end of the world all men will rise again, and soul and body will be re-united, when she spoke the words to Christ: "I know he will rise again in the resurrection, on the last day" (Jn. 11:24). Since usually the body has a share in the good or evil of the soul during life, it is fitting that the body share the reward or punishment of the soul.

After this resurrection on the last day: 1) All shall have the same bodies as now; 2) the bodies of those who died in God's friendship will be in a glorified state, and the bodies of the wicked in a repulsive state; 3) all will live forever. The deformed person, if he has led a good life will rise with a beautiful body; while the body of the most beautiful person, if he has died in mortal sin, will appear hideous.

It was Saint Paul who spoke of this resurrection with the words: "The dead will be raised incorruptible, and we shall be changed" (I Cor. 15:52).

At the very instant of death, each particular soul is judged by Christ, and its destiny determined forever. This is called the particular judgment. There will be another judgment at the end of the world when all men will be gathered before Christ, for the sentence to be pronounced before the sight of all. This will be the general judgment, and will not change the lot of each soul determined at the moment of death. At the moment of the particular judgment, the soul will receive the sentence of heaven, hell or purgatory according to the merits of life.

HELL

With the thought of heaven we are particularly impressed with God's goodness and mercy. But we must not forget that God is also infinitely just. We hear many jokes and anecdotes about hell and the devil. But for all the joking done about them, we can never forget that they are realities.

Did you ever hear a man lightly brush off certain laws with the remark: "Oh, they are merely laws without teeth!" We know what they are — laws that are on the books but which few bother keeping. They cannot be enforced because there is no penalty attached to their violation. People are not afraid to ignore such laws because they know nothing can happen to them. The laws as a result have become dead letters.

If a law or command is to work, it must have something behind it. We see it exemplified with high school pupils who will be out of control with one teacher whom they know may make threats and shout but never back up her commands with any penalty; with another teacher they will obey because they know she means what she says.

This is basically why Catholics see the existence of hell as most reasonable. If hell does not exist, the ten commandments have no teeth, and human nature being what it is, they would be no more than pious words. That is one reason why Catholics believe in hell; because it is the most logical thing in the world. But to back that logic up, we have abundant proof from Christ's own lips. He referred to hell as an "unquenchable fire" (Mk. 9:44), because the punishment of burning is

At the Sea of Tiberias, Jesus showed himself to the disciples. —John 21:1

The Sea of Tiberias in Israel today

photo by Paul J. Hayes

one of the pains of hell. Christ speaks of it as the "dark," for those there will never see the light of God; it is the place where there will be "wailing and grinding of teeth" (Mt. 8:12).

It was Christ who described the scene for us of the last judgment at the end of the world. He will sit in judgment and to those who lived a good life He will say: "Come. You have my Father's blessing! Inherit the kingdom prepared for you from the creation of the world" (Mt. 25:34). But to those who died with even a single mortal sin on their soul: "Out of my sight, you condemned, into that everlasting fire prepared for the devil and his angels!" (Mt. 25:41).

There will be in hell several punishments. First of all, the pain of sense, for those in hell will suffer indescribable torments; the pain of loss, being banished from God forever — with an intense desire for God (much more than we have even in this life) yet knowing that the sight of God will never be given. Those in hell will be tortured with envy of those in heaven. They will have no connection with those in heaven, though they may see them in some way. We recall the story in the gospel of the rich man and Lazarus. The rich man led an evil life and was sent to "the abode of the dead where he was in torment" (Lk. 16:23). He could see Lazarus far off in Abraham's bosom and cried out: "Send Lazarus to dip the tip of his finger in water to refresh my tongue, for I am tortured in these flames" (Lk. 16:24).

The fire of hell is not fire as we know it since it will affect soul as well as body, and will not destroy. In speaking of hell, Christ uses the words: "The fire is never extinguished," and says that those in that state "will be salted with fire" (Mk. 9:48-49). When a housewife puts crackermeal on meat and cooks it, it remains on the outside of the meat; if she puts salt on meat and cooks it, the salt permeates the whole piece of meat, does not just stay on the outer layer. When Christ referred to being "salted with fire," He meant that every part of one's being would receive the pain of hell.

Saint Theresa was favored not only with an extraordinary knowledge of heaven, but with a vision of hell. Her words give us pause to think of the results of mortal sin:

"While one day absorbed in prayer, I was suddenly, and without realizing how it came about, translated body and soul, to the regions of hell. I realized that God desired to show me the abode Satan had prepared for me, the abode that was to be eternally mine, if I would not change my sinful life for the better. The experience lasted a short time, but I shall never forget it no matter how many years I have yet to live. The entrance to this abode appeared to me like a long and narrow alleyway, or rather, like a very low, dark, narrow baker's oven. The floor was covered with the most repelling filth and mire giving off an unbearable stench, and alive with venomous vermin. At the end of this entry-way there was a wall with a narrow box-like opening through which I was forced. All that I had thus far seen — and I have given but a weak description of it — was actually delightful in comparison with the sight that greeted me within this cell-like enclosure. Words cannot convey the slightest conception of this utterly incomprehensible abode of torture. I felt within my soul a stinging fire which defies my powers to describe. At the same time my body fell prey to the most terrible pains. I have endured fearful pains in my earthly life, pains which were, according to the testimony of physicians, the most severe one can endure here below. In the period when I was lame, my entire nervous system suffered most excruciating twitchings and contortions. I suffered numerous other evils, besides, many of which had the devil for their author. Yet all these were as nothing in comparison with the tortures I now underwent. But most terrible of all was the thought that these horrible pains were without end, without the possibility of alleviation. And yet, even these awful pains of the body were insignificant as against those of the soul. Oh! these embraced such fear, such oppression, and such agonies of heart; they were so hopelessly and bitterly sorrowful that I should strive in vain were I to attempt to describe them. If I were to say that one endures here, in this wretched place, the trials of an unending death struggle, I should be stating it far too mildly. For, whereas at the last moment of earthly life a force that lies outside us seems to take the breath of life from us, the soul in hell seems to take its own life, to mutilate itself. No, never, never could I succeed in describing this internal fire, this sense of despair, the most terrible of all the pains and torments. I could not see who it was that tortured me, and yet I could feel myself being crushed and burned. But the pain of all pains was this interior flame, this despair of the soul. In this terrible place there is no hope of relief."

    Only those who die in unforgiven sin will receive these punishments of hell. But even one such mortal sin, however secretly it may have been committed, is sufficient to merit eternal punishment. Hell is not an argument for the hardness of God, but an indication of the horrible evil of sin.

PURGATORY

A Catholic doctor once remarked to a priest the complete reasonableness of purgatory, wondering why it is seldom taught and very often denied outside the Catholic Church. He observed that when a man stands on trial before a civil judge there are three possible verdicts: 1) acquittal, so that he will be completely set free; 2) a verdict of guilty, and if the crime is serious enough, life-imprisonment; 3) if the charge is too serious for acquittal but not serious enough for life-imprisonment, a punishment proportionate to the crime. As we stand before the judgment seat of Christ, there also may be one of three alternatives: heaven, hell or purgatory. Just as we could not do away with any of the three alternatives in a civil court, and still preserve justice, we cannot eliminate any of the three states in the after-life and not violate the justice of God. We cannot do away with purgatory, any more than we can demand that any person brought into civil court should either be sentenced to life in prison or be set free.

And we have the words of the Bible itself to back this up. It is a holy and pious thought to pray for the dead. "It was a holy and pious thought. Thus he made atonement for the dead that they might be freed from this sin" (II Mc. 12: 45-46). If we are urged to pray for the dead, it is not for those in heaven — they do not need our prayers. It is not for those in hell — they are beyond help. It is for those in a middle state, being prepared for heaven. That state we call purgatory.

Those souls who die with venial sin unforgiven or without having made up for the punishment due to sin completely, but without mortal sin, will be detained in purgatory for a time. It includes the punishment of being excluded from God and other pains for a time. The amount and time of suffering in purgatory will depend on the sins.

The doctrine of purgatory and the need for a means of remitting the temporal punishment due to sin has been reaffirmed by Vatican Council II and by Pope Paul:

"Very much aware of the bonds linking the whole Mystical Body of Jesus Christ, the pilgrim Church from the very first ages of the Christian religion has cultivated with great piety the memory of the dead. Because it is 'a holy and wholesome thought to pray for the dead that they may be loosed from sins,' she has also offered prayers for them." (Vatican II, *Dogmatic Constitution on the Church,* No. 50).

"That punishment or the vestiges of sin may remain to be expiated or cleansed and that they in fact frequently do even after the remission of guilt is clearly demonstrated by the doctrine on purgatory. In purgatory, in fact, the souls of those 'who died in the charity of God and truly repentant, but before satisfying with worthy fruits of penance for sins committed and for omissions' are cleansed after death with purgatorial punishments" (Pope Paul VI, *Apostolic Constitution on Indulgences,* January 1, 1967, No. 3).

And Pope Paul gives a reminder to all members of Christ's Mystical Body in the Church of their relationship to those who have gone before them:

"Let us pause here for a moment to reflect that this tribute of love for the deceased may be a duty for a number of reasons — a duty of gratitude. How much we owe our dead! We are debtors for such a heritage of love, memory and example. Then there is the duty of fidelity, for life is history, and history is tradition. For the believer and the civilized, tradition must be reasonable, must tend to continuity and development, must see to it that the lessons, experiences, undertakings, and sacrifices of our forebears on our behalf are not made futile. Moreover, there is the duty of love and reverence. Few other duties are more compelling than the classic remembrance of the departed. Few others so ennoble the heart in its fulfillment" (Pope Paul VI, Homily on November 2, 1966).

HEAVEN

If we took a poll among the various types of people, asking the one question: "What is heaven like?" we should probably get a good many different answers. From the little schoolboy we might hear: "Heaven is where you can have all the candy and ice cream you want and never get sick!" The man working eight or ten hours a day to support a large family might remark: "Just give me rest and relaxation." The chronically sick woman might remark: "There I'll have my health back." Behind many passing thoughts of heaven, there lurks in the mind of some the picture of angels in white robes and harps. Not that most people believe heaven is this, but with that picture so often presented, people very often slip into the mental conviction that heaven is a place of everlasting boredom. On the contrary, it is a place of never-ending joy. If God had prepared a place of white robes and harps, with people just *existing* — heaven indeed would be a dull place. But God knows us completely — after all, He made us, and knows what we want to make us perfectly happy.

Heaven is a place of indescribable happiness. Any words we

might use could give a very little idea of what heaven is. Saint Catherine was privileged with several visions. After one of them a priest asked her to describe it. Saint Catherine replied: "I would be making a most grievous blunder were I to attempt this; human words cannot express the value and the splendor of the heavenly treasures."

The happiness of heaven will be proportioned in the merits of each individual. "God will render to each according to his works." Heaven is well worth working for. And heaven will not be gained without penance and self denial, without working for it.

Only they will gain entrance into heaven who are free of all sin and from punishment due to sin.

Saint Theresa was miraculously given some understanding of the happiness of heaven and could only say: "The things I beheld were so great and wonderful that the very least of them would suffice to daze the soul. . . . No human being can properly conceive them."

The happiness of heaven consists chiefly in seeing God face to face and sharing his joy and happiness forever. There are other joys, such as union with friends and relatives, greater knowledge, no suffering whatsoever — but the one supreme happiness is union with God.

When we speak of heaven, no matter what we can say we can get little more knowledge than Saint Paul gave us: "Eye has not seen, ear has not heard, nor has it so much as dawned on man what God has prepared for those who love Him" (I Cor. 2:9).

Pope Paul VI and the Vatican Council in more than one place speak of the intimate relationship between our ultimate goal and the type of lives we should be transformed into because we live the truths of the Gospel:

"When we look at the lives of those who have faithfully followed Christ, we are inspired with a new reason for seeking the city which is to come (Heb. 13:14; 11:10). At the same time we are shown a most safe path by which, among the vicissitudes of this world and in keeping with the state in life and condition proper to each of us, we will be able to arrive at perfect union with Christ, that is, holiness. In the lives of those who shared in our humanity and yet were transformed into especially successful images of Christ (cf. 2 Cor. 3:18), God vividly manifests to men his presence and his face. He speaks to us in them, and gives us a sign of his kingdom, to which we are powerfully drawn, surrounded as we are by so many witnesses (cf. Heb. 12:1), and having such an argument for the truth of the Gospel" (Vatican II, *Dogmatic Constitution on the Church,* No. 50).

In view of the teachings and emphasis of the Catholic Church on the Communion of Saints, the resurrection of all on the last day, and eternal life after death, we might well put into practice the words of the inscription on a bridge in India: "The world is a bridge. Pass over it, but do not build on it."

Church of Dormition dedicated to Mary in Jerusalem. The colorful mosaic was used by soldiers for target practice during the Arab-Jewish conflict and bullet scars remain.

photo by Paul J. Hayes

Chapter 22

Mary, Mother of the Church

> We believe that the Blessed Mother of God, the New Eve, Mother of the Church, continues in heaven her maternal role with regard to Christ's members, cooperating with the birth and growth of divine life in the souls of the redeemed. — Pope Paul VI, *Credo of the People of God.*

The small town of Oberammergau in Bavaria has become famous throughout the world for its Passion Play. Every ten years as Lent approaches, preparations begin once again for the drama of Christ's passion and death. For months in advance, the spare time of most of the citizens is spent in arrangements for the great Passion Play. Their aim is to reproduce the last hours of the life of Christ as realistically as possible.

A few years ago, an American priest was attending the play and related an incident in connection with the representation of Judas' despair after the betrayal of Jesus. The audience was tense. Judas saw the full horror of his deed and it overwhelmed him; in despair he rushed to the temple and said to the chief priests and elders: "I did wrong to deliver up an innocent man!" And the only reply was: "What is that to us? It is your affair!" (Mt. 27:4). Judas flung the money into the temple and rushed out in despondency. At that point a little girl in the audience shouted: "Mother, why doesn't he go to Mary?" Perhaps if Judas had gone to Mary, things would have turned out much differently.

In the remark of that small girl, there is reflected the Catholic position on devotion to Mary. Even to the child, to have recourse to the Mother of Christ in difficulties seemed most natural. So, too, the Church, over the long centuries of her existence, has never hesitated to turn to Mary, to call upon her for help and guidance in bringing Christ and his message to all men.

It was no coincidence, for example, that the Second Vatican Council opened on the feast of the Maternity of Mary and closed on the feast of the Immaculate Conception, or that its sessions were entrusted to her protection. In fact, the role of the Blessed Virgin Mary "in the mystery of Christ and the Church" was the subject of an entire chapter in the *Dogmatic Constitution on the Church*. The document clearly encouraged Catholics to turn to Mary:

> Let the entire body of the faithful pour forth persevering prayer to the Mother of God and Mother of men. Let them implore that she who aided the beginnings of the Church by her prayers may now, exalted as she is in heaven above all the saints and angels, intercede with her Son in the fellowship of all the saints. May she do so until all the peoples of the human family, whether they are honored with the name of Christian or whether they still do not know their Savior, are happily gathered together in peace and harmony into the one People of God, for the glory of the Most Holy and Undivided Trinity (No. 69).

When the *Dogmatic Constitution on the Church* was promulgated on November 21, 1964, Pope Paul took the opportunity to proclaim Mary the Mother of the Church. "Knowledge of the exact doctrine of the Church on Mary will always be the key to a precise understanding of the mystery of Christ and his Church," the Holy Father said. "For the glory of the Virgin Mary, and for our own consolation, we proclaim Mary Mother of the Church, i.e., of the whole People of God, of the faithful as well as of the pastors. And we wish that through this title the Mother of God should be still more honored and invoked by the entire Christian people. . . . We trust, then, that with the promulgation of the *Constitution on the Church,* sealed with the proclamation of Mary as Mother of the Church, that is to say, of all the faithful and all the pastors, the Christian people may, with greater confidence and ardor, turn to the Holy Virgin and render to her the honor and devotion due to her."[1]

There are many good reasons why we should go to Mary. Let us discuss three of them: 1) She is unique among all the women of the universe in that she was conceived without original sin, gave birth to a Child without losing her virginity, and was taken up, body and soul, into heaven. 2) She was given the greatest of all relationships to Jesus — the relationship of mother to son. 3) She has demonstrated her deep love and concern for mankind by numerous appearances on earth, especially in recent centuries.

There is probably no way that we can really appreciate Mary's feelings when the angel Gabriel informed her that she was to be the mother of God, of the Messiah for whom the Jews had been waiting

---

[1] Pope Paul VI, Closing Speech of the Third Session of Vatican II, November 21, 1964.

for many centuries. The Gospels tell us that the humble Jewish maiden was "deeply troubled" by the angel's words and asked: "How can this be since I do not know man?" (Lk. 1:34). The angel replied that "the Holy Spirit will come upon you and the power of the Most High will overshadow you" (Lk. 1:35). With her fear that she would have to break her vow of virginity now allayed, Mary responded: "I am the servant of the Lord. Let it be done to me as you say" (Lk. 1:38).

And so it was, after the prescribed time had passed, that Mary gave birth to Jesus, "who did not diminish his mother's virginal integrity but sanctified it, when the Mother of God joyfully showed her first-born Son to the shepherds and Magi" *(Dogmatic Constitution on the Church,* No. 57). Some have interpreted the phrase "first-born Son" to mean that Mary had other children. This is incorrect. Among the Jews the phrase was used to indicate the preferential status of the eldest son to mark his rights and duties under the Mosaic Law. In the fourth century, Saint Jerome addressed himself to the contention that Mary had other children by pointing out that "every only-begotten is a first born, though not every first born is an only son. First-born does not mean him after whom came others, but him before whom no child is born."[2] The perpetual virginity of Mary has remained a constant teaching of the Church and the phrase "ever virgin" can be found in the Penitential Rite and the Roman Canon of the Mass.

Other extraordinary privileges granted to Mary because she was the Mother of God include freedom from original sin and from the corruption of the grave. The reason for both is not difficult to ascertain. One could hardly expect Christ to take his human nature from a source that had been stained by sin. By the same token, it was only fitting that the body in which the Son of God was conceived and nurtured should never experience the decay that follows death.

That the dogmas of the Immaculate Conception and the Assumption are basic tenets of Catholicism is undeniable. Both have been infallibly defined — the Assumption, as we noted in Chapter 12, by Pope Pius XII in 1950, and the Immaculate Conception by Pope Pius IX in 1854. The pertinent section of the latter pronouncement states:

"We declare, pronounce, and define that the doctrine which holds that the most Blessed Virgin Mary, in the first instant of her Conception, by a singular grace and privilege granted by almighty God, in

---

[2]Adv. Helvidium, 10. cf. Giuseppe Ricciotti, *The Life of Christ,* Milwaukee: Bruce, 1947, p. 241 fn.

view of the merits of Jesus Christ, the Savior of the human race, was preserved free from all stain of original sin, is a doctrine revealed by God and therefore to be believed firmly and constantly by all the faithful."

Mary's exceptional holiness, then, was absolutely necessary for the role she was to play in the salvation of mankind. Just as Eve had helped to bring death to man, so Mary helped to bring life. Saint Irenaeus summed it up well in these words, written in the second century: "The knot of Eve's disobedience was untied by Mary's obedience. What the virgin Eve bound through her unbelief, Mary loosened by her faith" *(Dogmatic Constitution on the Church,* No. 56).

If Mary's unique holiness is a reason for us to go to her, whether in difficulties or successes, so, too, is her special relationship with Jesus, the closeness of a mother to a son. Christ spent thirty years of his life with Mary. Between the two there was all the love and favor that exists between the best of mothers and her child. There was nothing He could refuse her. The prompt cooperation with her least wish was shown at the marriage feast at Cana.

Mary was already at Cana when Jesus and his disciples arrived and had probably been involved in the preparations for the wedding feast. Because such celebrations were rare, they were always very festive occasions. One of the highlights of the affair was the wine. It was not an ordinary wine but one which had been set aside for a long time and saved especially for this feast. At a certain point, however, Mary noticed that the wine had run out. Realizing what a catastrophe this could be for the family hosting the event, she went to Jesus and told Him: "They have no more wine." But Jesus replied that this was no concern of his, since "my hour has not yet come" (Jn. 2:3-4).

Jesus knew that if He did something about Mary's request, He would be setting in motion a chain of events that would lead unwaveringly to the hour of his passion, death, resurrection, and ascension. He felt that the time had not yet come for Him to perform the miracles that would authenticate his divine mission.

But Mary, who knew her Son better than anyone else, was not dismayed. She instructed those who were waiting on the tables to "do whatever He tells you" (Jn. 2:5). There were six stone water jars nearby, each one holding fifteen to twenty-five gallons. "Fill those jars with water," Jesus ordered, and it was done. "Now," He said, "draw some out and take it to the waiter in charge." As we know, the waiter was astonished at the superior quality of the wine and even called the

MARY, MOTHER OF THE CHURCH

groom aside to ask him why he had kept the good wine until the end of the dinner. We do not know what transpired after this, but we can surmise that Jesus' role was known to all the guests in a very short time. The evangelist tells us that "Jesus performed this first of his signs at Cana in Galilee. Thus did He reveal his glory, and his disciples believed in Him" (Jn. 2:6-11).

Christ showed toward his mother a willingness to grant her every request. Mary in heaven has not ceased to be the Mother of Christ. She still retains her maternal relations. How better can we ask a favor of Him than by presenting it through Mary's hands? One of the surest ways of gaining access to the Son is through his mother. "By her maternal charity, Mary cares for the brethren of her Son who still journey on earth surrounded by dangers and difficulties, until they are led to their happy fatherland. Therefore the Blessed Virgin is invoked by the Church under the titles of Advocate, Auxiliatrix, Adjutrix, and Mediatrix. These, however, are to be so understood that they neither take away from nor add anything to the dignity and efficacy of Christ the one Mediator" *(Dogmatic Constitution on the Church,* No. 62).

While many people are attracted to Mary because of her holiness and her singular relationship to Jesus, many more have been drawn by her repeated visitations to earth.[3] So significant have been these apparitions that we are living in what has been called the Marian Age. Each year millions and millions of people flock to the famous Marian shrines at Guadalupe in Mexico, La Salette and Lourdes in France, Fatima in Portugal, and Beauraing and Banneux in Belgium. Many of the pilgrims are seeking Mary's help with a personal problem, whether physical or spiritual. Others are heeding her urgent pleas for prayer, penance, and reparation for the sins which are being commited against her Son.

Time after time, in apparition after apparition, Our Lady warned that God is displeased with man's rejection of Him and his teachings and that unless all the people of the earth returned to a life of prayer and obedience to God, she would not be able to dissuade Him from punishing the world. At La Salette, in 1846, she declared that "if my people will not obey, I shall be compelled to loose my Son's arm. It is so heavy, so pressing that I can no longer restrain it. How long have I suffered for you! If my Son is not to cast you off, I am obliged to entreat Him without ceasing. But you take no least notice of that. No

---

[3] Belief in these apparitions is not required of Catholics as part of the "deposit of faith" left by Christ, but many are well authenticated, and have been recognized by Popes.

matter how well you pray in the future, no matter how well you act, you will never be able to make up to me what I have endured for your sake."

At Fatima, in 1917, the Blessed Virgin predicted World War II and the spread of the scourge of Communism throughout the world. "To prevent this," she said, "I shall come to ask for the consecration of Russia to my Immaculate Heart and the Communion of reparation on the First Saturdays. If my requests are heard, Russia will be converted and there will be peace. If not, she will spread her errors throughout the entire world, provoking wars and persecution of the Church. The good will suffer martyrdom; the Holy Father will suffer much; different nations will be annihilated."

This is precisely what happened and is still happening. But Mary also held out some hope for us: "But in the end my Immaculate Heart will triumph. The Holy Father will consecrate Russia to me,[4] and it will be converted and some time of peace will be granted to humanity."[5] But who knows when this period of peace will come? Or how much violence and suffering will precede it? Or how many souls will be lost for all eternity because they refused to stop offending God?

Mary has given us the only prescription for peace: prayer, penance, and reparation for sin. Nothing else can remedy the ills of the world. Out of her bountiful love for us, the love of a mother for her children, she has also pointed out the road that each of us must follow if we are to reach heaven. She is pleading with us, begging us to remain on that road. How tragic it is that so many of us refuse her wishes! How sad that we do not go quickly to her that she might bring us to her Son!

The Church, as we noted earlier, has always encouraged devotion to the Blessed Virgin. The bishops of Vatican II specifically directed that "practices and exercises of devotion toward her be treasured as recommended by the teaching authority of the Church in the course of centuries, and that those decrees issued in earlier times regarding the veneration of images of Christ, the Blessed Virgin, and the saints, be religiously observed" *(Dogmatic Constitution on the Church,* No. 67).

Two years later, Pope Paul VI declared that this passage from Vatican II "clearly referred to the Rosary," the greatest of all devo-

---

[4]This was done by Pope Pius XII in 1942.
[5]For information on eight apparitions of the Blessed Virgin, including those at La Salette and Fatima, see *A Woman Clothed with the Sun,* ed. John J. Delaney, New York: Image Books, 1961.

tions to Mary. And he urged "devout recitation of the Rosary" as a practice "well suited to God's people, acceptable to the Mother of God, and powerful in obtaining gifts from heaven."[6]

For centuries the Rosary has held a high place in the spiritual life of the Church. The Popes have written numerous encyclicals praising the devotion and recommending its widespread practice. Rosary crusades have led to major victories for Christian civilization — the overthrow of the dangerous Albigensian heresy in the thirteenth century and the defeat of the Turks at Lepanto in the sixteenth century, thus saving Europe from being overrun by Muslims. That the defeat of world Communism has not yet been achieved is due not to any lessening of the power of the Rosary but to the failure of men to carry out the request of Our Lady of Fatima to pray the Rosary.

The Rosary has been called "the Gospel in miniature" because it dwells on the important events in the life of Jesus and Mary. Pope John, who said all fifteen decades every day, expressed it this way:

"The Rosary, as is known to all, is a very excellent means of prayer and meditation in the form of a mystical crown in which the prayers "Our Father," "Hail Mary" and "Glory Be to the Father" are intertwined with meditation on the greatest mysteries of our faith. It presents to the mind, like many pictures, the drama of the Incarnation of our Lord and the Redemption."[7]

A good way to see what the Holy Father meant would be to recite the sorrowful mysteries while meditating on the material contained in Chapter 7.

There are some who scoff at the Rosary, who think of it as a devotion only for old people or for the unlearned and illiterate. They might be interested in the story that is told of the "sophisticated" university student who found himself sharing a train compartment in France with an old man whose shabby clothes and unkempt appearance gave him the look of a French peasant. When the youth noticed the Rosary beads in the old man's hands, he remarked contemptuously: "I see you still believe in that medieval fetish, the rosary beads, and I guess you still hold to the Virgin Mary and all the superstitious nonsense that priests tell you."

"Yes, my boy," the man said with a pained expression, "I do believe it all. Don't you?"

[6] Pope Paul VI, "Rosaries to the Mother of Christ" *(Christi Matri Rosarii)*, September 15, 1966
[7] Pope John XXIII, "Grateful Memory" *(Grata Recordatio)*, September 26, 1959.

The student laughed. "Are you serious, old man? Me believe in prayer and such religious hog-wash? I should say not. I learned different at college . . . and if you're smart you'll throw those silly beads away and learn something about the new thought."

"The new thought?" the old man said with tears in his eyes. "I'm afraid I don't understand. Perhaps you could help me."

The young man softened a bit and seemed to take pity on his traveling companion. "Well, if you can read," he said, "I'd be glad to send you some of my literature. You do read?"

The peasant nodded. "I read a little when I am not too busy."

"Splendid!" the college student exclaimed. "To what address shall I send it?"

Reaching into his pocket, the man who looked like a peasant drew out a card and handed it to the youth. The name printed on it was that of the famous French chemist who developed vaccines against hydrophobia and anthrax and discovered a way to sterilize milk — Louis Pasteur.[8]

True Christians, followers of Christ, look with reverence on any object or place associated with Our Lord. Palestine is honored as "The Holy Land," for its soil was pressed by his footprints. At Bethlehem, tourists feel a profound reverence, for *there* was born the Savior of the world. The Holy Shroud has long been the object of special honor as the cloth that wrapped Christ's body in the tomb. If lifeless places and objects can claim so much reverence, with how much more veneration would we approach the living persons who were associated with Christ? Important as any of them were, they fall into mere insignificance in comparison with the role of Mary.

This role — as Mother of God, the New Eve, and Mother of the Church — has never been clearer than it is today. Nor has devotion to Mary ever been more important than it is today. In the words of Pope Paul, spoken on the feast of the Assumption, August 15, 1971:

"We must not lessen our devotion to the Virgin Mary, we modern people who more than ever demand evangelical authenticity or who seek out the mysterious ways toward divine transcendence. We must remain faithful and fervent in the cult, in the love, in the imitation, in the invocation of Blessed Mary. Due devotion to Our Lady is a sign of the correct interpretation of the Christian religion, and of our Catholic religion in particular."

---

[8] "The Student and the Peasant," *The Immaculate,* October, 1969, p. 12

One of the best tributes that we can give to Christ is to show our devotion to Him through his mother. He willed it that way. And one of the surest ways of gaining God's help in attaining eternal life is through Mary, the "Gate of Heaven."

Proclaim the good news to all creation—Mark 16:15.

Chapter 23

Random Remarks on the Catholic Church

> The disciple is bound by a grave obligation toward Christ his Master ever more adequately to understand the truth received from Him, faithfully to proclaim it, and vigorously to defend it, never — be it understood — having recourse to means that are incompatible with the spirit of the gospel. At the same time, the charity of Christ urges him to act lovingly, prudently and patiently in his dealings with those who are in error or in ignorance with regard to the faith. — Vatican II, *Declaration on Religious Freedom*, No. 14.

Having examined the claims and credentials of the various churches today, we have seen the reasons why a Catholic is proud of what his Church stands for. We do not mean an arrogant and overbearing sense of pride, but rather a reasonable and justifiable self-respect. For as Vatican II warned: "All the sons of the Church should remember that their exalted status is to be attributed not to their own merits but to the special grace of Christ. If they fail moreover to respond to that grace in thought, word, and deed, not only will they not be saved but they will be the more severely judged" *(Dogmatic Constitution on the Church,* No. 14).

How can any man claim to be educated who is ignorant of the history of the Catholic Church, which has been a most potent factor in shaping the life and the thought of civilization? She established schools and universities throughout the world, and inspired painters, sculptors, and musicians in the achievement of their masterpieces. She fostered a love of literature and encouraged investigation of the secrets of nature, and thus laid the foundations of modern science.

What other religion can point to as many hospitals, homes for the aged, poor, orphans, and unfortunate, as Catholics have established? Catholics through those endeavors certainly fulfill Christ's injunction: "Love your neighbor."

The Catholic Church has always been the patroness of literature and the fostering mother of the arts and sciences. She founded and endowed nearly all the great universities of Europe. Without her we should be deprived today of the priceless treasures of ancient literature, for, in preserving the languages of Greece and Rome from destruction, she rescued classical writers of those countries from oblivion. Were it not for the diligent labors of the monks in the Middle Ages, our culture and learning today would never have reached its present level.

The Church has been accused of opposing progress. The truth is that she has been far ahead of her time in learning, culture, the arts and sciences.

We hear much about the great Renaissance of the Middle Ages — the revival of learning. How often do we hear the Church's part spoken of? As early as in the days of Popes Nicholas V (1447) and Leo X (1513) there were outstanding contributions to the various fields of the Renaissance. Boniface VIII in the thirteenth century was a patron of the arts. When the Popes were at Avignon, they were renowned for their work as patrons of the arts and sciences. Nicholas V brought the great Fra Angelico to Rome. Even at that time the Vatican library was the greatest in the world. It had some 5,000 volumes, while the entire royal library of France had at that time only 900. Even before the Renaissance began in Europe the Church had made great strides.

And so it has been through the ages. Far from holding back progress, the Church has given to the world some of the greatest contributions it has known.

Catholics are proud of the fact that their title is not a mere name but a reality. She has a just claim to the title of "Catholic," universal. At any ecumenical or world-wide council of the Church there are bishops from practically every nation and race. At the Second Vatican Council, bishops came from England, Germany, and the United States, from Africa, South America, and Australia, from the Near East and the Far East. The bishops came from every form of government, from republic to absolute monarchy. Their faces were marked by every shade and color that distinguish the human family. All knelt side by side under the same roof.

One of the inspiring sights through the years has been the arrival of refugees in New York. They were strangers to our customs and language. Every object that met their eyes was a sad reminder of the land they had left. But when a Catholic saw the cross over a Catholic church, there was a note of familiarity and warmness. In this church, once more they were at home, with the same Mass and sacraments, the same doctrines, the same familiar images of saints they had reverenced from childhood; they saw the baptismal font and confessionals. They saw the priest at the altar in the sacred vestments. They observed a multitude of worshipers kneeling around them, and they felt in their heart of hearts that they were once more among brothers and sisters, with whom they had "one Lord, one faith, one baptism, one God and Father of all."

The English historian Macaulay (1800-1859), non-Catholic though he was, paid the following tribute to the Catholic Church:

"There is not, and there never was on this earth, a work of human policy so well deserving of examination as the Roman Catholic Church. The history of that Church joins together the two great ages of human civilization. No other institution is left standing which carries the mind back to the times when the smoke of sacrifice rose from the Pantheon, and when camelopards and tigers bounded in the Flavian amphitheater. The proudest royal houses are but of yesterday, when compared with the line of the Supreme Pontiffs. That line we trace back in an unbroken series, from the Pope who crowned Napoleon in the nineteenth century to the Pope who crowned Pepin in the eighth; and far beyond the time of Pepin the august dynasty extends, till it is lost in the twilight of fable. The republic of Venice came next in antiquity. But the republic of Venice was modern when compared with the Papacy; and the republic of Venice is gone, and the Papacy remains. The Papacy remains, not in decay, not a mere antique, but full of life and youthful vigour. The Catholic Church is still sending forth to the farthest ends of the world missionaries as zealous as those who landed in Kent with Augustine, and still confronting hostile kings with the same spirit with which she confronted Attila. . . . She saw the commencement of all the governments and of all the ecclesiastical establishments that now exist in the world; and we feel no assurance that she is not destined to see the end of them all. She was great and respected before the Saxon had set foot on Britain, before the Frank had passed the Rhine, when Grecian eloquence still flourished at Antioch, when idols were still worshipped in the temple of Mecca. And she may still exist in undiminished vigour when some traveller from New Zealand shall, in the midst of a vast solitude, take his stand on a broken arch of London Bridge to sketch the ruins of St. Paul's."[1]

The Catholic Church is most remarkable in its history. It had its

[1] Lord Macaulay, *Essay on L. Von Ranke's History of the Popes.*

origin in a remote and insignificant corner of a great empire. It began with a group of unlearned men. Of these men one was a traitor, another a perjurer and a coward, and nine of the remainder deserted. Only one, John, was faithful. They preached doctrines completely foreign to the world around them under a banner representing disgrace and failure, a cross. Their teachings of love penetrated the mighty Roman Empire. In spite of bitter persecutions and seemingly overwhelming odds, they and their successors changed the face of the world.

Who were the men used by Christ to conquer the pagan world? Who were the men assigned to stand up against the fierce persecution and cruelty of the Romans? They were a small band of simple Jewish fishermen!

This group, seemingly so inept by all natural standards, was charged to effect the greatest, the most radical, and the most far reaching revolution in thought and conduct which the world has ever known. The results are the most phenomenal in all history. During their own lifetime they witnessed the birth of the Church in almost every land of the civilized world. This has no parallel in all history. The Catholic Church has triumphed, where by every human standard it should have failed.

The Catholic Church either was propagated with miracles or without them. If it was propagated with miracles, it is clearly divine. If it were propagated without the miracles, it bears even more strongly the stamp of the divine, for its propagation without the aid of miracles was of itself the greatest miracle of all.

The question often arises concerning the fact that many outside the Church, and even agnostics, seem to live better lives than Catholics. The answer is to be found in the fact that such persons living in a society permeated with Christian ideals are profoundly influenced, consciously or unconsciously, by the moral standards and the code of ethics inspired by the teachings of Christ. It will usually be found, upon analysis, that every trait which commends them in the eyes of their fellow citizens is traceable to the standards of conduct inculcated by the religion of Christ. They are good citizens not because of their agnosticism or atheism but in spite of it.

"How is it," one may then ask, "that there are persons in the Catholic Church whose lives are by no means exemplary?"

Remember Christ chose men, not angels to take care of his Church. This seems like a rather elementary observation, but if we keep it in mind, we shall have little trouble in understanding priests who perhaps do not live up to standards demanded of them, and Catholic people who lead anything but exemplary lives.

Remember, too, that among the twelve Apostles, Judas sinned mortally in betraying Our Lord; Peter denied Him with an oath. Both were sins, that of Judas and that of Peter. The others, except John, ran away when they were needed most.

It is not fair to judge the Church by those who fail to live up to the norms of the Church. It is only fair to judge the Catholic Church, or any organization, by those who live in accordance with the rules of that organization.

Yes, we have had bad Catholics — Catholics who have been a scandal to the Church. Hitler was a Catholic before he became a persecutor of the Church. Goebbels, another persecutor of the Church, was educated in the household of a priest. Stalin, though not a Roman Catholic, was a seminarian in a Greek Orthodox school, studying to be a priest. Mussolini was born a Catholic and baptized in the Faith. Cardenas of Mexico, God-hater and ruthless underminer of the Faith, was born of ancient Catholic stock. Castro of Cuba, oppressor of the Church in the predominantly-Catholic island nation, was educated in Jesuit schools.

It is easy to single out fallen-away or lax Catholics. But consider the countless souls who have given themselves wholeheartedly to the Faith. The Catholic Faith is to be judged by the lives of those who are faithful members, who abide by the laws and follow its ideals, not by those who reject its laws.

As a matter of fact, if we did not have some questionable Catholics, we should have something to wonder about. If you recall, Christ, on one occasion, in speaking of his kingdom, referred to the good and bad living side by side, when He compared them to wheat and weeds growing in the same field. It is not until harvest time that the wheat will be gathered into barns, and the weeds set aside for burning.

There is a vast difference between merely being a Catholic and wholeheartedly living as a Catholic. Through baptism a person becomes a member of the Church, but that fact itself does not make him either a good Catholic or bad one. The way in which a person lives his life, not the mere fact of baptism, makes him a good, bad or indifferent member of Christ's Church. By physical birth we become members of a family. But that fact does not force us into being the kind of children our parents desire. Our own free will determines that. Similarly, by our spiritual birth we are not forced into being the kind of children that God as our Father and the Catholic Church as our mother would desire us to become.

The modern world sometimes challenges the Catholic Church with the idea summed up in some such phrase as: "Your Church had its chance and lost it."

The correct answer is that our Church had its chance and took it, and that the world has been much the better for it.

People who declare that the Church has had only a negligible influence on civilization are lacking in a knowledge of history. They have no notion of what the Faith did accomplish, for they have no notion of what the world was like when Christianity came into it, and so they do not realize the work of regeneration and renewal that the Church did and continues to do in our own day. But to realize this, those who criticize would have to have more knowledge of history than they now have or are likely to take the trouble to acquire.

Is the Catholic Church a failure, as so many of its enemies charge? The ones who bring up the charge so persistently and loudly are merely advertising the fact that it is not a failure. They would not pay such great attention to a failure!

"THE BLOOD OF MARTYRS"

There is an ancient Christian phrase which modern Catholics might well make their own. It is the triumphant cry of Christians many centuries ago: "The blood of martyrs is the seed of Christians." It well may be used by the Catholic Church in our own day, for there have been in our time more martyrs than there were in the Roman persecutions of old. In our time, in Spain, Russia, China, Mexico, Cuba, and elsewhere, a greater number than of old have died for the Faith.

Only a short time before his death, Christ spoke of the world's hatred of Him. Then He told his followers simply: "No slave is greater than his master. They will harry you as they harried me" (Jn. 15:20). Why is it that the Catholic Church is pursued, age after age, with an unreasonable hatred? No other church can boast of such a number of martyrs in every generation. The reason is not far to seek if we remember Christ's prediction. Look for the religion today which is constantly suffering persecution, and you have the religion of Christ.

From the very origins of Christianity, not only men, but women and children also were thrown to wild beasts, or beheaded or burned to death because they would not deny their faith. The martyrs stood in the arena before thousands, and their courage left the bitterest of their enemies in awe.

The courage of the men and women martyred during the Anglican Reformation was equally remarkable. St. Thomas More, the merry martyr, even jested with the man who was about to behead him. "Assist me up, if you please," he said to the executioner. "Coming down I can shift for myself."[2] Or consider the final words of the Welshman David Lewis, who was canonized by Pope Paul in 1970:

"Here is a numerous assembly — may the great Savior of the world save every soul of you all. I believe you are here met not only to see a fellow-native die, but also to hear a dying fellow-native speak. My religion is the Roman Catholic; in it I have lived above these forty years; in it I now die, and so fixedly die, that if all the good things in this world were offered me to renounce it, all should not remove me one hair's breadth from my Roman Catholic faith. A Roman Catholic I am; a Roman Catholic priest I am; a Roman Catholic priest of that religious order called the Society of Jesus I am; and I bless God who first called me. I was condemned for reading Mass, hearing confessions, and administering the sacraments. As for reading the Mass, it was the old, and still is the accustomed and laudable liturgy of the holy Church; and all the other acts are acts of religion tending to the worship of God, and therefore dying for this I die for religion."[3]

In each century there are stories of heroic sacrifices and suffering for the Catholic Faith. And as we come nearer to our own time, the words of Christ concerning his followers are no less fulfilled: "They will harry you."

It was G.K. Chesterton, the English convert-author, who declared that the constant diabolical hatred of the Catholic Church, the bigotry and prejudice directed against this Church, would have been more than sufficient to persuade him of the truth of the Catholic Faith even if he had not been intellectually convinced by other considerations to become a Catholic.

If you are seeking the Faith of Christ in the world today, then begin your search by seeking the Church that is most at odds with the world, just as Christ himself was at odds with the world. Seek the

[2]Phyllis McGinley, *Saint-Watching*, New York: Viking Press, 1969, pp. 111-112.
[3]John Cardinal Wright, *The Church: Hope of the World*, ed. Rev. Donald W. Wuerl, Kenosha, Wisconsin: Prow Books, 1972, p. 157.

Faith that is criticized for being old-fashioned and impractical as Christ was accused of being impractical; seek the Church which is looked down upon as being socially inferior as Christ was sneered at because of the place from which He came; seek the Church which is most accused of having designs on temporal power as Christ was falsely accused of making Himself a king. Seek the Church which the world jeers at, because she claims to be infallible, as Christ was mocked for declaring, "I am the truth." Seek the Church which many are seeking to destroy, as Christ was destroyed on Calvary. Seek the Church rejected by the world as Christ was rejected by worldly men.

These are some of the signs to look for if you would find the Church of Christ in the world today.

Christ's prophetic words concerning persecution and martyrdom have been living realities in only one Church, down through the years.

During the days of glory of the pagan republic Rome, the Roman would say with pride, "I am a Roman citizen." This was one of his greatest boasts. He was proud of the republic, and of his part in it. The Church has lasted for twenty centuries, and will continue to last until the very end of the world. Her members are citizens of every land and she numbers her saints and her martyrs by the thousands. Today over six hundred million people take pride in the simple phrase, "I am a Catholic."

The Apostles' Creed

I believe in God, the Father Almighty, Creator of heaven and earth; and in Jesus Christ, His only Son, our Lord; who was conceived by the Holy Spirit, born of the Virgin Mary, suffered under Pontius Pilate, was crucified, died, and was buried. He descended into hell; the third day He arose again from the dead; He ascended into heaven, sits at the right hand of God, the Father Almighty; from thence He shall come to judge the living and the dead. I believe in the Holy Spirit, the holy Catholic Church, the communion of saints, the forgiveness of sins, the resurrection of the body, and life everlasting. Amen.

The Nicene Creed

We believe in one God, the Father, the Almighty, Maker of heaven and earth, of all that is seen and unseen. We believe in one Lord, Jesus Christ, the only Son of God, eternally begotten of the Father, God from God, Light from Light, true God from true God, begotten, not made, one in Being with the Father. Through Him all things were made. For us men and for our salvation He came down from heaven: by the power of the Holy Spirit He was born of the Virgin Mary, and became man. For our sake He was crucified under Pontius Pilate; He suffered, died, and was buried. On the third day He rose again in fulfillment of the Scriptures; He ascended into heaven and is seated at the right hand of the Father. He will come again in glory to judge the living and the dead, and His kingdom will have no end. We believe in the Holy Spirit, the Lord, the giver of life, who proceeds from the Father and the Son. With the Father and the Son He is worshiped and glorified. He has spoken through the Prophets. We believe in one holy catholic and apostolic Church. We acknowledge one baptism for the forgiveness of sins. We look for the resurrection of the dead, and the life of the world to come. Amen.

The Credo of the People of God

Proclaimed by His Holiness, Pope Paul VI, at the closing of the Year of Faith, June 30, 1968.

With this solemn liturgy we end the celebration of the nineteenth centenary of the martyrdom of the holy apostles Peter and Paul, and thus close the Year of Faith. We dedicated it to the commemoration of the holy Apostles in order that we might give witness to our steadfast will to be faithful to the deposit of the faith[1] which they transmitted to us, and that we might strengthen our desire to live by it in the historical circumstances in which the Church finds herself in her pilgrimage in the midst of the world.

We feel it our duty to give public thanks to all who responded to our invitation by bestowing on the Year of Faith a splendid completeness through the deepening of their personal adhesion to the word of God, through the renewal in various communities of the profession of faith, and through the testimony of a Christian life. To our brothers in the episcopate especially, and to all the faithful of the holy Catholic Church, we express our appreciation and we grant our blessing.

Likewise, we deem that we must fulfill the mandate entrusted by Christ to Peter, whose successor we are, the last in merit; namely, to confirm our brothers in the faith.[2] With the awareness, certainly, of our human weakness, yet with all the strength impressed on our spirit by such a command, we shall accordingly make a profession of faith, pronounce a creed which, without being strictly speaking a dogmatic definition, repeats in substance, with some developments called for by the spiritual condition of our time, the creed of Nicea, the creed of the immortal tradition of the holy Church of God.

In making this profession, we are aware of the disquiet which agitates certain modern quarters with regard to the faith. They do not escape the influence of a world being profoundly changed, in which so many certainties are being disputed or discussed. We see even Catholics allowing themselves to be seized by a kind of passion for change and novelty. The Church, most assuredly, has always the duty to carry on the effort to study more deeply and to present, in a manner ever better adapted to successive generations, the unfathomable mysteries of God, rich for all in fruits of salvation. But at the same time the greatest care must be taken, while fulfilling the indispensable duty of research, to do no injury to the teachings of Christian doctrine. For that would be to give rise, as is unfortunately seen in these days, to disturbance and perplexity in many faithful souls.

It is important in this respect to recall that, beyond scientifically verified phenomena, the intellect which God has given us reaches *that which is,* and not merely the subjective expression of the structures and development of consciousness; and, on the other hand, that the task of interpretation — of hermeneutics — is to try to understand and ex-

[1] Cf. 1 Tim. 6:20.
[2] Cf. Lk. 22:32.

tricate, while respecting the word expressed, the sense conveyed by a text, and not to recreate, in some fashion, this sense in accordance with arbitrary hypotheses.

But above all, we place our unshakeable confidence in the Holy Spirit, the soul of the Church, and in theological faith upon which rests the life of the Mystical Body. We know that souls await the word of the Vicar of Christ, and we respond to that expectation with the instructions which we regularly give. But today we are given an opportunity to make a more solemn utterance.

On this day which is chosen to close the Year of Faith, on this feast of the blessed Apostles Peter and Paul, we have wished to offer to the living God the homage of a profession of faith. And as once at Caesarea Philippi the apostle Peter spoke on behalf of the twelve to make a true confession, beyond human opinions, of Christ as Son of the living God, so today his humble successor, pastor of the Universal Church, raises his voice to give, on behalf of all the People of God, a firm witness to the divine Truth entrusted to the Church to be announced to all nations.

We have wished our profession of faith to be to a high degree complete and explicit, in order that it may respond in a fitting way to the need of light felt by so many faithful souls, and by all those in the world, to whatever spiritual family they belong, who are in search of the Truth.

To the glory of God most holy and of our Lord Jesus Christ, trusting in the aid of the Blessed Virgin Mary and of the holy Apostles Peter and Paul, for the profit and edification of the Church, in the name of all the pastors and all the faithful, we now pronounce this profession of faith, in full spiritual communion with you all, beloved brothers and sons.

PROFESSION OF FAITH

We believe in one only God, Father, Son and Holy Spirit, creator of things visible such as this world in which our transient life passes, of things invisible such as the pure spirits which are also called angels,[3] and creator in each man of his spiritual and immortal soul.

We believe that this only God is absolutely one in His infinitely holy essence as also in all His perfections, in His omnipotence, His infinite knowledge, His providence, His will and His love. He is *He who*

[3] Cf. Dz.-Sch. 3002.

is, as He revealed to Moses;[4] and He is *love,* as the apostle John teaches us;[5] so that these two names, being and love, express ineffably the same divine reality of Him who has wished to make Himself known to us, and who, "dwelling in light inaccessible,"[6] is in Himself above every name, above every thing and above every created intellect. God alone can give us right and full knowledge of this reality by revealing Himself as Father, Son and Holy Spirit, in whose eternal life we are by grace called to share, here below in the obscurity of faith and after death in eternal light. The mutual bonds which eternally constitute the Three Persons, who are each one and the same divine being, are the blessed inmost life of God thrice holy, infinitely beyond all that we can conceive in human measure.[7] We give thanks, however, to the divine goodness that very many believers can testify with us before men to the unity of God, even though they know not the mystery of the most holy Trinity.

We believe then in the Father who eternally begets the Son; in the Son, the Word of God, who is eternally begotten; in the Holy Spirit, the uncreated Person who proceeds from the Father and the Son as their eternal love. Thus in the Three Divine Persons, *coaeternae sibi et coaequales,*[8] the life and beatitude of God perfectly one superabound and are consummated in the supreme excellence and glory proper to uncreated being, and always "there should be venerated unity in the Trinity and Trinity in the unity."[9]

We believe in our Lord Jesus Christ, who is the Son of God. He is the Eternal Word, born of the Father before time began, and one in substance with the Father, homousios to Patri,[10] and through Him all things were made. He was incarnate of the Virgin Mary by the power of the Holy Spirit, and was made man: equal therefore to the Father according to His divinity, and inferior to the Father according to His humanity;[11] and Himself one, not by some impossible confusion of His natures, but by the unity of His person.[12]

He dwelt among us, full of grace and truth. He proclaimed and established the Kingdom of God and made us know in Himself the Fa-

[4] Cf. Ex. 3:14.
[5] Cf. 1 Jn. 4:8.
[6] Cf. 1 Tim. 6:16.
[7] Cf. Dz.-Sch. 804.
[8] Cf. Dz.-Sch. 75.
[9] Cf. *ibid.*
[10] Cf. Dz.-Sch. 150.
[11] Cf. Dz.-Sch. 76.
[12] Cf. *ibid.*

ther. He gave us His new commandment to love one another as He loved us. He taught us the way of the beatitudes of the Gospel: poverty in spirit, meekness, suffering borne with patience, thirst after justice, mercy, purity of heart, will for peace, persecution suffered for justice sake. Under Pontius Pilate He suffered — the Lamb of God bearing on Himself the sins of the world, and He died for us on the cross, saving us by His redeeming blood. He was buried, and, of His own power, rose on the third day, raising us by His resurrection to that sharing in the divine life which is the life of grace. He ascended to heaven, and He will come again, this time in glory, to judge the living and the dead: each according to his merits — those who have responded to the love and piety of God going to eternal life, those who have refused them to the end going to the fire that is not extinguished.

And His Kingdom will have no end.

We believe in the Holy Spirit, who is Lord, and Giver of life, who is adored and glorified together with the Father and the Son. He spoke to us by the prophets; He was sent by Christ after His resurrection and His ascension to the Father; He illuminates, vivifies, protects and guides the Church; He purifies the Church's members if they do not shun His grace. His action, which penetrates to the inmost of the soul, enables man to respond to the call of Jesus: Be perfect as your Heavenly Father is perfect (Mt. 5:48).

We believe that Mary is the Mother, who remained ever a Virgin, of the Incarnate Word, our God and Savior Jesus Christ,[13] and that by reason of this singular election, she was, in consideration of the merits of her Son, redeemed in a more eminent manner,[14] preserved from all stain of original sin[15] and filled with the gift of grace more than all other creatures.[16]

Joined by a close and indissoluble bond to the Mysteries of the Incarnation and Redemption,[17] the Blessed Virgin, the Immaculate, was at the end of her earthly life raised body and soul to heavenly glory[18] and likened to her risen Son in anticipation of the future lot of all the just; and we believe that the Blessed Mother of God, the New Eve, Mother of the Church,[19] continues in heaven her maternal role with

[13] Cf. Dz.-Sch. 251-252.
[14] Cf. Lumen Gentium, 53.
[15] Cf. Dz.-Sch. 2803.
[16] Cf. Lumen Gentium, 53.
[17] Cf. Lumen Gentium, 53, 58, 61.
[18] Cf. Dz.-Sch. 3903.
[19] Cf. Lumen Gentium, 53, 56, 61, 63; Cf. Paul VI, Alloc. for the Closing of the Third

regard to Christ's members, cooperating with the birth and growth of divine life in the souls of the redeemed.[20]

We believe that in Adam all have sinned, which means that the original offense committed by him caused human nature, common to all men, to fall to a state in which it bears the consequences of that offense, and which is not the state in which it was at first in our first parents — established as they were in holiness and justice, and in which man knew neither evil nor death. It is human nature so fallen, stripped of the grace that clothed it, injured in its own natural powers and subjected to the dominion of death, that is transmitted to all men, and it is in this sense that every man is born in sin. We therefore hold, with the Council of Trent, that original sin is transmitted with human nature, "not by imitation, but by propagation" and that it is thus "proper to everyone.[21]

We believe that our Lord Jesus Christ, by the sacrifice of the cross redeemed us from original sin and all the personal sins committed by each one of us, so that, in accordance with the word of the apostle, "where sin abounded, grace did more abound."[22]

We believe in one Baptism instituted by our Lord Jesus Christ for the remission of sins. Baptism should be administered even to little children who have not yet been able to be guilty of any personal sin, in order that, though born deprived of supernatural grace, they may be reborn "of water and the Holy Spirit" to the divine life in Christ Jesus.[23]

We believe in one, holy, catholic, and apostolic Church, built by Jesus Christ on that rock which is Peter. She is the Mystical Body of Christ; at the same time a visible society instituted with hierarchical organs, and a spiritual community; the Church on earth, the pilgrim People of God here below, and the Church filled with heavenly blessings; the germ and the first fruits of the Kingdom of God, through which the work and the sufferings of Redemption are continued throughout human history, and which looks for its perfect accomplishment beyond time in glory.[24] In the course of time, the Lord

---

Session of the Second Vatican Council: AAS LVI [1964] 1016; Cf. Exhort. Apost. Signum Magnum, Introd.
[20] Cf. Lumen Gentium, 62; cf. Paul VI, Exhort. Apost. Signum Magnum, p. 1, n. 1.
[21] Cf. Dz.-Sch. 1513.
[22] Cf. Rom. 5:20.
[23] Cf. Dz.-Sch. 1514.
[24] Cf. Lumen Gentium, 8, 5.

Jesus forms His Church by means of the sacraments emanating from His plentitude.[25] By these she makes her members participants in the Mystery of the Death and Resurrection of Christ, in the grace of the Holy Spirit who gives her life and movement.[26] She is therefore holy, though she has sinners in her bosom, because she herself has no other life but that of grace: it is by living by her life that her members are sanctified; it is by removing themselves from her life that they fall into sins and disorders that prevent the radiation of her sanctity. This is why she suffers and does penance for these offenses, of which she has the power to heal her children through the blood of Christ and the gift of the Holy Spirit.

Heiress of the divine promises and daughter of Abraham according to the Spirit, through that Israel whose scriptures she lovingly guards, and whose patriarchs and prophets she venerates; founded upon the Apostles and handing on from century to century their ever-living word and their powers as pastors in the successor of Peter and the bishops in communion with him; perpetually assisted by the Holy Spirit, she has the charge of guarding, teaching, explaining and spreading the Truth which God revealed in a then veiled manner by the prophets, and fully by the Lord Jesus. We believe all that is contained in the word of God written or handed down, and that the Church proposes for belief as divinely revealed, whether by a solemn judgment or by the ordinary and universal magisterium.[27] We believe in the infallibility enjoyed by the successor of Peter when he teaches ex cathedra as pastor and teacher of all the faithful,[28] and which is assured also to the episcopal body when it exercises with him the supreme magisterium.[29]

We believe that the Church founded by Jesus Christ and for which He prayed is indefectibly one in faith, worship and the bond of hierarchical communion. In the bosom of this Church, the rich variety of liturgical rites and the legitimate diversity of theological and spiritual heritages and special disciplines, far from injuring her unity, make it more manifest.[30]

Recognizing also the existence, outside the organism of the Church of Christ, of numerous elements of truth and sanctification

[25] Cf. Lumen Gentium, 7, 11.
[26] Cf. Sacrosanctum Concilium, 5, 6; cf. Lumen Gentium, 7, 12, 50.
[27] Cf. Dz.-Sch. 3011.
[28] Cf. Dz.-Sch. 3074.
[29] Cf. Lumen Gentium, 25.
[30] Cf. Lumen Gentium, 23; cf. Orientalium Ecclesarum, 2, 3, 5, 6.

which belong to her as her own and tend to Catholic unity,[31] and believing in the action of the Holy Spirit who stirs up in the heart of the disciples of Christ love of this unity,[32] we entertain the hope that the Christians who are not yet in the full communion of the one only Church will one day be reunited in one flock with one only shepherd.

We believe that the Church is necessary for salvation, because Christ, who is the sole mediator and way of salvation, renders Himself present for us in His body which is the Church.[33] But the divine design of salvation embraces all men; and those who without fault on their part do not know the Gospel of Christ and His Church, but seek God sincerely, and under the influence of grace endeavor to do His will as recognized through the promptings of their conscience, they, in a number known only to God, can obtain salvation.[34]

We believe that the Mass, celebrated by the priest representing the person of Christ by virtue of the power received through the Sacrament of Orders, and offered by him in the name of Christ and the members of His Mystical Body, is the sacrifice of Calvary rendered sacramentally present on our altars. We believe that as the bread and wine consecrated by the Lord at the Last Supper were changed into His body and His blood which were to be offered for us on the cross, likewise the bread and wine consecrated by the priest are changed into the body and blood of Christ enthroned gloriously in heaven, and we believe that the mysterious presence of the Lord, under what continues to appear to our senses as before, is a true, real and substantial presence.[35]

Christ cannot be thus present in this sacrament except by the change into His body of the reality itself of the bread and the change into His blood of the reality itself of the wine, leaving unchanged only the properties of the bread and wine which our senses perceive. This mysterious change is very appropriately called by the Church *transubstantiation*. Every theological explanation which seeks some understanding of this mystery must, in order to be in accord with Catholic faith, maintain that in the reality itself, independently of our mind, the bread and wine have ceased to exist after the Consecration, so that it is the adorable body and blood of the Lord Jesus that from then on are

---
[31] Cf. Lumen Gentium, 8.
[32] Cf. Lumen Gentium, 15.
[33] Cf. Lumen Gentium, 14.
[34] Cf. Lumen Gentium, 16.
[35] Cf. Dz.-Sch. 1651.

really before us under the sacramental species of bread and wine,[36] as the Lord willed it, in order to give Himself to us as food and to associate us with the unity of His Mystical Body.[37]

The unique and indivisible existence of the Lord glorious in heaven is not multiplied, but is rendered present by the sacrament in the many places on earth where Mass is celebrated. And this existence remains present, after the sacrifice, in the Blessed Sacrament which is, in the tabernacle, the living heart of each of our churches. And it is our very sweet duty to honor and adore in the blessed Host which our eyes see, the Incarnate Word whom they cannot see, and who, without leaving heaven, is made present before us.

We confess that the Kingdom of God begun here below in the Church of Christ is not of this world whose form is passing, and that its proper growth cannot be confounded with the progress of civilization, of science or of human technology, but that it consists in an ever more profound knowledge of the unfathomable riches of Christ, an ever stronger hope in eternal blessings, an ever more ardent response to the love of God, and an ever more generous bestowal of grace and holiness among men. But it is this same love which induces the Church to concern herself constantly about the true temporal welfare of men. Without ceasing to recall to her children that they have not here a lasting dwelling, she also urges them to contribute, each according to his vocation and his means, to the welfare of their earthly city, to promote justice, peace and brotherhood among men, to give their aid freely to their brothers, especially to the poorest and most unfortunate. The deep solicitude of the Church, the Spouse of Christ, for the needs of men, for their joys and hopes, their griefs and efforts, is therefore nothing other than her great desire to be present to them, in order to illuminate them with the light of Christ and to gather them all in Him, their only Savior. This solicitude can never mean that the Church conform herself to the things of this world, or that she lessen the ardor of her expectation of her Lord and of the eternal Kingdom.

We believe in the life eternal. We believe that the souls of all those who die in the grace of Christ — whether they must still be purified in purgatory, or whether from the moment they leave their bodies Jesus takes them to paradise as He did for the Good Thief — are the People of God in the eternity beyond death, which will be finally conquered

---

[36] Cf. Dz.-Sch. 1642, 1651-1654; Paul VI, Enc. Mysterium Fidei.
[37] Cf. S. Th., III, 73, 3.

on the day of the Resurrection when these souls will be reunited with their bodies.

We believe that the multitude of those gathered around Jesus and Mary in paradise forms the Church of Heaven, where in eternal beatitude they see God as He is,[38] and where they also, in different degrees, are associated with the holy angels in the divine rule exercised by Christ in glory, interceding for us and helping our weakness by their brotherly care.[39]

We believe in the communion of all the faithful of Christ, those who are pilgrims on earth, the dead who are attaining their purification, and the blessed in heaven, all together forming one Church; and we believe that in this communion the merciful love of God and His saints, is ever listening to our prayers, as Jesus told us: Ask and you will receive.[40] Thus it is with faith and in hope that we look forward to the resurrection of the dead, and the life of the world to come.

Blessed be God Thrice Holy. Amen.

[38] Cf. 1 Jn. 3:2; Dz.-Sch. 1000.
[39] Cf. Lumen Gentium, 49.
[40] Cf. Lk. 10:9-10; Jn. 16:24.

Bibliography

The following is a list of some works used in the preparation of this volume and which the reader or teacher may find of use. The authors do not necessarily agree with the contents or approach of every reference book.

Abbott, Walter M., S.J., *The Documents of Vatican II*, New York: Herder and Herder, 1966.
Adam, Karl *The Son of God*, New York: Sheed and Ward, 1940.
Adam, Karl *The Spirit of Catholicism*, New York: The Macmillan Company, 1935.
Aron, Robert *The Jewish Jesus*, Maryknoll: Orbis Books, 1971.
Bandas, Rev. Msgr. R. G. *Christ the Truth*, Saint Paul, Minnesota: E. M. Lohmann Company, 1969.
Barbet, Pierre, M.D. *A Doctor at Calvary*, New York: Image Books, Doubleday & Company, Inc., 1963. Translated by The Earl of Wicklow.
Bea, Augustin Cardinal *Unity in Freedom*, New York: Harper & Row Publishers, 1964.
Bea, Augustin Cardinal *The Unity of Christians*, New York: Herder and Herder, 1963.
Behind the Dim Unknown, New York: G. P. Putnam's Sons, 1966. Edited by John Clover Monsma.
Bishop, Jim *The Day Christ Died*, New York: Perennial Library, Harper & Row, Publishers, Inc., 1965.
Blenkinsopp, Joseph *Jesus Is Lord*, New York: Paulist Press Deus Books, 1965.
Boros, Ladislaus *Meeting God in Man*, New York: Herder and Herder, Inc., 1968.
Caldwell, Taylor *Dear and Glorious Physician*, New York: Doubleday & Company, Inc. (Book Club Edition), 1959.
Caldwell, Taylor *Great Lion of God*, New York: Doubleday & Company, Inc. (Book Club Edition), 1970.
1970 *Catholic Almanac*, Paterson, New Jersey: St. Anthony's Guild, 1970. Edited by Felician A. Foy, O.F.M.
Ciszek, Walter J., S.J. *With God in Russia*, New York: Image Books, Doubleday & Company, Inc., 1966.
Clifford, John W., S.J. *In the Presence of My Enemies*, New York: W. W. Norton & Company, Inc., 1963.

Connell, Francis J., *Father Connell Answers Moral Questions*, Washington, D.C.: The Catholic University of America Press, 1959.

Connell, Francis J., *Morals in Politics and Professions*, Westminster, Maryland: The Newman Press, 1951.

Connell, Francis J., *More Answers to Today's Moral Problems*, Washington, D.C.: The Catholic University of America Press, 1965.

Connell, Francis J., *New Baltimore Catechism No. 3* (Confraternity Edition), New York: Benziger Brothers, Inc., 1962.

Connell, Francis J., *Outlines of Moral Theology*, Milwaukee: The Bruce Publishing Company, 1964.

Connell, Francis J., *The Seven Sacraments*, Glen Rock, New Jersey: Paulist Press, 1966.

Cranston, Ruth *The Miracle of Lourdes*, New York: McGraw-Hill Book Company, 1955.

Dalrymple, John *The Christian Affirmation*, Denville, New Jersey: Dimension Books, 1971.

Daniel-Rops, Henri *The Book of Mary*, New York: Image Books, Doubleday & Company, Inc., 1963. Translated by Alastair Guinan.

Daniel-Rops, Henri *Daily Life in the Time of Jesus*, New York: Hawthorn Books, 1962.

Daniel-Rops, Henri *Jesus and His Times*, New York: E. P. Dutton Co., 1956.

Danielou, Jean *God's Life in Us*, Denville, New Jersey: Dimension Books, 1969.

Danielou, Jean *Great Religions*, Notre Dame, Indiana: Fides Publishers, Inc., 1967.

D'Aubigne, J. H. Merle *History of the Reformation of the Sixteenth Century*, New York: Robert Carter & Brothers, 1879.

Daughters of St. Paul *The Catechism of Modern Man*, Boston: The Daughters of St. Paul, 1968.

Daughters of St. Paul *The Faith We Live By*, Boston: The Daughters of St. Paul, 1969.

Daughters of St. Paul *The Sixteen Documents of Vatican II*, Boston: The Daughters of St. Paul, 1966.

Daughters of St. Paul *The Church's Amazing Story*, Boston: The Daughters of St. Paul, 1969.

Documents of Vatican II, The, New York: The America Press, 1966. Edited by Walter M. Abbott, S.J.

Durant, Will *Caesar and Christ,* New York: Simon and Schuster, Inc., 1944.
Evely, Louis *We Are All Brothers,* New York: Herder and Herder, 1967.
Evidence of God in an Expanding Universe, The, New York: G. P. Putnam's Sons, 1958. Edited by John Clover Monsma.
Farrell, Walter *A Companion to the Summa,* New York: Sheed & Ward, 1952.
Flood, Edmund *Parables of Jesus,* New York: Paulist Press, 1971.
Foley, Leonard *Signs of Love,* Cincinnati: St. Anthony Messenger Press, 1971.
Franzen, August, and Dolan, John P. *A History of the Church,* New York: Herder and Herder, 1969. Trans. from the German by Peter Becker.
Fulda, Edeltraud *And I Shall Be Healed,* New York: Simon and Schuster, Inc., 1961.
Galter, Albert *The Red Book of the Persecuted Church,* Dublin: M. H. Gill and Son Ltd., 1957.
Garcia-Diego, James *Approaches to Catechesis,* New York: Seton Press, 1965.
Gihr, Nicholas *The Holy Sacrifice of the Mass,* St. Louis: B. Herder Book Co., 1941.
Gillis, James M. *So Near Is God,* New York: Charles Scribner's Sons, 1953.
Giordani, Igino *Catherine of Siena,* Milwaukee: The Bruce Publishing Company, 1959. Translated by Thomas J. Tobin.
Goldstein, David *Autobiography of a Campaigner for Christ,* Boston: Catholic Campaigners For Christ, 1936.
Goodier, Alban *The Passion and Death of Our Lord Jesus Christ,* New York: P. J. Kenedy & Sons, 1944.
Goodier, Alban, Archbishop *The Public Life of Our Lord Jesus Christ,* New York: P. J. Kenedy & Sons, 1936.
Gorman, Ralph *The Trial of Christ,* Huntington, Indiana: Our Sunday Visitor, Inc., 1972.
Grollenberg, Luke H. *A New Look at an Old Book,* New York: Newman Press, 1969.
Guide to Reading the New Testament, A, Chicago: Acta Foundation, 1963.
Hardon, John A., S.J. *The Protestant Churches of America,* New York: Image Books, Doubleday & Company, Inc., 1969.

Häring, Bernard *Marriage in the Modern World,* Westminster, Maryland: The Newman Press, 1965.
Häring, Bernard *What Does Christ Want?,* Notre Dame, Indiana: Ave Maria Press, 1967.
Häring, Bernard *Shalom: Peace,* New York: Image Books, 1969
Harney, Martin P., S.J. *The Legacy of Saint Patrick,* Boston: The Daughters of St. Paul, 1972.
Hatch, Alden *Pope Paul VI,* New York: Random House, Inc., 1966.
Hayes, Edward J. Rev., Hayes, Paul J. Rev Msgr. and Kelly, Dorothy Ellen *Moral Principles of Nursing,* New York: The Macmillan Company, 1969.
Healy, Edwin F. *Moral Guidance,* Chicago: Loyola University Press, 1957.
Herberg, W. *Protestant, Catholic and Jew,* New York: Doubleday & Company, Inc., 1953.
Hill, John J. & Stone, Theodore C. *A Modern Catechism,* Chicago: Acta Foundation, 1965.
Hughes, Philip *The Church in Crisis: A History of the General Councils, 325-1870,* New York: Image Books, Doubleday & Company, Inc., 1964.
Hughes, Philip *A Popular History of the Catholic Church,* New York: The Macmillan Company, 1947. Macmillan Paperbacks Edition, Third Printing, 1968.
Hughes, Philip *A Popular History of the Reformation,* New York: Image Books, Doubleday & Company, Inc., 1960.
Jeremias, Joacheim *The Parables of Jesus,* New York: Charles Scribner's Sons, 1962.
John, Eric *The Popes,* New York: Hawthorn Books, Inc., 1964.
Kavanaugh, James J. *Man in Search of God,* New York: Paulist Press Deus Books, 1967.
Kerrison, Raymond *Bishop Walsh of Maryknoll,* New York: G. P. Putnam's Sons, 1962.
Knox, Ronald *The Belief of Catholics,* New York: Image Books, Doubleday & Company, Inc., 1958.
Krull, Vigilius H. *Christian Denominations,* Chicago: M. A. Donohue & Company, 1940.
Kubler-Ross, Elizabeth *On Death and Dying,* New York: The Macmillan Company, 5th printing, 1971.
Larsen, Earnest and Calvin, Patricia *Will Morality Make Sense to Your Child?,* Liguori, Missouri, 1971.

BIBLIOGRAPHY

Lewis, C. S. *The Case for Christianity,* New York: The Macmillan Company, 1943.

Long, Valentine, O.F.M. *The Angels in Religion and Art,* Paterson, New Jersey: St. Anthony Guild Press, 1970.

Lortz, Joseph, and Kaider, Edwin G. *History of the Church,* Milwaukee: The Bruce Publishing Company, 1938-1939.

Luijpen, William *What Can You Say About God?,* New York: Paulist Press, 1971.

Lunn, Arnold, and Lean, Garth *Christian Counter-Attack,* New Rochelle, New York: Arlington House, 1970.

MacArthur, Douglas, General of the Army *Reminiscences,* New York: The McGraw-Hill Book Company, 1964.

Manton, Joseph E., C.SS.R. *Happiness Over the Hill,* Huntington, Indiana: Our Sunday Visitor, 1970.

Manton, Joseph E., C.SS.R. *Pennies from a Poor Box,* Boston: The Daughters of St. Paul, 1962.

Manton, Joseph E., C.SS.R. *Sanctity on the Sidewalk,* Boston: Privately Printed, 1969.

Manton, Joseph E., C.SS.R. *Straws from the Crib,* Boston: The Daughters of St. Paul, 1964.

Maryknoll Catholic Dictionary, The, New York: Dimension Books, Grosset & Dunlap, 1965. Compiled and Edited by Albert J. Nevins, M.M.

Maynard, Theodore *Saints for Our Times,* New York: Image Books, Doubleday & Company, Inc., 1955.

Maynard, Theodore *The Story of American Catholicism,* New York: The Macmillan Company, 1960.

McFadden, Charles J. *Medical Ethics,* Philadelphia: F.A. Davis Co., 1961.

McGinley, Phyllis *Saint-Watching,* New York: The Viking Press, Inc., 1969.

McKenzie, John L. *Authority in the Church,* New York: Sheed and Ward, Inc., 1966. New York: Image Books, 1971.

McKenzie, John L. *Dictionary of the Bible,* New York: The Bruce Publishing Company, 1965.

McKenzie, John L. *Mastering the Meaning of the Bible,* Denville, New Jersey: Dimension Books, 1966.

McKenzie, John L. *The Roman Catholic Church,* New York: Holt, Rinehart, Winston, Inc., 1969. New York: Image Books, 1971.

McKenzie, John L. *Vital Concepts of the Bible,* Denville, New Jersey: Dimension Books, 1969.
Mead, Jude, C.P. *The Hours of the Passion,* Milwaukee: The Bruce Publishing Company, 1956.
Morton, H. V. *In the Steps of the Master,* New York: Dodd, Mead and Company, Inc., 1971.
Morton, H. V. *Through Lands of the Bible,* New York: Dodd, Mead and Company, 1970.
New Catechism, A, Catholic Faith for Adults, New York: Herder and Herder, 1967.
New Catholic Encyclopedia, New York: The McGraw-Hill Book Company; copyright 1967; 15 vols. and index, eds. Most Rev. William J. McDonald, Rt. Rev. James A. Magner, Martin R. P. McGuire, Rev. John P. Whalen.
O'Brien, John A., Rev. *Giants of the Faith,* New York: Image Books, Doubleday & Company, Inc., 1960.
O'Brien, John A., Rev. *The Road to Damascus,* New York: Image Books, Doubleday & Company, Inc., 1955.
O'Shea, Kevin, and Meehan, Noel *A Human Apostolate,* Liguori, Missouri: Liguori Publications, 1971.
Oursler, Fulton *The Greatest Story Ever Told,* New York: Doubleday & Company, Inc. (Book Club Edition), 1949.
Oursler, Fulton, and Armstrong, April Oursler *The Greatest Faith Ever Known,* New York: Doubleday & Company, Inc. (Book Club Edition), 1953.
Padovano, Anthony, Rev. *Who Is Christ?* Notre Dame, Indiana: Ave Maria Press, 1967.
Pope John XXIII *Ad Petri Cathedram,* 1959.
Pope John XXIII *Grata Recordatio,* 1959.
Pope Paul VI *Ecclesiam Suam,* 1964.
Pope Paul VI *Christi Matri Rosarii,* 1966.
Pope Paul VI *Apostolic Constitution on Indulgences,* 1967.
Pope Pius XII *Mystici Corporis Christi,* 1943.
Pope Pius XII *Humani Generis,* 1950.
Quoist, Michel *Christ Is Alive,* New York: Image Books, 1971.
Rahner, Karl *The Christian Commitment,* New York: Sheed and Ward, 1961.
Rahner, Karl *Everyday Faith,* New York: Herder and Herder, 1968.
Rahner, Karl *Servants of the Lord,* New York: Herder and Herder, 1968.

BIBLIOGRAPHY

Ricciotti, Giuseppe *The Life of Christ,* Milwaukee: The Bruce Publishing Company, 1947. Translated by Alba I. Zizzamia.
Rigney, Harold W., S.V.D. *Four Years in a Red Hell,* Chicago: Henry Regnery Company, 1956.
Sacred Congregation for the Clergy, *General Catechetical Directory,* Washington, D.C.: United States Catholic Conference, 1971.
Saints, The, New York: Guild Press, Inc., 1958. Edited by John Coulson.
Sarno, Ronald A. *The Story of Hope,* Liguori, Missouri: Liguori Publications, 1972.
Schneider, Nicholas *To Burn With the Spirit of Christ,* Liguori, Missouri: Liguori Publications, 1971.
Sheed, F. J. *Theology and Sanity,* New York: Sheed and Ward, 1947.
Sheed, F. J. *What Difference Does Jesus Make?,* New York: Sheed & Ward, 1971, cloth. Huntington, Indiana: Our Sunday Visitor, Inc., paperbound.
Sheen, Fulton J., Archbishop *Life of Christ,* New York: The McGraw-Hill Book Company, Inc. (Book Club Edition), 1958.
Sheerin, John B. *A Practical Guide to Ecumenism,* New York: Paulist Press, 1967.
Smith, George D. (ed.) *The Teaching of the Catholic Church,* New York: The Macmillan Company, 16th printing, 1964 (2 v.).
Spirago, Francis, and Clarke, Richard F. *The Catechism Explained,* New York: Benziger Brothers, 1927.
Stoddard, John L. *Rebuilding a Lost Faith,* New York: P. J. Kenedy & Sons, 1922.
Sullivan, Peter *Christ the Answer,* Boston: The Daughters of St. Paul, 1964.
Tanquerey, Adolphe *The Spiritual Life,* Tournai, Belgium: Desclée & Co., 1930.
Trese, Leo J. *Wisdom Shall Enter,* Notre Dame, Indiana: Dome Books, Fides Publishers, Inc., 1964.
Turro, James *Reflections . . . Paths to Prayer,* Paramus, New Jersey: Paulist Press, 1972.
United States Catholic Bishops *The Church in Our Day,* Washington, D.C.: 1968.
Van Kaam, Adrian *Religion and Personality,* Englewood Cliffs: Prentice-Hall, Inc., 1964. New York: Image Books, 1968.
Walsh, John, *The Shroud,* New York: Echo Books, Doubleday & Company, Inc., 1965.

Walsh, John, S.J. *This Is Catholicism,* New York: Image Books, Doubleday & Company, Inc., 1959.
Walsh, William Thomas *Our Lady of Fatima,* New York: Image Books, Doubleday & Company, Inc., 1954.
Werfel, Franz *The Song of Bernadette,* New York: Pocket Books, Inc. (Cardinal Edition), 1952. Translated by Ludwig Lewisohn.
Wilhelm, Anthony J. *Christ Among Us,* New York: Newman Press, 1967.
Willke, Dr. & Mrs. J. C. *Handbook on Abortion,* Cincinnati: Hiltz Publishing Co., 1971.
Wilson, Alfred *Pardon and Peace,* New York: Sheed & Ward, 1947.
Woman Clothed with the Sun, A, New York: Image Books, Doubleday & Company, Inc., 1961. Edited by John J. Delaney.
Wright, Cardinal John *The Church: Hope of the World,* Kenosha, Wisconsin: Prow Books, 1972. Edited by Rev. Donald W. Wuerl.
Wuerl, Rev. Donald W. *The Forty Martyrs,* Huntington, Indiana: Our Sunday Visitor Inc., 1972.
Zimmerman, Paul A. *Creation, Evolution and God's Word,* St. Louis: Concordia Publishing House, 1972.

Index

Actual Grace 198ff
Actual Sin 178
Angels 170ff
Anointing of Sick 123
Apostles 42, 69, 83ff, 89
Apostolicity, Church of the 102, 115ff, 119ff
Ascension 188
Assumption 219
Astronaut 25
Authority, Church 122, 127

Barbet, Pierre, M.D. 76ff
Bible 39, 137ff
Blessed Trinity 162ff
Blessed Virgin 174, 219ff

Cana 222
Capital Sins 183
Catholic Faith 14
Chain of Faith 153
Charity 199
Chesterton, G. K. 24, 235
Christ 47ff, 55ff, 61ff, 67ff, 91ff, 187ff
Christ, Credentials 61ff
Christ, Divinity of 55ff, 124, 153
Christ, Miracles of 61ff
Christ, Natures of 189
Christ, Redeemer 190ff
Christianity 37
Church 91ff, 101ff, 115ff, 127ff, 137ff, 147ff, 229ff
Church, Authority 123, 127ff
Church, Credentials 122ff
Church, Head of 93ff, 103ff, 127ff, 153
Church, Marks of the 102ff, 153
Communion of Saints 206
Confession 124
Corporal Works of Mercy 205
Council, Vatican II 13, 14, 35, 39, 134, 135, 147ff, 174, 175
Creation 169ff
Creed 117, 237ff
Crucifixion 61, 75ff

Death 173, 209
Divine Tradition 144
Divinity of Christ 55ff
Divorce 122

Ecumenism 147ff

Eternity 159, 203ff
Eucharist 124
Evil 177ff

Faith 123, 199
Faith, Catholic 14ff
Faith, Chain of 153
Fasting 123
Flagellum 74ff
Freedom, Religion of 150ff

Gifts of Holy Spirit 199ff
God 19ff, 153, 155ff, 187ff
God, Qualities of 156ff
God, Search for 19ff
Goodness, God of 160
Gospel 39ff
Grace 173, 193ff
Grace, Actual 198
Grace, Sanctifying 173, 197ff

Head, Church of the 103ff, 127ff
Heaven 125
Hell 210ff
Herod 73
Holiness, Church of the 102, 106ff
Holy Shroud 69
Holy Spirit 132, 199ff
Holy Spirit, Gifts of 199ff
Hope 199

Immaculate Conception 174, 220ff
Immutability 160
Incarnation 188, 192
Infallibility 127, 131ff
Infinity 159

Jesus 47ff, 55ff, 183ff
Josephus 43, 60
Justice, God of 161

Knowledge 160

MacArthur, Gen. Douglas 16, 17
Man, Creation of 171ff
Martyr 109, 127, 166, 234ff
Mary 174, 219ff
Mercy, God of 160
Mercy, Works of 205
Marks of the Church 101ff, 153ff

Messiah 48, 49, 55ff, 71
Miracle 61ff, 81ff, 110ff
Missionary 108, 109, 131
Mohammed 34, 48
Moral Virtues 200ff
Mortal Sin 181
Morton, H. V. 44, 60
Mother of the Church 219ff
Mueller, Bishop R. 14

Nature, of Christ 189ff
New Testament 37, 39ff, 63, 131, 137ff, 153

Old Testament 44, 137
Omnipresence 159
Original Sin 173, 178

Paraclete 132
Passion of Christ 67ff
Penance 123, 208
Pilate, Pontius 71, 74, 75
Plunkett, Joseph Mary 26
Plutarch 31
Pope 127ff
Pope John XXIII 14, 36, 134, 147
Pope John Paul II 90, 169
Pope Paul VI 147, 175, 180
Prayer 30ff
Profession of Faith 239
Prophecy, Fulfillment of 55ff
Purgatory 214

Real Presence 124
Redeemer 190ff
Redemption 192
Reformation 143
Religion, in Life 29ff, 32
Religion, Place of 29ff, 32
Religious Differences 29ff, 142, 143
Religious Freedom 150ff

Resurrection 81ff, 153
Revelation 137ff
Rock, The 81ff, 130
Rosary 224ff

Saints 109
Saint Paul 37
Saint Peter 42, 43, 94ff, 123, 130ff
Salvation 196
Sanctifying Grace 173, 197ff
Scripture 137ff
Seneca 33
Sermon on the Mount 52
Sheen, Bishop Fulton J. 68
Sign of Cross 162
Sin 173, 178ff
Sin, Consequences of 180ff
Sin, Mortal 181
Sin, Venial 181
Space Missions 25
Stoddard, John L. 32, 33
Succession of Popes 110ff

Temptations 182ff
Theological Virtues 199ff
Tradition 144
Trinity 162ff
Truth 13

Unity 102ff
Universality, Church of the 102, 115ff

Vatican II 13, 14, 35, 39, 134, 135, 147ff 174, 175
Venial Sin 181
Virtues 193ff
Virtues, Moral 200ff

Walsh, Bishop James, M.M. 108
Works of Mercy 205